Education in Nineteenth-Century British Literature

Sheila Cordner traces a tradition of literary resistance to dominant pedagogies in nineteenth-century Britain, recovering an overlooked chapter in the history of thought about education. This book considers an influential group of writers—all excluded from Oxford and Cambridge because of their class or gender—who argue extensively for the value of learning outside of schools altogether. From just beyond the walls of elite universities, Jane Austen, Elizabeth Barrett Browning, Thomas Hardy, and George Gissing used their position as outsiders as well as their intimate knowledge of British universities through brothers, fathers, and friends, to satirize rote learning in schools for the working classes as well as the education offered by elite colleges. Cordner analyzes how predominant educational rhetoric, intended to celebrate England's progress while simultaneously controlling the spread of knowledge to the masses, gets recast not only by the four primary authors in this book but also by insiders of universities, who fault schools for their emphasis on memorization. Drawing upon working-men's club reports, student guides, educational pamphlets, and materials from the National Home Reading Union, as well as recent work on nineteenth-century theories of reading, Cordner unveils a broader cultural movement that embraced the freedom of learning on one's own.

Sheila Cordner, Ph.D., teaches at Boston University. She has published articles on authors such as Charles Dickens and Elizabeth Barrett Browning, and has presented research on Victorian literature, Irish literature, service learning, and digital humanities.

Education in Nineteenth-Century British Literature

Exclusion as Innovation

Sheila Cordner

LONDON AND NEW YORK

First published 2016
by Routledge
2 Park Square, Milton Park, Abingdon, Oxon OX14 4RN

and by Routledge
711 Third Avenue, New York, NY 10017

Routledge is an imprint of the Taylor & Francis Group, an informa business

© 2016 Sheila Cordner

The right of Sheila Cordner to be identified as author of this work has been asserted by her in accordance with sections 77 and 78 of the Copyright, Designs and Patents Act 1988.

All rights reserved. No part of this book may be reprinted or reproduced or utilised in any form or by any electronic, mechanical, or other means, now known or hereafter invented, including photocopying and recording, or in any information storage or retrieval system, without permission in writing from the publishers.

Trademark notice: Product or corporate names may be trademarks or registered trademarks, and are used only for identification and explanation without intent to infringe.

British Library Cataloguing in Publication Data
A catalogue record for this book is available from the British Library

Library of Congress Cataloging-in-Publication Data
A catalog record for this book has been requested

ISBN: 978-1-4724-6747-8 (hbk)
ISBN: 978-1-315-57884-2 (ebk)

Typeset in Times New Roman
by Apex CoVantage, LLC

For my parents, Helen and Terence Cordner,

and for Jaffrie

Contents

List of Figures   viii
Acknowledgments   ix

1   Educational Machinery   1
2   "Scrambling" into an Austen Education   22
3   Radical Education in *Aurora Leigh*   45
4   "I Will Do without Cambridge": Thomas Hardy's Autodidacts   59
5   Neither Inside nor Outside in George Gissing   82
    Conclusion   100

Appendix 1: Excerpt from The Loiterer; *facsimile of issue 8 (1789)*   115
Appendix 2: Excerpts from The Popular Educator; *facsimile of 1.2 (1852)*   126
Appendix 3: National Home Reading Union program (1890)   137
Appendix 4: Excerpt from George Gissing's Thyrza *(1887)*   141
Works Cited   146
Index   157

Figures

Cover Image James David Smillie, *A Corner at Home* (1883); Photograph © 2015 Museum of Fine Arts, Boston.
4.1 Page from *The Popular Educator* (1855); Source: The Bodleian Libraries, The University of Oxford (OC) 260 h.8 (vols 5–6), p. 494. 65
4.2 National Home Reading Union Program (1890); Source: The Bodleian Libraries, The University of Oxford 26271 e.3, pp. 1–2. 66
6.1 "One Page of Girton's History Anticipated" (1875); Source: The Mistress and Fellows, Girton College, Cambridge. 108
6.2 "The Study of History" from *The Fritillary* (1897); Source: The Principal and Fellows of St. Hilda's College, The University of Oxford. 111

Acknowledgments

I extend many thanks to Ann Donahue at Ashgate, who encouraged me to pursue the publication of this book. From our first meeting looking out over a piazza in Venice to countless emails since then, I have appreciated her commitment to the project. I also want to thank Autumn Spalding for being extremely helpful during the final stages. *Victorian Review* published an earlier version of Chapter 3. I thank them for permission to reprint this material. The Boston University Center for the Humanities provided a Publication Production Award.

As I wrote this book, I could not help but reflect on my own education. Julia Prewitt Brown reminded me of the importance of independent thinking in today's academic world. Her wisdom and brilliance have inspired this book in so many ways, and her mentorship has meant a great deal to me. At every stage of this project, I have benefitted from Anna Henchman's very generous intellectual insight and professional advice. I have learned so much from the way that she seeks to break down existing barriers to intellectually elite circles. Both Anna Henchman and Julia Prewitt Brown have shown me what true teacher-scholars look like.

I was privileged to be a member of Susan Lanser's wonderful Graduate Consortium in Women's Studies Dissertation Workshop, and I feel fortunate that her support of my work has continued beyond the workshop. Members of the group—particularly Njelle Hamilton, Sadaf Jaffer, Andy Reyes, and Phyllis Thompson—read early drafts and shared ideas about the writing process.

There are too many generous professors in the Boston University English department to name them all here, but I thank them for providing such a stimulating environment in which to study. My thanks go especially to Joseph Bizup, William Carroll, William Huntting Howell, Laura Korobkin, Maurice Lee, Susan Mizruchi, Erin Murphy, Anita Patterson, Carrie Preston, John Paul Riquelme, and James Winn. During graduate school, I benefitted from many conversations with fellow students, especially those also working in the nineteenth century, including Leslie Simon and Andrew Christensen, who shared feedback on a number of drafts.

I remember the exciting moment when I discovered Laura Green's first book, and I thank her for her very helpful suggestions about the project. My initial interest in the nineteenth century took shape in English classes at Smith and at Oxford, and under the guidance of Nicholas Dames at Columbia, who has continued to encourage my work in the field. Gill Evans shared with me much insight about British education. I appreciate Michele Martinez's willingness to read and offer suggestions about my work on Elizabeth Barrett Browning.

At B.U.'s College of General Studies, I have been surrounded by many wonderful colleagues who have supported this project, especially Regina Hansen, Natalie McKnight, Megan Sullivan, and Meg Tyler, as well as fellow Victorianists Kathleen Martin, Joellen Masters, and Aaron Worth. Stephanie Byttebier, Lydia Fash, and Kyle Wiggins gave excellent writing group feedback.

I also want to thank Claire and Allan Damon, Amy Davison, Diana Pasculli, and Jay Boggis. I am thankful for ongoing conversations with Lindsey Benitz, Abby Egginton, Ari Fort, Christina Gosack, Elizabeth Maynard, Michaela Page, Patricia Park, Michelle Ploutz, Christina Steinel, and Monika Verma. Richa Jha provided a fabulous London home during my research trips there. Maryellen Benedetto and the "California team" have never been too far away to express interest in my work, and it has been great sharing the experiences of academic life with Michele Benedetto Neitz and Dave Schafer. I appreciate the continued support of my extended family.

My most enduring education came from my parents. Their genuine intellectual curiosity and love of books have always been contagious. Words cannot express the respect I have for them and how grateful I am for the enthusiasm they have shown for this book as well as my other endeavors. My father's comments on drafts of this book were very valuable. I am constantly impressed by my brother, Terence, and Meg, my sister, who have always been models for me of well-rounded people. I thank Jaffrie for both his gourmet meals and encouragement, which fueled me in writing this book.

1 Educational Machinery

Throughout the nineteenth century, politicians, religious leaders, and literary authors celebrated the expanded educational opportunities for women and the working classes in Britain. Yet a persistent tradition of writers tells a dramatically different story. This book captures an overlooked chapter in the history of thought about education in which literary authors remind us of the value in learning outside of schools. Jane Austen, Elizabeth Barrett Browning, Thomas Hardy, and George Gissing were all excluded from elite universities because of their class or gender.[1] Their position as outsiders and their intimate knowledge of Oxford and Cambridge through brothers, fathers, and friends gave them a unique perspective from which to critique existing institutions. This study tells the story of how these writers—these "educational outliers"—imagined alternatives to educational systems. Whereas most schools focused on only one class or gender, these authors experimented with pedagogical approaches that could be universally accessible. Barrett Browning's "novel-poem" *Aurora Leigh* (1856), for instance, explores the idea that the working-class Marian Erle, who learns to read by piecing together fragmentary texts "toss[ed]" to her by a "pedlar," can adopt an experiential pedagogy like that of the privileged-class Aurora (III.972, 969). Educational outliers also satirize pedagogies of rote memorization, which they identify in schools for the masses as well as in universities for the elite, offering instead new strategies to open students' minds. In *Tess of the D'Urbervilles* (1891), for example, Hardy describes the "mental limitations" of Angel's Cambridge-educated brothers in mocking them as "such unimpeachable models as are turned out yearly by the lathe of systematic tuition," and he explores a model of autodidacticism instead (156). Departing from institutional learning that can prevent people like Angel's brothers from associating with "persons who were neither University men nor churchmen," the writers in this book stress the cultivation of empathy as an essential component of broader reform (156).

What sets educational outliers apart from other writers who critique institutional learning is that they envision going outside of institutions.[2] They imagine what it would be like to abandon existing educational models by "unteaching," that is, the act of educating with the specific aim of dismantling habits commonly learned in schools. These writers attempt to undo the modes of reading and learning with which nineteenth-century readers were often inculcated by educational institutions.

Educational outliers "unteach" in two different ways. Austen and Barrett Browning write in a style that encourages readers to let go of their reliance on widespread approaches to reading. Hardy and Gissing depict specific characters who realize they need to "obliterate" what they have been previously taught (Hardy, *Tess of the D'Urbervilles* 116). By calling attention to our own habits of reading and absorbing knowledge, educational outliers help us grasp the ways we expand our minds to think imaginatively. They also show the danger of shutting off this potential. In doing so, they investigate the role literature plays in unteaching readers.

The radicalism of these authors becomes clear when we read them alongside the rhetoric of nineteenth-century educational discourse, which relies relentlessly on the metaphor of educational systems as machines that eliminate the possibility of students' imaginative thinking. In order to demonstrate the extraordinary pervasiveness of this rhetoric, this study considers not only educational writings but also workingmen's club reports, university examinations, parliamentary debates, student guides, and college newspapers. Given the preoccupation with education as a subject of debate in the nineteenth century, it is surprising that more scholars of nineteenth-century Britain have not explored the ramifications of educational reform on the period's literature.[3]

The authors at the heart of this book concern themselves with education on many levels of schooling. This study focuses on their explicit critiques of elite secondary and university education, encapsulated by "Oxbridge," because that is where these authors register most sharply the manifestations of a system that reinforces class, gender, and racial biases. The term "Oxbridge" was originally used in nineteenth-century literature to describe a fictional university, but starting in the twentieth century, it became more broadly used to discuss the unique education offered by Oxford and Cambridge as distinguished from that of other universities (*OED*). It often becomes difficult for writers to critique Oxbridge without also faulting the newer schools that have emulated the older system's emphasis on examinations. In the chapters that follow, the authors' critiques of specific Oxbridge schools as well as educational reform more generally become inextricably linked. Their work demonstrates the spectrum of literary writers' engagement with education reform. Barrett Browning's ideas, for instance, inspired interest in nineteenth-century supporters of women's education such as Barbara Leigh Smith Bodichon and Clara Collet (Dalley 538–9). *The Times Educational Supplement* lists Hardy—rather ironically, but tellingly nonetheless—as a member of "the Provisional Committee to further University Education in the South-West" (400).

Stepping Outside of School

Educational outliers offer insight that can only come from outsiders. Scholar-educators today face challenges when thinking critically about institutions in part because they cannot easily adopt the position of an outsider. The authors discussed in this project are poised for educational innovation because they occupy a position outside of the academy. They call attention to the habits of academics within institutions.[4] Recent studies of the history of reading—particularly reading in the nineteenth century—have urged literary scholars to become attuned to their professional investment in their own reading practices (Best & Marcus; Price; Dames 2011). These studies encourage academics to evaluate their own institutionally rewarded modes of encountering texts. Much like these scholars on reading, the nineteenth-century authors discussed in this book attempt to make the academic practices ingrained in educational institutions more transparent.

Almost all of the authors in this study condemn the classism that institutional approaches to learning perpetuate on a visible or invisible level. These writers critique an Oxbridge education that honors students who display most prominently what Pierre Bourdieu would call "ease" (Bourdieu 21). Bourdieu highlights the class biases enabled by universities that congratulate privileged students. Though one may enter an elite college, one's earlier educational background never really becomes irrelevant. He analyzes obituaries of professors, noting that those who originated from lower classes are described not in terms of intellect or brilliance but in terms of the intense labor they had to complete in order to become successful (46–7). Even self-evaluations by professors, Bourdieu notes, echo this pattern. When professors talk about "ease" or "natural" talent, he says, they are really referring to the "particular mode of acquisition" (21). What we call "ease," Bourdieu reminds us, is privilege. Those who grew up with academic culture in their family—for whom this is the native culture—feel more at ease. Bourdieu's ideas are useful for analyzing the work of writers who criticize schools that promote a curriculum reflecting the goals and cultural values of the privileged classes. The chapters that follow show that by establishing a personal connection with the material they learn, educational outliers try to counteract the detached ease of Oxbridge students operating as part of an academic "machine."

The Age of Machinery

Witnessing the proliferation of schools on the elementary, secondary, and higher education levels throughout the nineteenth century, educational outliers register the alarming mechanization of education. In his 1829 "Signs of the Times," Thomas Carlyle echoes Jane Austen's work and foresees the later critiques by Elizabeth Barrett Browning, Thomas Hardy, and George Gissing. He discusses how the "Age of Machinery" has impersonalized and systematized even the "internal and spiritual" aspects of life: "everything has its cunningly devised implements, its pre-established apparatus; it is not done by hand, but by machinery" (34, 35). The individual no longer controls her own thoughts; impersonal institutions dictate her thinking. Carlyle turns to the example of educational systems, alluding to Joseph Lancaster, who promoted the monitorial system as a way to streamline education for the masses: "thus we have machines for Education: Lancastrian machines; Hamiltonian machines; monitors, maps, and emblems" (35).[5] Carlyle satirizes England's approach to education as something that happens outside of oneself, set apart from the individual. His characterization of education in terms of industrial machinery anticipates the many reprises of schools as machines later in the century.

4   *Educational Machinery*

Throughout the nineteenth century, we observe the attempt to recover what Carlyle had earlier warned would be lost. He describes the state of education in his time:

> Instruction, that mysterious communing of Wisdom with Ignorance, is no longer an indefinable tentative process, requiring a study of individual aptitudes, and a perpetual variation of means and methods, to attain the same end; but a secure, universal, straightforward business, to be conducted in the gross, by proper mechanism, with such intellect as comes to hand.
>
> (35)

In Carlyle, we notice skepticism toward the current brand of institutional learning. Carlyle suggests that by accepting the new systems of mass education, society loses an "indefinable tentative process" focused on "individual aptitudes" with varied "means and methods." Under the new one-size-fits-all model, students lose an opportunity to explore ideas using their own unique learning styles. They no longer have a chance to experience education on a personal level. Many of the authors considered in this study use their outsider status from institutions to recover in their writing the approaches that Carlyle mourns as lost. Whereas subsequent chapters focus on literary writers outside of schools who critique the widespread standardization and reliance on rote memorization, this chapter reveals that a similar movement took shape within new and old educational institutions.

Literature That Unteaches Readers

The authors discussed here are part of a broad tradition of nineteenth-century literature responding to institutional education. By the early nineteenth century, a debate was already brewing between advocates of Romantic self-education such as Jean-Jacques Rousseau and William Wordsworth and reformers in favor of fact-based education including Patrick Colquhoun, author of *A New and Appropriate System of Education for the Labouring People* (1806), Andrew Bell, Joseph Lancaster, and, in the second half of the century, Robert Lowe.[6] From as early as Romantic writers such as Jean-Jacques Rousseau and William Wordsworth, we see how authors imagine ways literature can unteach their readers. Rousseau's Émile learns from experience that he gains apart from books, and Wordsworth's speaker in "The Tables Turned" (1798) resists a pedantic focus on books, emphasizing experiential education instead. He cries, "Up! up! And Quit your Books," making the suggestion to "Let Nature be your teacher" (Wordsworth, "Tables Turned" 1, 16). Wordsworth incites readers to consciously work against the modes of learning in which they have been trained. In *The Prelude* (1850; first version 1805), he went on to explore experiential education in more detail. Like Wordsworth, who invites us to "quit" the ways in which we have been taught, later writers recount experiences that have helped them dismantle their academic modes of reading. For example, Wordsworth's poetry has the effect of unteaching John Stuart Mill, prompting him to let go of the habits of analysis that stand in the way of cultivating his emotional life.

Numerous authors recall negative encounters with institutional education, recounting experiences that constrict their minds. Writing as insiders within ancient universities, Cambridge-educated Alfred Lord Tennyson and Oxford-educated Matthew Arnold complain about the stifling effects of their university education. In an 1828 letter to his aunt, Tennyson writes about the lack of inspiration he feels as a student at Cambridge:

> I am sitting Owl-like and solitary in my rooms (nothing between me and the stars but a stratum of tiles) the hoof of the steed, the roll of the wheel the shouts of drunken Gown and drunken Town come up from below with a sea-like murmur. . . . [author's ellipsis] I know not how it is but I feel isolated here in the midst of society. The country is so disgustingly level, the revelry of the place so monotonous, the studies of the University so uninteresting, so much matter of fact—none but dryheaded calculating angular little gentlemen can take much delight in [Logarithms] . . .
>
> (22–3)

In the midst of an academic community, Tennyson feels isolated from his "dryheaded" classmates. This isolation discourages him instead of inspiring him to develop his intellectual independence.

Arnold laments the lack of his generation's creative potential in "The Buried Life" (1852): "But hardly have we, for one little hour, / Been on our own line, have we been ourselves—/" (59–60). Having received an extensive classical education from a very young age as the son of Rugby School's headmaster, Arnold expresses the burden he feels from previous traditions of knowledge. In "The Scholar-Gipsy" (1853), Arnold paints a portrait of modern society as diseased, describing "its heads o'ertax'd" and the "strong . . . infection of our mental strife" (205, 222). He adapts a seventeenth-century "story of the Oxford scholar poor, / Of pregnant parts and quick inventive brain, / Who, tired of knocking at preferment's door" left the university to "learn the gipsy-lore" with that "wild brotherhood" (33–5, 37, 38). Arnold capitalizes on this story that takes as its starting point the unfortunate situation of needing to leave Oxford because of financial circumstances and uses it to imagine what one would learn if one abandoned Oxbridge altogether. In "Stanzas from the Grande Chartreuse" (1855), the speaker describes how his education constrained his potential: "For rigorous teachers seized my youth, / And purged its faith, and trimm'd its fire" (67–8). Arnold has received an education of "trimming" and "purging." His schooling has robbed him of something.

In order to arrive at their individual revelations, John Stuart Mill and John Henry Newman both needed to step outside their trained academic modes of thinking. They turned to literature, which had the effect of unteaching what they had been previously taught. In his *Autobiography* (1873), when Mill describes the period of his breakdown, he recounts how he read "accidentally, Marmontel's 'Mémoires,' and came to the passage which relates his [Marmontel's] father's death" (99). He continues, "a vivid conception of the scene and its feelings came over me, and I was moved to tears. From this moment my burthen grew lighter. The oppression of the thought that all feeling was dead within me, was gone. I was no longer hopeless . . ." (99). Mill's "accidental" reading, so very different from the prescribed reading by his father, lets him break free from the constraints imposed on him by academic training. Through this new type of reading, he can connect intellect with emotion. Just before this passage describing his accidental reading, Mill recounts the kind of thinking to which he had grown accustomed: "I went on with them [his usual occupations] mechanically, by the mere force of habit. I had been so drilled in a certain sort of mental exercise, that I could still carry it on when all the spirit had gone out of it" (98). The intellectual exercises he describes carry the air of mechanical rote learning and thinking. His language is that of a detached student, fueled merely by "habit," as a result of "drilling." By reminding us of the ways in which his mind had been trained—just before relaying his discovery of accidental reading—he juxtaposes these two modes of reading. This juxtaposition reappears in every chapter of this book: accidental reading that is affective and self-directed versus academic modes of reading and thinking that involve rote learning, memorizing, cramming, and feeling detached from what one reads.

Mill ultimately turns to poetry—to Wordsworth—which has the effect of unteaching him. "I took up the collection of his poems from curiosity, with no expectation of mental relief from it, though I had before resorted to poetry with that hope," he describes (103). Mill finds in Wordsworth's poems a "medicine for [his] state of mind" because "they expressed, not mere outward beauty, but states of feeling, and of thought colored by feeling, under the excitement of beauty. They seemed to be the very culture of the feelings, which I was in quest of" (104). It is through poetry that Mill experiences a deeply personal relationship to a text—he is able to combine thought and feeling.

Newman recounts his own transformative reading; he describes how his reading of the *Monophysites* and the *Arian History* haunt him, pushing him further toward conversion to Catholicism. He arrives at this revelation also by accident: "Wonderful that this should come upon me! I had not sought it out; I was reading and writing in my own line of study" (114). Two great minds of the nineteenth century achieved intellectual, personal, and spiritual growth by allowing themselves to veer off from their formal training. These discoveries came from unteaching through accidental reading—a moment of exploratory self-education not rewarded by universities.

The idea of accidental reading resurfaces throughout the nineteenth century at a time when many leaders sought to make learning more standardized. While reading was often associated with physical and emotional feeling, formal institutions of learning sought to separate students and keep them at a distance from texts (and the intellectual traditions they embody).[7] Academically trained men like Newman and Mill needed to remove themselves, even momentarily, from their formal training in order to have this physiological or emotional connection with the text. Men who were trained at elite universities or through extensive tutoring were very much aware of the expectations they faced. The structure of Oxbridge in particular, as I discuss, left little room for deviating from the examination-driven curriculum and little room for reading freely—for being attuned to the *effect* of the text on themselves. Mill and Newman stress how the lack of standardization afforded to them in moments of exploratory self-study allowed them to have individual moments of intellectual contemplation. They define accidental reading in direct contrast to academic modes. What Newman's accidental reading allows him—to pursue his "own line of study"—is exactly what Arnold laments that he has missed as part of his institutional education when he says "hardly have we . . . / Been on our own line" (114, 59–60). The idea of accidental reading preserves what is lost amidst the increasingly mechanized systems of education.[8]

If we think about Carlyle's idea that learning should be an indefinable, tentative process, the idea of accidental reading allows for a space where learning is not clearly prescribed. It is more in tune with a physiological, empathic reading than the kind of rote learning that authors critique. Amidst education reform that often used literary texts to reinforce the class system and to perpetuate an elite intellectual tradition, some writers imagined literature as a means of breaking out of these models.

Educational Machinery for the Masses

What were the institutional approaches that Arnold lamented? They often resembled the methods of learning that were discussed publicly in relation to "educational machinery" for the working classes, which will be discussed over the next few pages before turning to an analysis of the rhetoric emerging from Oxbridge. The authors studied react to the focus on rote learning in both elite universities and working-class schools, and they emphasize the similarities in pedagogy. Educators relied on rote memorization of facts because it ensured that working-class students acquired just enough literacy to be useful but not enough to alter the existing class structure. As a result, teachers often did not transform minds or spark students' imaginations. It was not uncommon for students to memorize out loud one book for the entire year in preparation for a standardized test (Altick 156–8).[9] As Richard Altick notes, "The best child (assuming he was not struck mute on examination day) was the one who had memorized the whole book" (157). Charles Dickens's *Hard Times* (1854) famously satirizes an education devoted to memorizing facts in Mr. M'Choakumchild's schoolroom: "Now, what I want is, Facts. Teach these boys and girls nothing but Facts. Facts alone are wanted in life. Plant nothing else, and root out everything else" (5).[10] Parliamentary debates, government reports, and educational pamphlets confirm that Dickens's satirical depictions of schoolrooms in novels including *Hard Times*, *Nicholas Nickleby* (1838), and *Our Mutual Friend* (1864) were not far from the truth of the educational situation for the working classes. Schools focused even more tightly on rote learning once Robert Lowe introduced the Revised Code in 1862, which established that schools would receive a government grant based on the number of students who passed an examination in reading, writing, and arithmetic (Parry). Lowe summarized his plan for parliament as "that which is called payment by results, on a strict examination of children grouped according to age, the payments depending on that examination, and on nothing else" (*Hansard*, House of Commons, 5 May 1862, column 1268).

8   *Educational Machinery*

Matthew Arnold, Inspector of Schools as well as an insider of elite school culture, often criticized the "payment by results" as embodied in the Revised Code. In his "General Report for the Year 1867," he writes:

> In a country where everyone is prone to rely too much on mechanical processes and too little on intelligence, a change in the Education Department's regulations, which, by making two-thirds of the Government grant depend upon a mechanical examination, inevitably gives a mechanical turn to the school teaching, a mechanical turn to the inspection, is and must be trying to the intellectual life of a school . . .
>
> (Maclure 81)

Arnold laments the reliance on "mechanical processes," blaming this at least in part on government regulations. He sets this mechanization—the "mechanical turn to the school teaching"—in opposition to the "intellectual life of the school." He suggests that teachers have figured out ways to prepare their students to pass examinations in grammar, geography, and history "without their really knowing any one of these three matters" in what he calls "the game of mechanical contrivances" (Maclure 81). What does Arnold suggest that schools need at this point in the century? He calls for "more free play for the inspector, and more free play, in consequence, for the teacher" (Maclure 81). Arnold echoes Carlyle's thoughts several decades earlier that the learning process has become increasingly mechanized.

By midcentury, the rhetoric of educational machinery was commonly used to describe the project of educating the masses. Drawing upon one of the established definitions of the word "machinery"—in use since the eighteenth century to refer to a large system—politicians and education reformers used it, not surprisingly, to talk about a new universal system of education (*OED*). But leaders also used the word "machinery" to refer to children as if they were industrial machines. What often underlay politicians' and educational leaders' rhetoric of educational "machinery," then, was the desire to control the education of the working classes as cogs of a larger factory-like machine by depending on pedagogies of rote learning.

Many believed that working-class students should be taught just enough to keep them out of public houses.[11] Parliamentary debates about mass education in the second half of the century returned repeatedly to discussions of "educational machinery" and students as "machines," often in support of the expansion of elementary education for the working classes (*Hansard*, House of Commons, 25 June 1857, column 409; 6 June 1890, column 186). This rhetoric was adopted by Oxbridge as well, as discussed later in the chapter. The extent to which this rhetoric was employed implies the overwhelming focus on educational apparatuses—on external devices and systems that drive learning—instead of on the learning processes of individuals.

A quotation from the *Proposed National Arrangements for Primary Education* (1870) exemplifies the fear many felt in providing education for the masses, especially as they witnessed the proliferation of educational "machines": "The masses will certainly use their power in the great changes which are rapidly coming upon the country, and unless intelligence guides their energy and strength, the results may be disastrous to the nation at large, as well as to class interests and privileged orders" (quoted in Hurt 68). This passage indicates the trepidation many felt about what the "masses" might do with their education and how they could threaten existing national systems. It also reminds us that fear must have often driven those who determined the curriculum and pedagogy for the working classes. Members of Parliament as well as many educators felt that the spread of knowledge needed to be highly controlled.

Colleges founded for the working classes sparked debates about whether or not members of the lower classes should gain access to a college education at all and if so, what they should study. At the forefront of these debates were the Working Men's College, founded in 1854 by a group of Christian socialists including Frederick Denison Maurice and Thomas Hughes, and the University Extension movement, sponsored by the University of Oxford starting in 1878, which made lectures available to working-class students in towns and cities throughout England.

Some also feared the effects of allowing women access to higher education, but proponents of women's education reform typically did not question established institutional models any more than supporters of working-class education did. The founding of Girton College in 1869, the first women's college at Cambridge, took place in the larger context of debates about women's education throughout the century. Both Austen and Barrett Browning criticize learning methods for middle-class girls that rely on the transfer of existing schools for men to educational institutions for women, as well as the learning approaches that emphasize the acquisition of frivolous accomplishments. *Mansfield Park*'s Fanny, for example, encounters the latter pedagogical model when she goes to live with her wealthy relatives; her cousins have learned just enough to compete on the marriage market by memorizing disjointed information such as the "principal rivers in Russia" (Austen 15). In the 1860s, roughly a decade after Barrett Browning's satire of accomplishments in *Aurora Leigh*, the Schools Inquiry Commission addressed the superficiality of girls' education. Educationists such as Emily Davies, the founder of Girton College; Dorothea Beale, leader of Cheltenham Ladies College; and Frances Buss, who directed the North London Collegiate School for Ladies, were all involved in the Commission.[12]

While women's education was being taken more seriously in some quarters, others expressed concerns about the detrimental effects of studying on women's minds and overall health. Even advocates of women's education like Charles Dodgson, who tutored girls and captured the imaginative capacity of women in his writing, were ambivalent about women entering the Oxbridge system.[13] In an 1885 response to a mother's letter regarding the education of her daughter, he expresses concern that the girl "*does* work too hard," in preparation for university training, "and is in danger of defeating her own object" (564). "If there is one subject less adapted than another to be got up by 'cram,'" he writes, "it is Mathematics" (564). Commenting on the girl's efforts to "cram," he adds: "I am no great advocate for *regular* work—i.e. so many hours a day all the year round. I believe in periods of *intense* work followed by periods of *perfect* idleness: I think your daughter needs to be driven to the latter more than the former!" (565). Whether or not Dodgson advised against "cramming" her mathematics in preparation for college, the girl in question would have undoubtedly needed to adopt a mode of "cramming" upon entering Girton or Somerville because of Oxbridge's emphasis on examinations.

Oxbridge Machinery

Although standardization and rote learning were often discussed publicly in relation to educational machinery for the working classes, writings and records reveal that much of a student's life at Oxford or Cambridge was shaped by similar pedagogical practices. This book analyzes writings and sources related to Oxbridge education in order to uncover what someone like Matthew Arnold tried to abandon from his studies. The authors discussed in later chapters were familiar with the curriculum and pedagogy of elite universities, and in some cases reacted directly to them. Oxford and Cambridge shared many similarities in nineteenth-century Britain as well as some differences. This book focuses on Oxford, the basis of Jude's fictionalized Christminster in Hardy's novel, because public debates about reform—particularly examination reform—seemed to emerge more forcefully from Oxford than from Cambridge.

Pedagogies of rote learning prevalent at Oxford produced students who often felt distant from the texts in front of them and from the previous intellectual traditions that the texts embodied. Although this detachment obviously was not the case for every student who passed through the halls of Oxford and Cambridge, the evidence of rote learning and the subculture of students' resistance to it helps explain the turn towards alternative forms of learning by both university-trained intellectuals and autodidacts.

Universities and secondary schools for privileged men remained extremely influential in terms of shaping curriculum and pedagogy in new schools for women and the working classes.[14] In the midst of national reform, centuries-old schools stood poised on the brink of innovation, but they usually reinforced the idea of educational systems as machines. Despite the backdrop of seismic shifts in England's educational system, little changed within existing universities, particularly at Oxford. As one historian points out, "the only significant change" in the content of the "Responsion" examination—the first examination in the Oxford student's career—between 1808 and 1914 was that "after 1850 elementary mathematics was required from all candidates in place of logic" (M.C. Curthoys 356). Required divinity study remained present until 1930.[15] During a time when new populations of students joined the ranks of the educated, Oxbridge schools adhered to pedagogical traditions, missing out on the opportunity to capitalize on ideas from fresh students.

The required extensive preparation in Greek and Latin eliminated many applicants and helped ensure that for most students like Hardy's Jude who could not afford extensive training in classical languages, Oxford remained a place to be viewed only as a "gorgeous city" from afar (20). Before having even arrived at Oxford, the undergraduate would most likely have had to "show knowledge of certain Greek and Latin texts, be 'well grounded' in Greek and Latin grammar, translate from English into Latin, and have some knowledge of geometry, arithmetic, and divinity" (Darwall-Smith, *A History of University College, Oxford* 354). Although some scholarships did exist for qualified male students, they were rare.

Since many of the writers discussed here were familiar with the educational experience of an Oxford student, it is important to get a general sense of the format and subjects studied in the nineteenth century. A student who enrolled at midcentury Oxford would have taken most of his courses by lectures, one-on-one tutorials, and small group tutorials. His education would have centered on the study of Latin and Greek. A student at Brasenose College during the years 1856–1858, for example, would have studied the following authors and texts:

Divinity: John, Luke, Matthew, Mark, Gospels, Acts
Greek: Homer, Herod, Plato, Sophocles, Ethics, Thucydides, Ajax, Birds and Clouds, Logic, Pinder [*sic*]
Latin: Virgil, Cicero, Juvenal, Livy, Aeneid, Annals, De Officiis, Horace, Georgics (Boardman)

Starting in 1850, students had the option of taking courses in the natural sciences and law and modern history, but in order to do so they first needed to demonstrate proficiency in the classics. Concrete details about specific classes and material that students studied remain nebulous because of the scattered records kept by individual teachers, students, and colleges. At nineteenth-century Oxford, course catalogues, syllabi, and transcripts did not exist. Much information is available about end-of-term examinations, but extensive research at the university as well as correspondence with individual archivists at Brasenose, Christ Church, University College, Magdalen, Corpus Christi, and Balliol colleges at Oxford uncovered many gaps in our historical knowledge of what a typical day in the life of an Oxford student looked like (see information from Conway, Boardman, J. Curthoys, Darwall-Smith, Reid, and Sander).[16]

The 1852 Royal Commission of Oxford, which assessed the current practices and gave recommendations for Oxford's future in its Report, perhaps provides the most helpful insight into a student's learning experience. It is also a significant text because it sparked public dialogue about Oxford pedagogy; this is further evidence that the debate about university education was a public one, and that it is important to think about how authors were reacting to and engaging in this debate. From the Report we learn that a busy day in the life of an Oxford student in the 1850s might entail the student doing some private reading, attending a meeting with a college tutor, perhaps going to a meeting with a private tutor, and attending a lecture by a university professor. The College tutorials, which sometimes resembled what we might today consider to be lectures, accounted for most of the student's education (Oxford University Commission 86). In the tutorial, the tutor would often point out the important parts of a text and employ a catechetical, question-and-answer style of teaching.

In *Pass and Class, An Oxford guide-book through the courses of literae humaniores, mathematics, natural science, and law and modern history* (1861), written nine years after the Commission's Report, Montagu Burrows offered insight into the question-and-answer pedagogy of the college tutorial system:

> The general system of these lectures may be described as that of reading through the principal books of the course, (chiefly the Greek and Latin ones), chapter by chapter, book by book, the men construing in turns, the Tutor correcting, questioning, and illustrating. This may sometimes be varied by the Tutor taking a subject as a whole, and lecturing upon it more or less catechetically . . .
>
> (49–50)

Although the "lectures" with tutors that Montagu Burrows describes differed in degree from lessons in schoolrooms for working-class students, their catechetical, rote question-and-answer format shared a passive reliance on protocol and on testing. Oxbridge's emphasis on examinations resembled the weight given to testing in schools for the working classes, especially following the Revised Code of 1862. Burrows encouraged students to rely on the "machinery of University teaching," adopting the rhetoric of educational machinery to an Oxford setting (121).

Although the Royal Commission cast the catechetical question-and-answer method as an acceptable pedagogy, the Report alluded to the ineffectiveness of this method in generating original thinking. A student might excel on an examination if asked to translate a passage he has memorized, but often "the same youth, if required to translate off-hand a passage of common Greek which he has never seen before, commits great errors, and also shows by his translations of English into Latin and Greek that he has a very imperfect acquaintance with the principles of language" (Oxford University Commission 75). Students performed well, the Report implied, if they were evaluated on memorized material, but when they needed to rely on their own thinking and their own translation skills, the results could be poor. Despite some criticism, actual reform regarding pedagogy at Oxford was scarce. The alterations that were carried out focused on delivering traditional curriculum more effectively through existing methods.[17]

Exams and Cram at Oxbridge

From the beginning to the end of the nineteenth century, examinations occupied the central position in any undergraduate's Oxbridge education, resembling the emphasis placed on examinations in educational programs for the working classes.[18] The literary writers in this book reacted strongly to the centrality of examinations in institutional education. The focus on examinations forced students to learn in ways that allowed them to excel on tests; for most students, this meant memorizing and cramming. It is significant that *Examination Statutes* became the most important publication for students and faculty of the university in the nineteenth century.[19] Not completely unlike the contemporary course catalogues at American universities today, the *Examination Statutes* listed all requirements for examinations, degree courses, and recommended reading. *Examination Statutes* encouraged what we would now call teaching to the test, offering much detail pertaining to testable material. Instead of describing a course, they outlined examination content.

Examinations often tested information that could be easily memorized, as the following examples show:

1852

1. Give a map of Palestine, shewing its divisions at the time of our Saviour, and the situations of the principal places.
2. Give, in order, the leading events of our Saviour's life.

Historical

3. Give an account of the Samian War.
4. The policy pursued by Sparta from the battle of Aegos Potami to Leuctra.
5. The battle of Chaeronea.

1853

6. Trace the principal rivers of Europe, distinguishing those known in ancient geography.

1874

7. Describe the principal military routes from Italy into Gaul and Germany.[20]

These questions do not encourage critical thinking. Instead they reward students for memorizing facts and geography like the "principal rivers of Europe." Although factual information can be a necessary starting point for critical thinking, the examinations did not assess students in the latter.

The Royal Commission provides multiple accounts of the ways in which the examination system rewarded students for cramming instead of cultivating their intellectual curiosity. Professor J.M. Wilson remarked in the Report that "in order to distinguish between the Candidates, the Examiner is driven to ask questions out of the obscurer corners (so to speak) of the book; and the matter lurking in these corners is always the least valuable part" (Oxford University Commission 82). Private Tutors that are often employed by students consequently make these obscure passages the subject of their lessons, "handed down from Tutor to Tutor" (82). Wilson noted, "I have often found with great regret that the number of attendants on my Lecture in the Ethics is almost doubled, as I approach the analysis of the more technical and obscure passages of the work, which I know to be useless, or nearly useless, to the Student" (82).

The weight placed on examinations at Oxford created a test preparation industry resembling the one that exists today, including published practice examinations and cramming devices like the modern-day "Spark Notes." Students could purchase copies of examination papers and practice questions in books such as the 1856 *Examination Papers: Consisting of Passages selected from Greek and*

Latin Authors, Prose and Verse; with Questions on the Subject-Matter, History, Grammar &c. In addition, satirical writings by students and alumni, recounting experiences with rote learning, cramming, and test-taking, became very popular.

Critiques of Cram, Echoes of Educational Machinery

As the Royal Commission Report shows, the negative effects of the emphasis on examinations did not go completely unacknowledged; the authors studied here were in fact part of a larger movement of resisting pedagogies at elite universities. Through the writings of students and alumni of Oxbridge schools, we hear how detached they feel from the texts assigned to them and from the information they memorize for examinations.[21]

Those who attended Oxbridge sometimes resented the education they received for shutting down their independent thinking. For some, the education afforded them at Oxbridge sealed them off from the rest of society, at a time when that society was shifting radically and classes were increasingly mingled in urban areas. At the same time, the writings from male students at England's most elite universities show that at these schools, students felt that they were taught to memorize and cram facts—much like their counterparts in mass education schools set up to control the working classes. Ultimately I situate these student writings in the context of the larger cultural movement of resistance to dominant pedagogies that I am tracing throughout the nineteenth century.

One of the most popular writings of students and alumni that reflected the discontent with Oxbridge learning was a satirical treatise on how to "pluck," or fail, an exam. The preoccupation with testing became the subject of satire in the popular *A New Art Teaching How to Be Plucked, Being A Treatise after The Fashion of Aristotle; Writ for The Use of Students in The Universities* (1835), alternatively titled *The Art of Pluck*, by Scriblerus Redivivus, or, Edward Caswall. The first edition sold out in six days.[22] Instead of providing a guide for success, like that of Burrows, Caswall instructs students in how to fail an examination. He explains that "a man is said to be plucked from analogy to a bird. . . . The like analogy as a further proof is to be noted betwixt a man and a bird, not only at his Pluck, but also before and after; for he is said to be crammed first, and to have been well roasted by the examiner afterward" (vii–viii). Caswall joins the persistent dialogue about "cram" that runs throughout the century, and outlines the "art of plucking" in individual subjects.[23] He pays close attention to history because of its emphasis on facts and dates:

> In the reading of History for Pluck, let each be mindful to consider of chronology, as of a separate thing not to be mixed up with history, for indeed history is of things, but chronology of times.
>
> (7)

> Likewise this other, that if a person remember not one particular event of history, the first that he calleth to mind will do in its stead. The same for names

also, as to put for Alcibiades, Heliogabalus; for Julius Caesar, Og the King of Basan.

(8)

The Art of Pluck pokes fun at the energy Oxford and Cambridge students invest in mastering facts and dates. The book's popularity testifies to the predominant culture of testing at elite universities—an approach to learning in which memorization disguises the bankruptcy of thought and imagination.

The 1877 *ABRACADABRA: A Fragment of University History* mocks the rote learning still found at Oxford later in the century as well as the pretense that there exist multiple modes of study there:

> The modes of question and answer which were adopted, when the test came into actual operation, were such as to give room for the exercise of various powers of mind, and to encourage considerable varieties in the modes of study.
>
> Sometimes it was studied straightforwards, each letter of the combination leading up to and involving the study of the following letter, thus
>
> A—B—R—A—C—A—D—A—B—R—A.
>
> This was known as the *a priori* or Progressive Method.
> Sometimes it had to be studied backwards, thus
>
> A—R—B—A—D—A—C—A—R—B—A.
>
> This was known as the *a posteriori* or Regressive Method.

(6)

Written 25 years after the Royal Commission, this satirical piece highlights the existence of the same method of learning for every student. Students inherit stale intellectual traditions, the writer emphasizes. The author criticizes the expectation that Oxford students should set out to learn only what others had learned before. He goes on to describe a young generation of dissatisfied Oxford students: "It was absurd, they said, for persons to be pensioned for life merely for showing that they knew what their fathers knew before them. In fact, knowledge was a will-o'-the-wisp; it never could be attained. What was wanted was not knowledge, but investigation" (13). Students want to investigate, to think for themselves, instead of memorizing information inherited from their forebears.[24]

Further solidifying the image of the Oxford student as a passive receptor of knowledge, the speaker of the poem "Juvenal in Oxford" (c. 1877) compares "the reading man" to a sheep who merely follows the rest of the flock:

> The reading man! Oh, what a broad conceit
> Of sheep who need a pitchfork ere they bleat!
> A motley crew of every shape and size,
> Sheep—but with pigtails, scholarship, or prize.
> Note well the ample gown, the classic pile
> Of ancient tomes, the supercilious smile.

(8)

16 *Educational Machinery*

The speaker suggests that an Oxford student needs the "pitchfork," or prodding from a tutor, and that he remains content to follow the rest of the scholarly flock. Despite how different they may appear outwardly, the sheep—or rather the students—remain the same. The author renders the trappings of an Oxford man—"scholarship," "prize," "gown," and so forth—ridiculous when he invites his reader to envision them on a sheep.

The first women's college students joined this broader critique of pedagogies prioritizing memorizing and mastering. Anna Lloyd, a student at Girton College, wrote in 1870: "We are being worked hard this term. Our classical Master in the matter of study has no heart. I do not believe in being crammed like a Dorking fowl. I like to brood over knowledge, until it becomes a part of the mind" (63). Rote learning held its grip on university pedagogy from the beginning to the end of the century, from *The Art of Pluck* to the writings of the first women's college students.

"Cramming" became the subject of a larger debate about Oxbridge as well as elementary schools in the 1870s, reflected in numerous periodical articles.[25] Despite some resistance, cramming remained a central part of a student's life at Oxford or Cambridge into the twentieth century. Examinations remained firmly rooted in Oxbridge culture—and in British culture more generally. The discussions of "cram" exemplify the fascinating shift that happened over the course of the nineteenth century. The reform movement for elementary education prompted elite universities to codify their conservative practices, which then become enshrined in new schools. As a result, when writers critique the system in Britain, they often challenge not just the Oxbridge system but also the offspring of this system: mass education schools, public schools, girls' schools, women's colleges, and working men's colleges.

Chapter Review

The goal of this book is to trace a tradition that emerged from outside of institutions at a time when an increasing number of people attended school. This story begins in the early nineteenth century, when debates about mass education and schools for women began, and it ends after the passing of important Education Acts by the end of the century. Each subsequent chapter unfolds chronologically and pauses at a crucial moment or debate in the nineteenth-century's history of education.

Chapter 2 situates Jane Austen's works in opposition to the two competing strains of thought regarding education for women at the time: the idea that women should be given a more orderly education resembling the institutional education for men—suggested in treatises by Mary Wollstonecraft and Hannah More—and the notion that women should be taught with the narrow goal to acquire information for show in order to ensure their success on the marriage market. These two predominant notions of women's education endanger a form of learning Austen appreciates, which she wittily calls "scrambling" (Austen, *Emma* 18). An education of "scrambling" allows for a self-directed process of learning resulting in the development of one's judgment. In her novels, her ironic narrator subtly unteaches her readers, encouraging them to enact their own "scrambling." Novels, for Austen, can provide an even more effective education than Oxbridge in developing one's judgment. I trace Austen's critique of dominant educational models as early as her *History of England* (1791). Turning to her brothers' satires of Oxford pedagogy in *The Loiterer* (see Appendix 1), the college magazine they founded and published from 1789 to 1790, Chapter 2 considers the influence of their writing on Austen's own depictions of learning—and the attempt to unteach readers—in *Pride and Prejudice* (1813), *Mansfield Park* (1814), *Emma* (1816), *Persuasion* (1818), and *Northanger Abbey* (1818).

By midcentury, conversations about schools and colleges for women had intensified. Chapter 3 examines Elizabeth Barrett Browning's engagement with these developments in *Aurora Leigh* (1856). Barrett Browning criticizes both the predominant girls' school education of "accomplishments," anticipating the Schools Inquiry Commission's criticism a few years later, and the prevalent pedagogies at Oxbridge (I.426). As an alternative, she models an experiential approach to learning for women of different classes centered on what she calls "headlong" reading (I.707). Aurora, Barrett Browning suggests, engages her own empathic, bodily reading of texts that translates to an openness to other people. Barrett Browning encourages her own readers to adopt a "headlong" reading, paving the way for reform within themselves.

Chapter 4 shifts the focus to the public debates over education for working-class men. Despite the expanded access to schools in the second half of the century, autodidact culture continued to thrive, as shown in materials such as the National Home Reading Union Summer Assembly program (see Appendix 3) and *The Popular Educator* (see Appendix 2), a periodical for individuals learning on their own. Chapter 4 discusses the writings of the autodidact community alongside fictional depictions of autodidacts in novels by Thomas Hardy such as *A Pair of Blue Eyes* (1873), *The Woodlanders* (1887), *Tess of the D'Urbervilles* (1891), and *Jude the Obscure* (1895). The largely self-taught Hardy analyzed the energy of autodidacts and feared their models of learning would disappear. By using administrators' records and university examiners' notes, Chapter 4 shows that Hardy's concern— that both old and new schools would ignore the qualities he sees in autodidacts— was historically grounded. Hardy tests out the idea that a Cambridge-educated clergyman's son might be better off rejecting an Oxbridge education; the privileged-class Angel in *Tess of the D'Urbervilles* declares, "I will do without Cambridge" (115). At a crucial moment in the history of education in Britain, Hardy explores what it would mean for British society to "do without Cambridge."

By the late nineteenth century, more educational opportunities for women and the working classes existed, and the tradition shifts, as we see in works by George Gissing—most notably *Thyrza* (1887) (see Appendix 4), and also in *New Grub Street* (1891). Chapter 5 offers a reading of Gissing in the context of the nineteenth-century genealogy, exploring his departure from the emphasis on the binary between those who can easily be identified as insiders of educational institutions and those who are clearly outsiders. Gissing's social vision overcomes this binary in his portrayal of a class of intellectuals who are neither inside nor outside of educational systems as a result of the democratization of education. I pay particular attention to the ways in which Gissing's experience as a student, tutor, and teacher in an American public school shape his exploration of the figure of Egremont in *Thyrza*, an Oxford-educated man who reads the poetry of Walt Whitman, which has the effect of prompting him to unlearn his trained academic habits.

The conclusion offers a reading of Virginia Woolf, who famously proclaimed herself an institutional outsider, even though, as Gissing's work reminds us, this figure becomes less easy to define by the end of the nineteenth century. The conclusion focuses on Woolf's depictions of the figure of the institutional outsider in her short story "A Woman's College from Outside" (1926), her unpublished "novel-essay" *The Pargiters*, written in the early 1930s, and *The Years* (1937). Alongside Woolf, the conclusion examines how one group, in the second half of the nineteenth century and early twentieth century, negotiated its position within universities that had formerly excluded them: the first students at Oxford and Cambridge women's colleges. Although many historians' accounts of these "bluestockings" exult in their admittance to universities, much student writing—including poetry, satire, and autobiography—echoes male students' critiques of rote learning at Oxbridge earlier in the century as well as those offered by literary authors. The first Oxbridge women's college students confirmed what novelists and poets imagined in their fictional accounts. They provide insight into the difficulty that historically excluded groups face in entering institutions that fail to capitalize on their unique models of learning.

Notes

1 Although Gissing had educational opportunities through scholarships early on, he remained very much aware of the difficulties facing him in pursuing an Oxbridge education.
2 Charlotte Brontë and George Eliot both criticize educational institutions, for example, but their critique focuses on the lack of adequate schooling for women, which is in line with Wollstonecraft's critique of the disorder in available models of learning—instead of imagining going outside of the system.
3 Although several book-length studies about authors' own educations and their educational ideas exist, such as D.D. Devlin's *Jane Austen and Education*, which discusses Locke's influence on Austen, and Sara Atwood's *Ruskin's Educational Ideals*, few book-length studies of nineteenth-century literature place multiple writers in the context of the educational discourse of their time. See Elizabeth Gargano's *Reading Victorian Schoolrooms: Childhood and Education in Nineteenth-Century Fiction*, which focuses on elementary and secondary school narratives, Laura Green's *Educating Women: Cultural Conflict and Victorian Literature*, and Cathy Shuman's *Pedagogical Economies: The Examination and the Victorian Literary Man* for excellent book-length works of scholarship on the intersections of literature and education in the nineteenth century. Whereas both Green and Shuman focus on one gender, this book offers a study of authors who had in common not one class or gender but their position outside of schools and their visions of alternative education.
4 In a review of what he labels "conservative manifestos" on higher education, Nicholas Dames talks about how works by Martha Nussbaum and Louis Menand maintain the

status quo rather than unveiling a radical future for education. Analyzing why these books tend to lean in this direction, he poses the question: "What if the most urgent, most brilliant work academies can produce comes from an obsession that, in part at least, is an obsession with the institution that makes such work possible?" (167). Professors' investment in universities may help them to produce brilliant scholarship, but this same "obsession" renders it difficult for insiders of universities to imagine a truly alternative vision of education.

5 The monitorial system, for which Joseph Lancaster (1778–1838) advocated, deflected the responsibility of the teacher onto pre-adolescent students to cover lessons of all different levels in the same classroom (Altick 144–6). James Hamilton (1769–1829) proposed a method of teaching languages without teaching grammar; students taught themselves by relying solely on English translations of foreign texts (Birch 156, note 14).

6 See Altick for a helpful discussion of Bell, Lancaster, and Colquhoun (144–6), and of Lowe (155–7).

7 Rachel Ablow notes that "an attention to the historical specificity of Victorian reading" often "returns us to the issues of physical and emotional feeling" (4).

8 During the nineteenth century, as the sciences established themselves within universities, scientists needed to practice a kind of accidental reading—or accidental learning—that allowed them to step outside of the institution and forge new discoveries. Charles Lyell wrote to Darwin: "Fancy exchanging Herschel at the Cape for Herschel as President of the Royal Society—which he so narrowly escaped being! . . . [author's ellipsis] Work exclusively for yourself and for science . . . [author's ellipsis] Do not prematurely incur the honour or penalty of official dignities" (quoted in Holmes 463). "Herschel at the Cape" represents the freedom of autodidacticism and the freedom captured in Newman and Mill's accidental reading, whereas "Herschel as President of the Royal Society" embodies the stifling effects of "learned bodies"—the obligation to work within inherited intellectual traditions, as Arnold bemoans.

9 Ginger S. Frost's *Victorian Childhoods* provides a helpful sketch of what a typical nineteenth-century classroom would have looked like (38–41). See Robson's *Heart Beats: Everyday Life and the Memorized Poem* for an exploration of some of the positive effects of rote memorization.

10 Whereas Dickens focuses on critiquing elementary and secondary schools for the masses, educational outliers focus their critiques on rote memorization in schools for the elite. Educational outliers, I argue, were shaped more by their exclusion specifically from Oxbridge than Dickens was, and they explore alternative educational approaches outside of institutions more persistently than Dickens does.

11 Others stressed more rigorous technical and scientific education in new universities. In his 1852 lecture for the Government School of Mines and of Science applied to the Arts titled "Technical Education on the Continent," Lyon Playfair analyzes the industrial education in continental European countries such as Germany, France, Belgium, and Denmark, urging England to adapt some of their pedagogical practices in order to compete in industry. Departing from the humanistic study that Matthew Arnold advocates in both *Culture and Anarchy* (1869) and "Literature and Science" (1882), Thomas Huxley calls for a new type of university in his 1868 address to students at the South London Working Men's College titled "A Liberal Education; and Where to Find It": "the best of our schools and the most complete of our university trainings give but a narrow, one-sided, and essentially illiberal education—while the worst give what is really next to no education at all. The South London Working-Men's College could not copy any of these institutions if it would; I am bold enough to express the conviction that it ought not if it could" (108).

12 See De Bellaigue (113). Buss's model was unique in that it offered schooling for women of any religious denomination or class (Coutts).

13 See Robson's "Reciting Alice: What Is the Use of a Book without Poems?" for a discussion of Dodgson's recasting of pedagogy emphasizing memorization as creativity in *Alice in Wonderland* (107). We can read Dodgson as someone who critiques the system by playing with it.
14 Even a popular novel such as Thomas Hughes's *Tom Brown's Schooldays* (1857), which tells the tale of a boy at Rugby School in the era of its legendary headmaster Thomas Arnold, exemplifies the far-reaching effect of exclusive school culture; the readership extended far beyond schoolboys in elite schools, selling 28,000 copies in 1862 and went through 53 editions by 1892 (Mitchell).
15 Students who were not of the Anglican faith were able to be examined in "a miscellaneous selection of 'substituted matter'" after 1855 (M.C. Curthoys 357).
16 It is telling that the very thorough and insightful histories of Oxford, such as those by Evans and by Brock and Curthoys, give little detailed information about what specific texts students studied and what specific classes and tutorials they took.
17 See Rothblatt 164. Copleston, a tutor at Oriel, articulated a widely accepted idea that it was less crucial to cultivate a few talented students "exploring untrodden regions" than to ensure "an annual supply of men, whose minds are . . . impressed with what we hold to be the soundest principles of policy and religion" (quoted in Rothblatt 164).
18 Burrows provides an overview of the examinations an Oxford student was required to take in 1861:

   1. Responsions, commonly called 'Little go.'
   2. The First Public Examination, or Moderations.
   3. The Second Public Examination, First School, or First Final School, commonly called 'Great go.'
   4. The Second Public Examination, Second School, or Second Final School, distinguished by its particular subject, as Mathematical School, Law and Modern History School, or Natural Science School. (9)

19 In addition, a publication such as the 1873 *Student's Handbook to the University and Colleges of Oxford* was really more of a guide to examination requirements.
20 These examples are taken from examinations students took to obtain scholarships at Wadham College and Christ Church College; they were similar to questions given on university-wide examinations.
21 In giving a context for the critiques of exam culture, I focus on satirical writings that were distributed to the public as independent publications. Paul Deslandes has helpfully studied many college periodicals, noting that student writers often use the examination as a literary trope, which reminds us of the importance of the examinations as "rites of passage" in their lives (Deslandes 141, 152). Although it might be tempting to dismiss student writings about dissatisfied college experiences as complaints from disgruntled students, as Deslandes nearly does, I suggest that they help shape our understanding of rote learning at Oxbridge, especially given the surprisingly little concrete information we have about actual learning habits and pedagogies (152–3).
22 See note and preface to the second edition, which is included in the third edition.
23 The use of the word "to cram" in the sense "to fill quite full, overfill (with facts, knowledge, etc.)" was used as early as Shakespeare in *The Winter's Tale*: "Cram's with prayse, and make's As fat as tame things" (i.ii.93, *OED*). Cramming in terms of preparing a person "for an examination or special purpose, in a comparatively short time, by storing his memory with information, not so much with a view to real learning as to the temporary object aimed at" or "To 'get up' (a subject) hastily for an occasion, without any regard to its permanent retention or educative influence" came into more common usage in the nineteenth century (*OED*). These usages of "cram" are closely related to—and derived from—the definition of cram "to feed with excess of food (*spec.* poultry, etc., to fatten them for the table" (*OED*).

24 The narrator then goes on to satirize the premise of reform; university leaders get together and decide on nothing besides gaining more revenue (13).
25 The same year as Lloyd laments her cramming, Arnold writes a letter to the Editor of the *Pall Mall Gazette* and warns against spreading the focus on testing for fellowships: "The rivalry for fellowships is already the animating principle of our university education. When the Civil Service is entirely open to competition, we shall be, in fact, throwing a vast additional weight into the same scale and offering a similar incentive to schools of the lower grades" (*Letters* 440). Echoing Arnold, A.H. Sayce, fellow of Queen's College, Oxford, writes: "Originality, bold speculation, unremunerative study, are anthithetic to all the qualities fostered by an examination" (M.C. Curthoys 367). These comments follow the 1852 Royal Commission and the debates in the 1830s and 40s, already critical of the propensity of Oxford examinations to promote cram. See Shuman for an extensive discussion of the place of examination in British culture.

2 "Scrambling" into an Austen Education

We recall that by 1829, Thomas Carlyle was lamenting that "we have machines for Education" ("Signs of the Times" 35). He was nostalgic for "Instruction" as "an indefinable tentative process, requiring a study of individual aptitudes, and a perpetual variation of means and methods" (35). Fifteen years before Carlyle wrote "Signs of the Times," Austen anticipated the beginnings of what he refers to as the "machines" of education. She resisted the idea that women should be given a more orderly education resembling the institutional model for men as well as the notion that women should be taught with the narrow goal to acquire information for show in order to ensure their success on the marriage market. These models of learning prevented the kind of individualized process Carlyle describes.

Austen joined a conversation about education that was enlivened by Mary Wollstonecraft's call for equality in *A Vindication of the Rights of Woman* (1792):

> To do every thing in an orderly manner, is a most important precept, which women, who, generally speaking, receive only a disorderly kind of education, seldom attend to with that degree of exactness that men, who from their infancy are broken into method, observe.
>
> (Wollstonecraft 25)

Wollstonecraft, in criticizing the education commonly given to women in eighteenth-century Britain, claims that the problem lies in the *disorder* of women's education. A woman's education, Wollstonecraft argues, often lacks the order and "method" of a man's education. Austen takes this negative idea of a disorderly education and modifies it; she does not dismiss completely the benefits of the education Wollstonecraft describes but rather suggests that a successful learning approach may have an element of disorder, akin to Carlyle's "indefinable tentative process" (Carlyle 35). She rejects the idea that the gendered pedagogical models of elite schools for men should be transferred to schools for women. In *Mansfield Park* (1814), Austen also criticizes the kind of education that encourages the Bertram sisters' acquisition of "accomplishments" in order to achieve a socially successful marriage (364). This common model of women's education focuses too much on a narrow goal of garnering external polish for the marriage market instead of an inner transformation resulting in the cultivation of one's own judgment.

Taking into account the influence of her brothers' satirical writings about education in *The Loiterer* (1789–1790) on her own writing and educational ideas, this chapter analyzes Austen's critiques of these two strains of thought about women's education in her *History of England* (1791) and in her novels.

The two predominant notions of women's education in her time threatened a form of learning Austen valued. She explored a model of education that she cleverly calls "scrambling," which allows for a self-directed process of learning resulting in the development of one's judgment. An education of "scrambling" has the potential, for Austen, to take its students on an unconventional course of learning. The narrator of *Emma* (1816) describes Mrs. Goddard's school and its peculiarities—including its encouragement of "scrambling":

> Mrs. Goddard was the mistress of a School—not of a seminary, or an establishment, or any thing which professed, in long sentences of refined nonsense, to combine liberal acquirements with elegant morality upon new principles and new systems—and where young ladies for enormous pay might be screwed out of health and into vanity—but a real, honest, old-fashioned Boarding-school, where a reasonable quantity of accomplishments were sold at a reasonable price, and where girls might be sent to be out of the way and scramble themselves into a little education, without any danger of coming back prodigies.
>
> (18)

By using the verb "to scramble" to describe a type of learning, Austen suggests an acquisition of knowledge that is self-directed and hands-on. An education of "scrambling" relies on the student to make her own decisions instead of memorizing lessons assigned by an instructor. There is no way of determining exactly how and what one will learn at Mrs. Goddard's school. Austen analyzes the possibilities of a self-directed education of "scrambling" that can result in the development of one's judgment, as in the character of Fanny Price in *Mansfield Park*; she sets "scrambling" in opposition to the Bertram sisters' acquisition of memorized information for show. Fanny receives some guidance in her "scrambling" from her cousin Edmund Bertram and Emma Woodhouse from Mr. Knightley, but both female characters reap the benefits of their learning approach most fully when they learn to contemplate on their own.

I align Austen's use of the word "scrambling" with the definition of "to scramble": "to make one's way by clambering, crawling, jumping, etc. over difficult ground or through obstructions" (*Oxford English Dictionary*). Austen applies this word—often used at the time to describe a physical act—to education in order to emphasize the active qualities she values in a learning process that is, at least in part, self-directed.[1] Implicit in her use of the word is the reliance on oneself to forge a route; the "clambering" and "crawling" suggest an element of unpredictability because there exists no predetermined path. Austen values that unpredictability. By approaching education as a process of active self-discovery—one that combines fancy and judgment—students can focus on transforming themselves from within instead of congratulating themselves for acquiring the trappings of education noticeable only on the surface. Inherent in an education of "scrambling" is a process of learning that contributes to the development of what lies "within," as a result of honing one's judgment (*Mansfield Park* 364). Austen contrasts this "scrambling" with an education that emphasizes one fixed goal.

She does not then offer a simple treatise on women's education. In her novels, Austen subtly unteaches her readers through both plot and style, coaxing them away from oversimplified thinking about the process of learning. We see her depictions of learning as a "tentative process," as Carlyle describes it, which often leads to her heroines' development of judgment (35). We read and reread the passages describing Elizabeth Bennet making sense of Darcy's letter, for example, witnessing the formulation of her own thoughts about the letter and about Darcy (*Pride and Prejudice* 150–60). Austen puts her heroines in states of chaos in order to explore how one must rely on inward knowledge. She uses the novel form to work in the stages of reflection that result in becoming truly learned.

As active readers of her novels, we must rely on our own judgment to navigate the simplistic morals she gives us ironically. In this way, Austen uses her novels to unteach us as readers from reading passively, requiring us to "scramble" into a reading that tests our own judgment. Her ironic narrator never lets the reader rest. By repeatedly withholding information, for instance, Austen teaches us to read actively. In *Pride and Prejudice* (1813), we must first hear the townspeople's impressions of Mr. Darcy before he appears in the novel. Austen uses her irony to pull us away from expecting an authoritative treatise or work of sentimental fiction that leaves readers with a simplistic moral. Readers are often suspended, waiting to find out the solution the heroine will choose because she has realized—along with her readers—that there exists no "right" solution or easy way of finding it. This is a very different reading experience from that of reading a treatise; readers of treatises are rarely disrupted in their own thinking because they encounter straightforward arguments from the authoritative writer.

Hannah More's treatises on women's education, including *Essays on Various Subjects, Principally Designed for Young Ladies* (1777), *Strictures on the Modern System of Female Education* (1799), and *Hints Towards Forming the Character of a Young Princess* (1805), offer teachings that are hinged upon her ideals of the Christian woman.[2] By giving us ironic truths, Austen forms her narratives of education against authoritative, orderly proclamations about what a good education—and a good piece of writing—looks like. Unlike More and Wollstonecraft, she focuses her educational arguments for women on the premise that they should take advantage of their opportunity for a less methodical, less predictable education. Austen calls into question the educational ideals of her time, as well as the modes of conveying those ideals, including treatises and moralistic novels; she hints at a more tentative, less dogmatic approach to the experience of learning.

Although several studies have addressed the subject of education as a theme in Austen's works, none of them have explored the value that Austen places on learning outside of schools and how this shapes her conception of what a novel can do.[3] At a time when treatises on education—and women's education in particular—flooded the market, Austen offers antitreatises on women's education. We can better understand her novels as antitreatises by considering her early ironic writing on history; this writing requires readers to synthesize information instead of learning history sequentially to memorize facts and dates. Furthermore, Austen experiments with the novel as an even more effective form of education than Oxbridge. Novels can provide an education in developing one's judgment, Austen hints, in ways that Oxford and Cambridge cannot.

Austen's Oxbridge Connections

Austen's skepticism about institutional learning—and any model of formal education that purports to accomplish mastery of the individual—was undoubtedly influenced by her knowledge of the two dominant pedagogical institutions of her time: Oxford and Cambridge. Her ideas about education were informed by her intimate knowledge of these universities through her father, brothers, nephews, and family friends who attended these schools. The closest she ever came to being a student in Oxford was her experience at age seven as a pupil at Mrs. Cawley's Oxford school, which must have presented a peculiar learning experience for a young girl studying in the university town and led on tours of Oxford colleges that she would never be able to attend because of her gender (Honan 31). Although she could not enroll in schools such as Oxford, Cambridge, Eton, Rugby, or Winchester, she came into contact regularly with the culture of elite male pedagogies. In many of her letters, Austen mentions privileged schools and men who attend them, whether it is "J. Bridges," whom she writes in 1808 "left us for London in his way to Cambridge, where he is to take his Master's Degree" (Austen, *Letters* 142), or "Mr. W.," whom she describes in 1813 as an "easy, talking, pleasantish young Man" "of St. Johns, Cambridge" (Austen, *Letters* 207). These multiple references to elite male schools remind us of their presence in her life, even though she never experienced them as a student.

Austen writes frequently about her nephews and corresponded with them about their experiences at Winchester, Rugby, and Oxford. She mentions her nephew Edward "going to Rugby" in 1809 and her nephew George at Oxford in 1814 (Austen, *Letters* 179–80, 264). She corresponds with Edward about school; in an 1816 letter, for instance, she writes to him to "give [him] Joy of having left Winchester" (*Letters* 336). In an 1817 letter to Caroline Austen, she notes, "I hope Edwd is not idle. No matter what becomes of the Craven Exhibition [a kind of scholarship] provided he goes on with his Novel. In that, he will find his true fame & his true wealth. That will be the honourable Exhibition which no V. Chancellor can rob him of" (*Letters* 349). She adds, "I have just recd nearly twenty pounds myself on the 2d Edit: of S & S—which gives me this fine flow of Literary Ardour" (*Letters* 349). Austen ironically separates her nephew's literary aspirations from university aspirations. She suggests that his main concern should be on writing—not on scholarships or awards bestowed by a "V. Chancellor." Her letters reflect not only a wry awareness of the kinds of schools her male relatives attended; they also show her working through the positives and negatives of what Wollstonecraft would describe as a more orderly education.

In addition to learning about schools through conversations and letters, she read *The Loiterer*, a periodical published at Oxford by her brothers James and Henry from January 1789 to March 1790 in 60 issues (Honan 59).[4] Austen not only discovered more about Oxford from *The Loiterer*; she also undoubtedly learned something about satire and about writing ironically on education. All that she read about Oxford was certainly not positive. In the satires of Oxford men in *The Loiterer*, she would have learned about "The orators of the coffee-house, the jockies of Port-meadow, and the champions of the High-street" (8.7). In "Disadvantages arising from misconduct at Oxford, in a letter from H. Homely" (1789), the writer wants to warn others of his own Oxford experience:

> As I understand that your design is, by a weekly distribution of wit and advice, to amuse and instruct the University, of which I was once a member; and as I have already perceived that you have resolution enough to expose the vices and follies, which have sprung up in a soil so friendly to each, I hope that you will not despise the communications of one, who in a former part of his life has been a considerable sufferer from both.
>
> (8.3–4)

The writer gestures towards the irreverent tone of *The Loiterer*, telling us a little bit about the publication. He goes on to offer a tale pretending to have a moral for future Oxford men. At first, he felt "enchantment" (5) and was "the happiest man alive" (5), but soon he fell into a routine that doomed him: "morning was dissipated in doing nothing, and the evening in doing what was worse; the first part wasted in idleness, the latter drowned in intemperance" (6). By the time he took his degree he "was as ignorant as emaciated, and as much in debt as the first peer of the realm" (6). In this story that sets up the expectation of offering a warning or moral, we learn that there is no clear lesson.

The writer cautions Oxford readers against meeting a fate like his own, but the payoff of spending more time on his studies is unclear. If someone devotes all of his time to pursuing an Oxford education, what will he get from it? This question regarding the value of institutional education is left suspended in a number of articles in *The Loiterer*, and Austen picks it up in her novels. We see echoes of the ambivalence about the benefits of an Oxford education in Austen's satires of pedantic Oxford graduates such as the overbearing John Thorpe in *Northanger Abbey* (1818), who pompously declares his opinions on every subject—even the drinking habits of undergraduates (47). Throughout *Northanger Abbey* we see Catherine Morland developing her own judgment of other people, but we see little indication that the Oxford-educated characters such as Thorpe and James Morland do the same. Even though Catherine's brother James does not exhibit the harmful effects of his education in the more accentuated ways that Thorpe does, he displays little understanding of character; he cannot perceive the Thorpes' faults, referring to John Thorpe as "Poor Thorpe," and says of Isabella Thorpe after she has jilted him, "I can never expect to know such another woman!" (167). Austen suggests that these highly educated male characters have not gained insight into themselves or others.

In *The Loiterer*, Austen would have read satirical accounts of Oxbridge men as well as mock treatises. Her brothers' publication of mock educational treatises perhaps influenced her to consider the limitations of the treatise form and to capitalize on what the novel can do that a treatise cannot. Take for example the satirical treatise in *The Loiterer* titled "Thoughts on Education—A new System recommended" (1789). The author explains that he responds to "the attempt of many zealous writers, who have variously employed their pens on the subject of education" (27.158). He declares that he thinks "them all more zealous than successful, and more plausible than true" (158). The writer prescribes a good education that consists of "objects totally independent of thought and reflection" (162). When he describes education for girls, he writes that from her youth, a girl must "look forwards to matrimony, as the sole end of existence, and the sole means of happiness; and that the older, the richer, and the foolisher her husband is, the more enviable will be her situation" (162). "Having taught her this truth," the writer continues, "it will be easy to make her act accordingly" (162).[5] *The Loiterer* satirizes predominant educational ideas as well as the treatises that convey them. In her *History* and her novels, Austen depends on satirical "truths" to test her readers' own judgment. *Pride and Prejudice*, for example, begins with the now famous "truth": "It is a truth universally acknowledged, that a single man in possession of a good fortune, must be in want of a wife" (1).

Influenced by the ironical writing about education in *The Loiterer*, Austen uses irony in the narration of her novels to unteach readers. Unlike these mock treatises, however, she uses the novel form to hint at an alternative method of learning. She does not simply critique pedagogical models; she imagines substitutes for them. Whereas *The Loiterer* author hopes that his piece "will induce all the married part of them, to remove their sons from Winchester, Westminster, or Eton, and place them (with a salary of 200L per ann.) under the direction of the *Loiterer*," Austen actually imagines what a desirable education would look like as a substitute for Winchester or Eton (27.158). Her brothers prefer the form of a satirical treatise about education, but Austen explores the possibly transformative effects of a positive approach to learning in the interiority of her fictional characters. The novels she writes can serve as an education in themselves outside of institutions.

In addition to the Oxford pedagogy she learned about through her brothers, her own educational background—a mixture of scattered formal schooling and learning at home—frames her model of learning by "scrambling." After attending the strict Mrs. Cawley's school in Oxford, she later experienced a more lenient approach to learning at the Reading Ladies Boarding School. Austen no doubt had the headmistress Sarah Hackett (who went by the name of Mrs. Latournelle) in mind when she described Mrs. Goddard's school (Honan 31–3). Mrs. Latournelle's school allowed for more independence than most boys' boarding schools.[6] Girls at Mrs. Latournelle's school were not expected to rely solely on the school for an all-encompassing education. This was important for Austen. The academic lessons constituted only part of their overall learning experience. Austen suggests in *Emma* that in order for a school to be successful, it must recognize that it cannot teach everything. A beneficial learning approach, for Austen, serves as a starting point for the process of further development.

The two different experiences at the two schools she briefly attended perhaps contributed to Austen's overall ambivalence about formal education. Many of Austen's heroines are shaped by the course of learning they pursue outside of schools, and Austen was influenced by the type of education she received at home. Like many women of her time, she took advantage of her intellectual freedom to read novels—a luxury that men studying at Oxford, for instance, did not always have because novels were not assigned as part of any institutional curriculum. Like the Dashwood sisters in *Sense and Sensibility* (1811), when girls were denied access to schools their brothers attended, women often formed their own intellectual milieu, educating themselves outside of schools. Girls became educated not only by listening in on their brothers' tutors but also by studying their household library, by learning from mothers and governesses, and especially through reading groups they formed when their brothers left for school (Hilton and Hirsch 7). The reading of novels reinforced this intellectual freedom outside of schools.

In addition to the education she received under the guidance of her father, she was exposed to her father's own pupils. Reverend George Austen, the former recipient of a Tonbridge fellowship to St. John's College, Oxford, had "embarked upon the usual recourse of scholarly but impoverished clerics, that of taking in boys to prepare them for university entrance by teaching them the necessary classical studies" (Austen-Leigh, *Family Record* 23). Her father's educational approach no doubt shaped her positive impressions of learning with a combination of freedom and guidance—and the potential for "scrambling" that this kind of education afforded.[7] The education that the Austens made available to their male boarders offered not just formal lessons but also an education of the individual. A good educator, as we shall see in *Mansfield Park*'s Edmund, encourages a student's own learning outside of organized lessons.

As a writer who did not receive university training, Austen embraced her self-education. In an 1815 letter, she explains to James Stanier Clarke, librarian and domestic chaplain to the Prince Regent, that she is not up to the task of taking his suggestions to develop a clergyman character in her future novels (Austen, *"My Dear Cassandra"* 109). The clergyman's conversation, she writes, "must at times be on subjects of science and philosophy of which I know nothing—or at least be occasionally abundant in quotations and allusions which a woman who, like me, knows only her own mother-tongue and has read little in that, would be totally without the power of giving" (Austen, *"My Dear Cassandra"* 128). Austen slyly explains that she cannot precisely depict a pedantic clergyman because she lacks the education that produces a person who places stock in authority and acquires knowledge to display for others by spouting familiar quotations. She makes the connection to education more explicit in the next sentence of her letter to Clarke:

> A classical education, or at any rate, a very extensive acquaintance with English literature, ancient and modern, appears to me quite indispensable for the person who wd. do any justice to your clergyman; and I think I may boast

myself to be, with all possible vanity, the most unlearned and uninformed female who ever dared to be an authoress.

(Austen, *"My Dear Cassandra"* 128–9)

Here Austen takes bemused pride in being "unlearned" and "uninformed," since it gives her an out; she celebrates herself as an author free from the pretentious trappings of a university or elite tutored education. She has not followed a prescribed course of reading, either from a tutor or from the expectations thrust upon her. Austen claims the literary style of the "unlearned," which gives her room to explore how people take in knowledge outside of formal education. Being "unlearned" leaves room for developing one's own opinions instead of relying on information one has absorbed from a "learned" authority. We see Austen attempting to reflect this freedom of the "unlearned" in the style of her novels; her ironic narrators constantly invite readers to rely on their own judgment instead of receiving maxims passively.

Austen uses her position as a privileged, well-read outsider of universities to critique conventional education. She tests out the idea of unteaching readers as early as her *History of England*, experimenting with a style of writing that pulls readers away from dogmatic modes of learning that encourage the reader to ingest facts passively. We see her experimenting with history as a form of storytelling that relies on the reader to make it come alive, and she later explores applying this ironic narration to the storytelling in her novels. In her *History of England*, Austen satirizes the notion of an authoritative version of history; she urges readers to compare different forms of historical narratives. Written at age 16, *History of England* attests to her early questioning of widely accepted histories. She criticizes the notion that any one author has the power to recount one version of history: "It is to be supposed that Henry was married, since he had certainly four sons, but it is not in my power to inform the Reader who was his wife" (177). Austen acknowledges the collective aspect of history; anyone, she suggests, can have access to historical knowledge and can actively take part in piecing together history. When she discusses Henry VIII, she writes: "It would be an affront to my Readers were I to suppose that they were not as well acquainted with the particulars of this King's reign as I am myself" (180). The author of this history does not assume an all-knowing voice; Austen makes it clear that she sees herself as just one part of a gathering of historical knowledge—just as much a part of it as her reader.

On one level, Austen's witty rewriting of British histories underscores the atrocities specific to British history and exposes the inevitable biases in recounting history in general. More relevant to this study, however, is Austen's reliance on the reader's own ability to recognize the disorder inherent in history. She shifts the focus away from facts and dates, announcing on the title page: "There will be very few Dates in this History." Austen characterizes history as chaotic. One can only learn history through an engagement with the disorder of it instead of memorizing historical facts by rote or passively accepting one account. Austen hints that writers could do more to capitalize on readers' engagement. *Northanger Abbey*'s Catherine Morland expresses her lack of interest in history, which she "read[s] a little as a duty" (87) and explains that it provides "torment" (88) instead of "instruction" for young readers (88). Catherine describes the flaws in existing accounts of history: "The quarrels of popes and kings, with wars or pestilences, in every page; the men all so good for nothing, and hardly any women at all—it is very tiresome" (87). She "think[s] it odd" that she finds history "so dull" because "a great deal of it must be invention" (87). Most versions of history bore Catherine because even though they might rely on "invention" they fail to capitalize on the lively potential of recounting history as a story that engages imaginative readers.

For Austen, history has the potential to be a good story, but it requires an active reader to unravel it. She views history as almost akin to literature. In her *History*, Austen ironically mingles factual versions of history with literary depictions: "the King made a long speech, for which I must refer the Reader to Shakespear's [sic] Plays" (177). We see Austen critiquing existing notions of history and of education but we also see her writing in an ironic way that begs for an attentive reader. We glimpse her early conceptualization of "scrambling" in her *History* that we later see in her fiction.

Learning history by "scrambling," Austen suggests, encourages students to grow in their own judgment. Austen anticipates the later social satire of Dickens, who in *Hard Times* (1854) condemns the emphasis on learning factual information at the expense of fostering sound moral judgment, and of John Ruskin, who censures the British reading public's poor moral judgment in *Sesame and Lilies* (1865). When discussing Queen Elizabeth, for example, Austen hints at the public's moral assessment of historical figures and events:

> I know that it has by many people been asserted and believed that Lord Burleigh, Sir Francis Walsingham, and the rest of those who filled the cheif [sic] offices of State were deserving, experienced, and able Ministers. But Oh! how blinded such Writers and such Readers must be to true Merit, to Merit despised, neglected and defamed, if they can persist in such opinions when they reflect that these men, these boasted men were such scandals to their Country and their sex as to allow and assist their Queen [Elizabeth] in confining [Mary Queen of Scots] for the space of nineteen years . . . and at length in allowing Elizabeth to bring this amiable Woman to an untimely, unmerited, and scandalous Death.
>
> (183–4)

To study history is to reassess one's own judgment—and that of historical writers—when necessary. Austen shows very clearly that she views history not as a methodical study of information but as something that invites opinions from many different people. She calls upon readers to form an opinion for themselves about the inaccuracies of these histories. In studying history, readers must look within.

History *should* be biased, according to Austen. She dismisses any expectations the reader might have about obtaining an unbiased account of Henry VI, for example, from her history: "I suppose you know all about the Wars between him and the Duke of York who was of the right side; if you do not, you had better read some other

History, for I shall not be very diffuse in this . . ." (178). Austen's history only adopts an authoritative tone satirically. She aims "not to give information" but instead to engage with readers who possess opinions different from hers—to "vent [her] spleen *against*, and shew . . . Hatred *to*" those people who do not agree with her (178).

In addition to ironically depicting an authoritative history that is passively received by readers, Austen rejects the common notion that women should study history as a polite form of knowledge from a safely removed distance.[8] She requires readers of her *History* to get involved in what they read and to be changed by it. Austen satirizes other versions of history while exploring what a fruitful study of history—what a productive education—can be. In order to learn history, one must not pursue the goal of attaining one, all-knowing account; instead the learning experience should invite the student to partake in the process of engaging with history. She not only critiques other models of education; in the form of her *History of England*, she is already offering a vision of what a meaningful education might look like—an education that requires the reader to actively pull together various sources while developing one's own judgment, often making sense out of chaos. In her fiction, she attempts to model this kind of learning.

Austen's novels record an internal history, set in contrast to the factual histories she satirizes in her *History of England*. *Persuasion* (1818), for example, begins with a factual history in its description of the history of English families. Sir Elliot reads about his family in the *Baronetage*: "Then followed the history and rise of the ancient and respectable family, in the usual terms: how it had been first settled in Cheshire; how mentioned in Dugdale—serving the office of High Sheriff . . ." (1). Reading a history of English families requires a different kind of reading from the one we must do to learn about her individual characters in *Persuasion* and her other novels—a kind of active reading she hints at in her *History*.

Austen's "Plan of a Novel" and Plan for Her Novels

Her *History* displays Austen's experimentation with the idea of unteaching readers through ironic narration, which she would use again and again in her novels. The narrator of *Northanger Abbey*, for instance, sounds much like the ironic narrator in her *History of England*, giving us factual information about characters but then avoiding making judgments, leaving it up to us as readers to decide. The narrator concludes the novel by stressing that she will not leave us with a clear moral: "I leave it to be settled, by whomsoever it may concern, whether the tendency of this work be altogether to recommend parental tyranny, or reward filial disobedience" (212). There exists no such thing as a simple moral in Austen's fiction—for her characters or for her readers. We must arrive at our own conclusions.

We might better understand how Austen tells the story of characters that learn through an "indefinable, tentative process" by studying her satirical "Plan of A Novel" (1816) for a fictitious book she never actually writes, in which she outlines everything she tries to avoid capturing in her novels (Carlyle 35). Scholars have argued that the "Plan of a Novel" suggests a parody of Gothic fiction such as Ann Radcliffe's *The Mystery of Udolpho*.[9] It is more likely, however, that Austen uses this parody to explore the type of heroine to which she imagines alternatives, especially in the context of her ideas about education. She takes as her starting point the suggestions made by James Stanier Clarke, which she renders absurd. At the outset of her satirical "Plan" she makes it clear that her hypothetical "Heroine" is very "accomplished" as a result of her education, prepared for any situation that might require her to display her competence in "modern Languages" or her ability to play the "Harp" (Austen, "Plan of a Novel" 226). But she has not developed her own judgment. Whenever she receives an offer of marriage, for instance, she "refers wholly to her Father," a clergyman (228). She is "often carried away by the anti-hero, but rescued either by her Father or by the Hero" (228). The heroine has learned to acquire accomplishments, but she cannot think for herself.

Whereas Austen capitalizes on her own education outside of universities, her proposed Heroine gains little from learning at home. She takes part in no substantive discourse, conversing with her father "in long speeches, elegant Language—& a tone of high, serious sentiment" (226). Fancy words mask any real dialogue. Here we see how Austen's ideas about education do not rely on a clear demarcation between institutional and noninstitutional education; not all learning outside of schools is beneficial, and not all institutional learning is harmful. The tutored education the Heroine receives as well as the Oxbridge training her father acquired prove undesirable because of their emphasis on learning for show. Austen turns Clarke's suggestions upside down, depicting the clergyman as learned to a fault: "The Father to be of a very literary turn, an Enthusiast in Literature, nobody's Enemy but his own" (227). He may be well-informed, but he has sparked little curiosity and initiative in his daughter. Even when they are forced to flee their home and travel to Europe, "driven from his Curacy by the vile arts of some totally unprincipled and heart-less young Man," the Heroine expresses no desire to observe other cultures and mingle with new people (227). They encounter "a wide variety of Characters—but there will be no mixture" (228). The Heroine has not gained knowledge of herself, and she does not expand her mind by learning about others.

Austen's satirical plan for a hypothetical novel does not make space for scenes of learning by self-discovery. In her actual novels, she values educational models that rely on one's judgment and, at times, one's imagination. She admired women, like her niece Fanny, who embody a combination of these qualities:

> Adieu my dearest Fanny. . . . [author's ellipsis] The most astonishing part of your character is, that with so much imagination, so much flight of mind, such unbounded fancies, you should have such excellent judgment in what you do!
> (Austen, *"My Dear Cassandra"* 146)

Fanny embodies a freedom to imagine and to think beyond the bounds of what lies in front of her—to give into flights of fancy—but this does not preclude her from also developing "excellent judgment." Austen capitalizes on the ability of the novel to encourage an education that fosters the attributes she celebrates in her niece. A good education, for Austen, does not shut down the imagination while fostering judgment; this is what she strives to show us again and again in her novels. "Scrambling" requires both imagination and judgment, and she expects this combination from her readers.

Austen emphasizes that the novel is an ideal platform for "scrambling" and an appealing alternative to dogmatic forms of learning. In her passage defending novel-reading in *Northanger Abbey*, she emphasizes that novels allow readers to push the boundaries of conventional histories, anthologies, poems, and periodicals. Novels provide innovation and insight into human nature: they are the form "in which the greatest powers of the mind are displayed, in which the most thorough knowledge of human nature, the happiest delineation of its varieties, the liveliest effusions of wit and humour, are conveyed to the world in the best-chosen language" (23). Austen puts the novel in opposition to outdated strains of knowledge, as represented in histories of England, anthologies, and the *Spectator*. In contrast to the liveliness inherent in the novel, Austen describes male-dominated genres that beg to be read passively. Like the writers of treatises that present authoritative arguments, the "nine-hundredth abridger of the *History of England*" and the "man who collects and publishes in a volume some dozen lines of Milton, Pope, and Prior, with a paper from the *Spectator*" have assumed the authority to make assessments about what is worth reading (22). Instead of presenting a wealth of material with which the reader can engage by drawing upon her own wisdom and imagination, they present orderly texts to be read in a scripted way. These forms of writing resemble the educational models Austen critiques because of their focus on learning from an authority to achieve a narrow goal.

Her jab in *Northanger Abbey* at the *Spectator*'s privileged position in relation to novels underscores the publication's inability to draw readers into its world: "the substance of its papers so often consisting in the statement of improbable circumstances, unnatural characters, and topics of conversation which no longer concern anyone living; and their language, too, frequently so coarse as to give no very favourable idea of the age that could endure it" (22–3). Readers cannot connect to it. The publication does not model for its readers an approach to taking in knowledge that they can relate to their lives. Readers cannot get involved with what they read, unlike the readers of Austen's novels, who must rely on their own judgment to "scramble" along with her characters.

Austen questions an intellectual tradition that excludes its female students instead of involving them actively in "scrambling" into greater self-knowledge. Her description of the *Spectator* ultimately suggests a scorn for a learning process in which the student receives wisdom passively. She certainly does not denounce the work of all previous male authors in these forms. But she recognizes that the novel can do what the *Spectator* and most histories cannot: the novel can put the reader in the position—sometimes along with Austen's heroines—of making meaning out of disorder, of relying on one's own perception and imagination.

Fake Scrambling

Novels, Austen suggests, can serve as a more successful education in developing one's judgment than Oxbridge does. In her novels, she continues the critique she begins in her *History* of the practice of passively receiving knowledge, a practice that limits the ability to judge for oneself. Austen often places her heroines—and her readers—in the position of distinguishing between characters who can navigate on their own (*Mansfield Park*'s Fanny Price) and characters who have learned only to regurgitate information received from others (Mary Crawford and the Bertram sisters in *Mansfield Park*, and Jane Fairfax and Emma Woodhouse in *Emma*). Resisting the way that some writers of eighteenth-century moralistic fiction aimed to impart simple morals to their female readers, she wants her readers to form their own opinions as they read.

Austen realizes that the approach to learning of receiving knowledge from one authoritative source in pursuit of a narrow educational goal fails to give students—particularly female students—the tools they need to navigate their contemporary age. The marriage market drives girls' education in *Mansfield Park*, for example; the pedagogy that Sir Thomas lays out for his daughters serves a capitalist function that will allow them to thrive as candidates for wedlock. This presents itself as another example of an educational model that precludes "scrambling"—and the inner transformation that comes with it—in favor of learning with a very limited purpose. His educational plan, then, depends on what the market for wives dictates that young ladies should learn. If, as Ruth Perry suggests, capitalism shifted the emphasis from family-centered notions of kinship to kinship based primarily on marriage (and specifically financially driven marriages), decisions about women's education were undoubtedly shaped by market-based demands for what constituted a desirable wife (Perry 4–5, 19–20). Austen clearly disapproves of the expensive new seminaries emerging in towns and cities and the tutoring for girls influenced by this trend. Instead of encouraging self-discovery as Mrs. Goddard's school does, new girls' schools subscribed to the limited goal of producing young women with "accomplishments" that would appeal to suitors on the marriage market (*Emma* 18).[10] In treating education as a product, these newer schools for young women promote a set of skills considered to be important for upper-middle and upper-class women to possess, not unlike the elite traditions of knowledge that privileged young men were expected to master at Oxford and Cambridge. Both groups—girls grooming for marriage and men preparing for lives as gentlemen—are encouraged to learn in ways that emphasize their external polish instead of developing what lies within.

Austen's critique of conventional girls' education appears throughout her fiction. The Musgrove sisters in *Persuasion*, for instance, "had brought from a school at Exeter all the usual stock of accomplishments, and were now, like thousands of other young ladies, living to be fashionable, happy, and merry" (28). In *Emma*, we see this limited approach to women's education manifest itself in both the receiver of a tutored education—Emma Woodhouse—as well as the trained governess, Jane Fairfax. Emma has memorized lists of books, but for much of the novel she is caught between falling short of pursuing a more orderly education to actually read these books and applying her own judgment to the information she has received from her governess. She struggles to combine imagination with the development of her own judgment, as we are reminded in Mr. Knightley's conversation with

Mrs. Weston. Mr. Knightley remarks, "I have seen a great many lists of her drawing up at various times of books that she meant to read regularly through" (29). He recalls admiring her potential in the "list she drew up when only fourteen," and "remember[s] thinking it did her judgment so much credit" (27). In this long passage uninterrupted by the narrator, the reader soon realizes that the development of Emma's judgment ended there. Mr. Knightley concludes that Emma did not expand her judgment beyond knowing what she should read. She knows the names of books but does not engage with their ideas. Emma's education has resulted in her formation of hierarchies and categories, showing a superficial level of patience (these "very good lists" were "very well chosen") and industry (they were "very neatly arranged—sometimes alphabetically, and sometimes by some other rule"), but we learn that ultimately she "will never submit to any thing requiring industry and patience, and a subjection of the fancy to the understanding" (29–30).

While Mr. Knightley concedes that Emma's work ethic begs for more sustained rigor, what Austen critiques most strongly is her lack of critical judgment and her inability to subject "the fancy to the understanding" (30). She possesses reading and organizational skills, and she knows in theory what she should read, but she does not actually read the books; she does not think critically and imaginatively about them. Austen partially criticizes her for not working hard enough—for not following through with her reading in any organized way—but she also criticizes Emma for seeing reading as only a labor to be fulfilled, an industrious activity that one can summarize in lists. Perhaps the fault lies not within Emma but in the method of learning that incited her to view education as a series of initial lists or titles to be memorized. There is no depth to Emma's knowledge. Her education, in effect, has endowed her with recognizable signs of learning in lists of famous literature, but it has not given her the opportunity to expand her own mind with reflection.

Emma's tutored education prevents her from embracing the disorder Austen calls for in her ideal pedagogical model. Furthermore, Emma tries to make her education regenerative by attempting to pass it on to Harriet, but it cannot be successfully passed on. Harriet, an alumna of Mrs. Goddard's school, turns out to be more the educator than the student. We encounter Harriet Smith's good judgment at the beginning of the novel, for example, when we hear her positive impressions of Mr. Martin's respectability and intellectual curiosity: "He had never heard of such books before I mentioned them, but he is determined to get them now as soon as ever he can" (23). Yet for much of the novel, we hear from Emma's perspective about Harriet as naïve and helpless, and about Mr. Martin as unworthy. Unlike Emma, Harriet is able to rely on her sound judgment from the beginning of the novel.

In *Emma*, Austen dismisses the idea of educating women for a narrow goal—whether that goal is to prepare women like Emma for successfully finding a husband or to train Jane Fairfax to pursue a job as a governess. Although Austen does not elaborate on the specifics of Jane Fairfax's education, she makes it clear that the outcome is undesirable. Her education has been limited to one professional goal: to become a governess. Jane is destined for the governess profession at an early age but dreads being an educator. She becomes a pawn in the education market. Others invest in Jane's education, presuming that it will produce returns when she becomes a governess and can support herself. "The plan was that she should be brought up for educating others," the narrator tells us matter-of-factly, "the very few hundred pounds which she inherited from her father making independence impossible" (128). Jane, trained to be a governess, loathes her future role as an educator. Instead of inspiring in her a desire to share her knowledge with others, her education has produced the opposite effect. She compares the governess trade to the slave trade when explaining her employment prospects: "When I am quite determined as to the time, I am not at all afraid of being long unemployed. There are places in town, offices, where inquiry would soon produce something—Offices for the sale—not quite of human flesh—but of human intellect" (235). When Mrs. Elton appears shocked by the analogy to the slave trade, Jane replies: "I did not mean, I was not thinking of the slave-trade . . . governess-trade, I assure you, was all that I had in view" (235).[11] She further compares the slave-trade to the governess-trade: "widely different certainly as to the guilt of those who carry it on; but as to the greater misery of the victims, I do not know where it lies" (235). Jane becomes enslaved in a profession that supposedly bears the responsibility of sparking inspiration in new generations of students.[12] Instead of allowing her the kind of "scrambling" that Austen suggests can prove regenerative, her education provided a narrow path to one profession determined by her social class.

Although Austen hints at educational questions in her other novels, it is in *Mansfield Park* that we hear repeatedly of education as a pressing concern. We are given maxims about education from the ironic narrator that emphasize the limited goals of women's education. From the very beginning of the novel, we learn that Mrs. Norris believes that education serves a practical, economical purpose for women: "Give a girl an education, and introduce her properly into the world, and ten to one but she has the means of settling well, without farther expense to any body" (5). Sir Thomas Bertram clearly subscribes to this philosophy of educating women. When he observes Fanny dancing at a party long after her arrival at his home, he congratulates himself on improving his lower-middle-class niece with education: "he was proud of his niece, and without attributing all her personal beauty, as Mrs. Norris seemed to do, to her transplantation to Mansfield, he was pleased with himself for having supplied every thing else;—education and manners she owed to him" (217). He focuses on the external markers of the education he has provided her—on the "manners" she learned from an educational model that aims solely to prepare women for display.

Later in the novel, Austen explores the reflections of Sir Thomas, who regrets his plan of education for his daughters:

> Something must have been wanting *within*, or time would have worn away much of its ill effect. He feared that principle, active principle, had been wanting, that they had never been properly taught to govern their inclinations and tempers, by that sense of duty which can alone suffice. They had been instructed theoretically in their religion, but never required to bring it into

daily practice. To be distinguished for elegance and accomplishments—the authorised object of their youth—could have had no useful influence that way, no moral effect on the mind.

(364)

His plan of education produces a superficial effect because his daughters never learned how to "govern their inclinations and tempers." The education his daughters received did not focus on what was "within." The Bertram girls never had the chance to develop their self-knowledge, which their cousin Fanny already possesses when she comes to Mansfield Park and develops further there. Sir Thomas realizes that the education he has provided has missed an opportunity to change the girls' "principle," and what his daughters have not been taught is the ability to "govern" their own character. The fancy tutored education Sir Thomas has arranged for his daughters has given them "accomplishments" to flaunt at parties but has clearly failed them in terms of their character: "Wretchedly did he feel, that with all the cost and care of an anxious and expensive education, he had brought up his daughters, without their understanding their first duties, or his being acquainted with their character and temper" (364). Just as Mr. Bennet reflects at the end of *Pride and Prejudice* on his role—perhaps failed role—as a father to his daughters, here Sir Thomas reflects on his failure as a father to encourage a different approach to learning.[13] Sir Thomas's failure as a father here is explicitly a failure of education.

Sir Thomas's realizations reflect our own challenge as readers of the novel; we must learn to distinguish for ourselves the accoutrements of learning displayed by many characters from the self-knowledge that several characters such as Fanny embody. The first reaction to Fanny at the Bertram household is one of dismay at her ignorance of factual information. The Bertram sisters and parents have come to confuse easily memorized facts with character. Sir Thomas warns them, "we shall probably see much to wish altered in her, and must prepare ourselves for gross ignorance, some meanness of opinions, and very distressing vulgarity of manner; but these are not incurable faults—nor, I trust, can they be dangerous for her associates" (8–9). Fanny arrives at Mansfield Park lacking the factual information pertaining to subjects such as geography that the Bertram sisters had come to adopt, mistakenly, as self-knowledge. They express shock when they find out that Fanny does not possess it. The narrator tells us that "Fanny could read, work, and write, but she had been taught nothing more; and as her cousins found her ignorant of many things with which they had been long familiar, they thought her prodigiously stupid . . ." (15). We then hear the voices of the Bertram sisters themselves:

"Dear Mamma, only think, my cousin cannot put the map of Europe together— or my cousin cannot tell the principal rivers in Russia . . ."

(15)[14]

"But, aunt, she is really so very ignorant!—Do you know, we asked her last night, which way she would go to get to Ireland; and she said, she should cross to the Isle of Wight. She thinks of nothing but the Isle of Wight, and she calls it *the Island*, as if there were no other island in the world . . ."

(15)

The examples the Bertram sisters use to express their dismay at Fanny's ignorance refer to facts and memorized geography.

Immediately after we hear the voices of the Bertram household in reaction to Fanny's "ignorance" of geography, the narrator informs us of how this orderly education has left them lacking in some crucial areas. We are given information with which to form our own judgments about education in the novel. The Bertram sisters, the narrator informs us, lack "self-knowledge":

Such were the counsels by which Mrs. Norris assisted to form her nieces' minds; and it is not very wonderful that with all their promising talents and early information, they should be entirely deficient in the less common acquirements of self-knowledge, generosity, and humility. In every thing but disposition, they were admirably taught.

(16)

Fanny, we learn as the novel progresses, retains the qualities of "self-knowledge, generosity, and humility" even as she receives a more formal tutored education as well as the education of reading she experiences under Edmund's guidance and on her own. Austen presents self-knowledge as something that can indeed be fostered, resisting the "nature versus nurture" debate and instead focusing on what education can and cannot do.[15]

Those who have received an education focusing on the veneer of knowledge for display cannot view the educational problem critically. Lady Bertram does not see the futility of possessing factual information without the intellectual and moral knowledge with which to frame it. She "paid not the smallest attention" to "the education of her daughters" and dismisses Fanny's "being stupid at learning" as "very unlucky, but some people *were* stupid, and Fanny must take more pains . . ." (16). Lady Bertram approaches the subject of education with simplistic conclusions, and in doing so, she mistakes "accomplishments" and facts with self-knowledge (364).

The kind of education that Lady Bertram and her daughters value prevents students from being able to think for themselves. Although Mary Crawford is well educated, she cannot readily form her own opinions or "judg[e] from herself" (87). Edmund acknowledges the extent to which others have influenced Mary's thinking, especially in terms of her ideas about the church: "I suspect that in this comprehensive and (may I say) common-place censure, you are not judging from yourself, but from prejudiced persons, whose opinions you have been in the habit of hearing. It is impossible that your own observation can have given you much knowledge of the clergy" (87). Her education has put her too much "in the habit of hearing" others' ideas (87). She has not been taught to think for herself, as Austen has enticed us to do as we read her novel.

Some forms of education, Austen warns, can even taint and injure. Fanny and Edmund discuss the potentially harmful "effect of education" on Mary:

> "I know her disposition to be as sweet and faultless as your own, but the influence of her former companions makes her seem, gives to her conversation, to her professed opinions, sometimes a tinge of wrong. She does not *think* evil, but she speaks it—speaks it in playfulness—and though I know it to be playfulness, it grieves me to the soul."
>
> "The effect of education," said Fanny gently.
>
> Edmund could not but agree to it. "Yes, that uncle and aunt! They have injured the finest mind!—for sometimes, Fanny, I own to you, it does appear more than manner; it appears as if the mind itself was tainted."
>
> (211)

Fanny refers to what she has observed in the Bertram sisters as "education," and Edmund remarks that the "education" the Bertram sisters received—intended to focus on "manner"—has actually injured the inner principle and capacity for judgment. Here Edmund uses the word "manner" to label the external manifestations of one's training instead of what lies within.[16] Austen suggests that even if the education serves to focus on what she deems as superficial "accomplishments," it can negatively affect the inner principle (364). The effect of education runs deeper than manners or "accomplishments" (364). Students who set out to attain skills and facts on a superficial level, Austen suggests, fall in danger of acquiring irreversible habits of mind.

We perceive the "effect of education" in a number of characters who are worse off for the attitudes about learning they embrace (211). These characters' lack of judgment, Austen suggests, is related to their lack of Christian self-government. If one possesses Christian self-government—through learning from sermons, parental guidance, or one's own suffering—one might be more receptive to an education of "scrambling" that encourages the development of judgment. Unlike the Bertram sisters and Mary Crawford, who have learned religious values only in theory, Fanny embodies Christian-based self-government in practice. Fanny's "self-knowledge" is partly a result of having suffered (16). For Austen, it is important that Fanny arrives with "self-knowledge" and Christian principle as a result of her own suffering (16). The Bertram sisters could have attained it through other means such as their father's guidance, but it cannot be fostered solely through their tutored lessons that focus on external "accomplishments" instead of inner transformation (364). An education— like the one given to Fanny's female cousins—can only do so much if students have not developed self-government. There is a limit to what an education can do for anyone, and Austen is skeptical of educational models that claim to extend a student beyond her intellectual and personal capacity.[17] Austen pays attention to what a student must possess—self-knowledge like Fanny's from suffering; self-government; and the right social circumstances—in order to get the most out of an education. Here and elsewhere in her writing, Austen suggests that one's temperament is not to blame; it is more a question of learning self-government.

The idea that a valuable education may be linked to religion is also apparent in Austen's portrayal of Edmund Bertram, who is training to be a clergyman and emerges as one of the productive educators in *Mansfield Park*. Unlike Mr. Collins in *Pride and Prejudice* who reads *Fordyce's Sermons* to the Bennets with "monotonous solemnity" and without any attentiveness to what his listeners take in, Edmund envisions his role not merely as lecturing to students who passively receive his messages (51–2). Whereas Mr. Collins's method of reading *Fordyce's Sermons* to women who listen passively would have been a conventional means of educating women at the time, Edmund envisions something different. Speaking to Mary Crawford during their visit to Sotherton, Edmund expresses an awareness of his role as a teacher attentive to his students:

> The *manners* I speak of, might rather be called *conduct*, perhaps, the result of good principles; the effect, in short, of those doctrines which it is their duty to teach and recommend; and it will, I believe, be every where found, that as the clergy are, or are not what they ought to be, so are the rest of the nation.
> (74)

Edmund envisions engaging his congregation by relating his teachings to practice. He notes the link between principle and what can be taught. In this way, he exhibits insight as an educator, informed by his training as a clergyman. Edmund—the family's wise son—has pursued much of his own reading in addition to receiving an Oxbridge education. This is important to Austen, as it is to the later writers in this study. An education received can only do so much; it remains essential to do one's own reading, sometimes under the guidance of another person. Edmund, as a result of the education he has pursued on his own, possesses an awareness of others as a clergyman and as an educator.

Scrambling in Austen

Even though her uncle prescribes a tutored education for her, Fanny Price manages to "scramble" into a meaningful education. Austen emphasizes repeatedly Fanny's ability to synthesize imagination and judgment. She learns from tutored lessons once she is at Mansfield Park as well as from the reading she does outside of her formal learning, and she continues to cultivate her self-knowledge. Fanny, who has been excluded not only from Oxford and Cambridge like the Bertram sisters, is also excluded from the tutoring that the Bertram sisters have received for much of their lives. She has been excluded on the basis of gender as well as class. Fanny's early exclusion from this form of education, Austen suggests, helps her pursue a path of learning to develop her own thinking instead of acquiring frivolous knowledge for display. Austen contrasts the true Christian self-government Fanny has developed as a result of her suffering with that of Mrs. Norris, for example, who puts on Christian beliefs for display.

Fanny receives help in her endeavor from her cousin Edmund, who focuses on developing his own judgment outside of his university education. Education, for Edmund, is regenerative; his education makes him want to share what he has learned, which is a positive "effect of education" also embodied in Fanny, who later teaches her younger sister (211). One who receives an authentic education will want to pass it on. Unlike Jane Fairfax who dreads teaching, Fanny becomes an educator herself when she visits her parents and siblings. She tries to infuse her sister with an enthusiasm for reading: "to be having any one's improvement in view in her choice! But so it was. Susan had read nothing, and Fanny longed to give her a share in her own first pleasures, and inspire a taste for the biography and poetry which she delighted in herself" (313). A valuable education motivates the learner to want to pass it on, even if not fully engaged by the student.

Unlike the other educators or overseers of education in the novel, such as Sir Thomas, Edmund cultivates both Fanny's intellectual education and her development of judgment. Recognizing "Fanny's mental superiority" (370), he encourages her to pursue an education of "scrambling," reminding her not just to read for factual information:

> He knew her to be clever, to have a quick apprehension as well as good sense, and a fondness for reading, which, properly directed, must be an education in itself. Miss Lee taught her French, and heard her read the daily portion of History; but he recommended the books which charmed her leisure hours, he encouraged her taste, and corrected her judgment; he made reading useful by talking to her of what she read, and heightened its attraction by judicious praise. (18)

Edmund's knowledge of character enables him to recognize Fanny's innate ability. He then fosters an education of positive disorder from multiple sources, helping her "fondness for reading" to become "an education in itself." Here Austen differentiates between the "History" and "French" Fanny learns along with her cousins and the "judgment" she develops outside of her tutor's lessons. Edmund serves as a different kind of tutor; instead of assisting Fanny in memorizing historical facts, he encourages open discussion and gives her "judicious praise." The pedagogy Edmund embraces is an education that takes as its starting point not an expert text but rather one that depends on "scrambling" by using multiple means of obtaining knowledge. Again we see the importance of reading beyond one's prescribed lessons in the education Fanny receives at Mansfield Park. Later writers try to preserve this unstructured reading as an essential component of the learning process because they see it threatened by the expansion of institutional education.

Although Austen's heroines learn from men who could be considered authority figures like Edmund and Mr. Knightley, they arrive at inner knowledge only when they find themselves reflecting in solitude. Mr. Knightley can incite Emma to pay more attention to her own conscience, for example, but ultimately she can only develop it herself. In the midst of a conversation with Harriet, Emma realizes her mistakes, but Austen includes this exclamation only after several pages describing Emma alone in reflection. Emma can then come to the conclusion that "her own conduct, as well as her own heart, was before her in the same few minutes.

She saw it all with a clearness which had never blessed her before. How improperly had she been acting by Harriet!" (320). Austen emphasizes that it is in these moments of self-directed, individual thought when her heroines experience their own most meaningful education. In long passages such as this one, Austen lets us experience as readers the deep reflection that comes from resisting the impulse to receive knowledge passively. As readers, we must rely on our own combination of fancy and judgment—our own "scrambling"—to appreciate an Austen novel. It is in the kind of education guided by regenerative learners such as Mr. Knightley or Edmund that Austen explores the possibility of an education of "scrambling" that does not have negative social consequences. Emma's and Fanny's educational experiences are guided by tutors who help them form their own judgment.

Austen anticipates later writers, like Hardy, who see the benefits of learning outside of elite schools but who also weigh the real consequences of missing out on the social literacy passed on to students through an education with some guidance. In *Pride and Prejudice*, for instance, we see in long passages describing Elizabeth's thought processes how "scrambling" serves her well, but we also see the negative effects of an education of "scrambling" in Lydia, who eventually relies on Elizabeth and Jane for money. Lydia's failures may be the result of her lack of developed Christian self-government, but they also may be a result of precarious social circumstances. The Bennet sisters have had the freedom to explore on their own, but Austen reminds readers how this can be disastrous if not given enough guidance. When her aunt and uncle ask if Lydia intends to live with Wickham without being married, Elizabeth responds, "she has never been taught to think on serious subjects . . . she has been given up to nothing but amusement and vanity. She has been allowed to dispose of her time in the most idle and frivolous manner, and to adopt any opinions that came in her way" (214). Here Austen presents the failure of an education without enough guidance. An education of "scrambling," then, cannot be enough for everyone. Perhaps women of Lydia and Elizabeth's class are especially susceptible to the negative effects of an education with too much freedom.

The resources at Fanny's disposal upon her arrival at Mansfield Park allow her to extend her learning beyond her academic lessons in a productive way. The Bertram sisters have failed to do this, but Fanny takes pleasure in going "beyond her knowledge": "Their road was through a pleasant country; and Fanny, whose rides had never been extensive, was soon beyond her knowledge, and was very happy in observing all that was new, and admiring all that was pretty" (64). Austen puts this model of observational, exploratory learning—beyond what one has learned formally either through tutored lessons or in school—in opposition to the approach of Mary Crawford, who "had none of Fanny's delicacy of taste, of mind, of feeling; she saw nature, inanimate nature, with little observation; her attention was all for men and women, her talents for the light and lively" (64). The repetition in the phrase "nature, inanimate nature" reflects the tiresome way Mary views the world outside of her textbooks and her immediate social circle: nature is repetitive and inanimate, instead of overflowing with what Fanny describes as "new" and "pretty." Austen's tone here, describing Mary's "talents" for the "light and lively" is clearly satirical; her characterization of what Mary is missing as "inanimate" suggests that Mary fails to notice what Fanny gains from going "beyond her knowledge." Mary Crawford cannot be an Austen heroine because as readers we cannot depend on her to help us to go beyond our own knowledge. We will never enter into new imaginative territories by following a character like Mary. She serves as an antiheroine like the satirical "Heroine" in Austen's "Plan of A Novel" because she never models the process of developing one's judgment. If Mary were a heroine, she would deny us the opportunity of "scrambling" as readers because she never allows herself to learn from disorder.

Whenever we think we are about to grasp a basic moral of her story, Austen warns us to stay alert—to train ourselves against reading a novel to simply receive ideas. In *Mansfield Park* we hear echoes of *The Loiterer* writer attempting satirically to give his reader an easy moral about education, warning of sloth at Oxford. Austen repeatedly offers overly simplistic educational theories in the characters of Lady Bertram and Sir Thomas—theories that test our own judgment of her characters. The only reason Sir Thomas's method failed his daughters was because he did not focus on the development of their character, and Fanny is "stupid at learning" (16), Lady Bertram concludes, because she has not been trained in rote memorization to acquire "accomplishments" (364). By calling our attention to easy ways out of the complex questions of education, Austen tunes us into a broader societal problem. Even though one father may realize the failure of an education driven by the marriage market, it will take a much more widespread realization to change the context of ideas about educating women and to reform accepted views of marriage.

At a time when women's education was widely debated, Austen remained ambivalent not only about "orderly" education but also about models of learning that purport to provide an all-encompassing education. Writing before the founding of the first institutions of higher education for women in Britain, she clearly rejects the idea that orderly, authoritative models of schools for men should be adopted for women, an idea that Elizabeth Barrett Browning also resists. Anticipating the other writers in this book, Austen was uncomfortable with the idea of discounting completely the benefits of being educated outside of schools in a model that embodies an "indefinable, tentative" process (Carlyle 35). Austen's ideal models of learning are forward thinking in their critique of traditional convention and also in their call for a positive disorder encompassing different learning strategies instead of one method. We are left "scrambling" to piece together a clearly defined educational approach in Austen's works, and we realize, ultimately, that no facile vision emerges. And that is the point. Even though we might be reading Austen's novels while sitting comfortably in an armchair, we are never quite at rest.

Notes

1 See, for example, two examples of this usage cited in the *OED*: T. Pennant *Tours Scotl.* (1774) 339, "The height was taken by a little boy, who scrambled to the top," and W. Irving *Adventures Capt. Bonneville* (1837) II.117, "Sometimes they scrambled from rock to rock, up the bed of some mountain stream."
2 Austen pokes fun at the pedantry she sees even in More's only novel, *Coelebs in Search of a Wife* (1809), which, as the title suggests, recounts the journey of Caleb to find the

perfect wife under the guidance of his mentor. Austen writes in a letter to her sister Cassandra that "the only merit it could have, was in the name of Caleb, which has an honest, unpretending sound; but in Coelebs, there is pedantry & affectation.—Is it written only to Classical Scholars?" (Austen, *Letters* 179).

3 For book-length studies of education as a theme in Austen's work, see especially D.D. Devlin, *Jane Austen and Education*; Barbara Horwitz, *Jane Austen and the Question of Women's Education*; and Laura Mooneyham White, *Romance, Language and Education in Jane Austen's Novels*.

4 See Honan's chapter on *The Loiterer* for a helpful overview of the publication (56–65).

5 Austen wrote "Love & Freindship" [*sic*] in 1790, the year after Issue 27 of *The Loiterer* was published, possibly picking up on the satirical note in *The Loiterer*: "Let her avoid love and friendship as she wishes to be admired and distinguished" (163).

6 In her biography of Austen, Elizabeth Jenkins sets the scene for the "easy-going" school: "The school buildings were romantic, formed in part as they were of the old gatehouse of the Abbey, and surrounded by a spacious, shady garden, very delightful to the girls on hot summer evenings. The régime was easy-going in the extreme" (13).

7 See Austen-Leigh's *A Family Record* (54–5) for more description of the education Austen's father encouraged.

8 See Christopher Kent's helpful discussion of Austen's depiction of history in the context of women's study of history (60–61).

9 See Austen, "Plan of a Novel" (689–90, note 1).

10 For a study of girls' schools emerging in Austen's time, see De Bellaigue (10–42).

11 For a more complete discussion of this analogy and for more detailed context of the governess profession, see Lynda A. Hall's "Jane Fairfax's Choice: The Sale of Human Flesh or Human Intellect."

12 If we view this in the context of a broader discontent among women at the time for becoming governesses, we might consider Austen's depiction of Jane as another example of an education that trains students to work only towards a narrow goal. For a book-length study of governesses and Victorian literature, see Kathryn Hughes, *The Victorian Governess*.

13 Mr. Bennet says to Lizzy: "Who should suffer but myself? It has been my own doing, and I ought to feel it. . . . You may well warn me against such an evil. Human nature is so prone to fall into it! No, Lizzy, let me once in my life feel how much I have been to blame. I am not afraid of being overpowered by the impression. It will pass away soon enough" (227). The failure of the father characters in terms of education is further evidence that Austen does not suggest that someone is completely hopeless because of temperament; Lydia Bennet, for instance, could have been taught self-government by her father.

14 What later writers such as Barrett Browning and Hardy pick up on is that the frivolous education for privileged girls, the mass education models for the working classes, and the elite university education offered at Oxford and Cambridge all emphasized rote memorization, such as mastering the "principal rivers of Europe" (Examination Papers 1853).

15 I argue that Austen anticipates later literary resistance to nineteenth-century educational institutions, departing from eighteenth-century conversations about education and upbringing. See Jenny Davidson's *Breeding: A Partial History of the Eighteenth Century* for an analysis of the conversation about how educational ideas evolved as part of the nature versus nurture debate.

16 Edmund uses the word in the sense of "outward bearing, deportment; a person's characteristic style of attitude, gesture, or speech" (*OED*).

17 Austen's idea that "scrambling" may benefit some women and not others is related to the idea that, as Julia Prewitt Brown states, "Jane Austen makes us acknowledge the undemocratic truth that those who are born unintelligent are at a terrible disadvantage in the world. Her belief in the importance of education, one of her most constant and serious concerns, is an extension of this awareness" (125).

3 Radical Education in *Aurora Leigh*

Whereas Austen hints at an education of "scrambling" and anticipates more explicit critiques of dominant pedagogies by later writers, nineteenth-century advocates of education for women often turned directly to Elizabeth Barrett Browning's "novel-poem" *Aurora Leigh* (1856) for inspiration. Barbara Leigh Smith Bodichon, instrumental in the founding of Girton College, uses a substantial quotation from *Aurora Leigh* as an epigraph to her 1857 essay "Women and Work," and Clara Collet's 1890 essay "The Economic Position of Educated Working Women" begins with a long passage from the poem.[1] Reformers such as Bodichon and Collet who use *Aurora Leigh* to support their arguments for women's education remind us that Barrett Browning's poem was as important for its educational ideas as for its innovations in poetic form. Despite the interest that her pedagogical insights sparked in the nineteenth century, however, no full study exists of Barrett Browning's important contribution to educational debates.[2] A recurrent tension in Barrett Browning scholarship stems from the fact that it urges us to think about her *either* as a reformer *or* as a gifted poet.[3] Exploring her educational project in *Aurora Leigh* allows us to see how her roles as reformer and innovative poet inform each other. By emphasizing the visceral and affective qualities of her poetry, Barrett Browning engages her readers empathically in her vision for reform, teaching us how to read her text while unteaching us from trained habits of reading.[4]

Barrett Browning goes further than many other nineteenth-century proponents of women's education by criticizing dominant pedagogies for both elite and working classes and by proposing a new experiential form of education grounded in what she describes as "headlong" reading (I.707).[5] Instead of pitting experiential education against book learning, as Romantic writers such as William Wordsworth and Jean-Jacques Rousseau often did, Barrett Browning's educational model emphasizes a kind of experiential approach to texts that is embodied in headlong reading. Reading becomes not just cerebral, but also bodily and emotional, as she shows by using images associated with spasmodic poetry such as pulsation.[6] "It is rather when / We gloriously forget ourselves and plunge / Soul-forward, headlong" into books, Aurora says, that we gain the most from reading (I.705–7). Barrett Browning's headlong reading requires readers to immerse themselves emotionally and viscerally in texts, remaining open to new meaning that might emerge instead of searching for one predetermined, "right" reading. Openness to texts leads to an openness—an empathy—for others. When Aurora feels texts "puls[ing]" and "beat[ing]" within her, she reads "for hope" instead of reading to memorize facts as her Oxbridge-educated cousin Romney does (I.896, 841, 730). Barrett Browning places headlong reading at the heart of her educational model intended for women of different classes. She suggests that poetry's physiological aspects, such as those Jason Rudy discusses, should be experienced by all classes. "Poetry in the spasmodic model," Rudy writes, "seems no longer limited to an elite few but is directed instead to the human body and universal experiences" (80). Barrett Browning links the privileged-class Aurora's headlong reading with her empathy for the working-class character Marian, who educates herself while "tramping" when the "pedlar" "would toss her down / Some stray odd volume from his heavy pack" (III.948, 969, 972–3). Aurora can recognize Marian's intellectual curiosity because her education has taught her more than facts. She can adapt her knowledge to new situations and connect with someone of a lower class.

Despite Aurora's and Marian's similar approaches to reading, however, Barrett Browning acknowledges that their class determines these two women's access to education. Marian lacks the intellectual framework that Aurora takes for granted. She remains "not in earshot of the things / Out-spoken o'er the heads of common men / By men who are uncommon" (III.1000–1002). Barrett Browning confronts this class disparity, urging us not to dismiss it as insurmountable. By depicting the possibilities—and limitations—for Marian and Aurora to adapt comparable educational models, Barrett Browning explores the educational possibilities for students from the working classes.

When Barrett Browning wrote *Aurora Leigh* in the 1850s, people of Marian's class were gaining increased access to education. Mass education programs enlarged the size of the literate population dramatically, and with many more people receiving elementary schooling, more students—particularly male students—sought higher education.[7] Educational reformers began asking the questions: What access should we give new populations of students to higher education and to elite intellectual traditions, and how and what should these students be taught? Barrett Browning raises these questions but avoids providing a simple solution. Like Austen, she refuses to set out a rigid methodology. Criticizing Tennyson's depiction of a women's college in *The Princess* (1847), she writes in an 1848 letter to her friend Mary Russell Mitford, "what woman will tell the great poet that Mary Wollstonecraft herself never dreamt of setting up collegiate states, proctordoms & the rest, . . [sic] which is a worn-out plaything in the hands of one sex already, & need not be *transferred* in order to be proved ridiculous?" (*Letters to Mary Russell Mitford* 240). Barrett Browning, herself excluded from Oxford and Cambridge because of her gender, sees the value in an education like her own, completely outside of schools; she deems all current institutional models "ridiculous."

Book Learning and Belatedness

Just as Barrett Browning did, Aurora pursues a mostly self-directed education outside of schools with some guidance from her father. Barrett Browning's unique education no doubt inspired Aurora's; Barrett Browning read extensively, devouring books by Thomas Paine, Voltaire, David Hume, Mary Wollstonecraft, and Rousseau (Mermin 18). She participated in her brother's Greek lessons and went on to master the subject through additional study, reaching a level of learning that set her apart from most women of the period and many men.[8] Barrett Browning uses Aurora, who encounters the British system as a foreigner, to challenge the privileged place of the traditional educational institution in British society.

Memorizing facts as a student at Oxford or Cambridge can harm more than enlighten, Barrett Browning warns. Oxbridge's educational method leaves Romney overly rational and creatively impotent. He "lives by diagrams, / And crosses out the spontaneities / Of all his individual, personal life / With formal universals" (III.744–7). Oxbridge has taught him charts and paradigms but at the cost of his independent thought. Instead of sparking intellectual excitement, Romney's education has heightened his sense of belatedness. He feels burdened by all of the ideas that others have generated before him. Romney says, "The world, we're come to late, is swollen hard," echoing Matthew Arnold's own belatedness in his 1852 "The Buried Life": "But hardly have we, for one little hour, / Been on our own line, have we been ourselves" (II.263; Arnold 59–60). Romney's and Arnold's educational experiences have encouraged them to absorb past traditions instead of creating their own meaning as they read. Despite their initiation into male British intellectualism, they feel out of place in their own literary and historical time. Romney feels far removed from the books in front of him, unlike Aurora who feels words "puls[ing]" in her as she reads (I.896). Barrett Browning links Romney's detached reading of texts to a detachment from other people; he memorizes "universals" instead of connecting with others on an individual level (III.747). As a result of his education, he will help perpetuate the power of existing systems instead of breaking down social barriers. In contrast, both Aurora and Marian become invigorated by their own potential for innovation at a time when a broader range of people can obtain access to learning. Barrett Browning's ideal readers discover their own meaning instead of simply absorbing others' ideas.

As a young girl in Italy, Aurora listens first-hand to a critique of traditional schools from her father—a critique that Barrett Browning maintains throughout *Aurora Leigh*. Aurora's father encourages her to consider learning as an intellectual adventure:

> —out of books
> He taught me all the ignorance of men,
> And how God laughs in heaven when any man
> Says 'Here I'm learned; this, I understand;
> In that, I am never caught at fault or doubt.'
> He sent the schools to school. (I.189–94)

In just a few lines, Barrett Browning criticizes the educational system that produces well-read, overconfident students who fear admitting to what they do not know. Aurora's father satirizes the notion that one can be "learned" in a specific subject. He trains her to become suspicious of educational systems that place too much authority in books. With the enjambment of "out of books," Barrett Browning sets up the expectation that books will bring greater knowledge; she surprises us when we learn that Aurora's father uses book learning to teach her "all the ignorance of men" (I.189–90). He renders foolish the notion that there exists *one* approach to acquiring knowledge. Aurora's father especially distrusts the self-congratulatory aspects of higher learning. For him, learning means doubting, questioning, and stumbling through one's own mistakes rather than mastering a specific body of knowledge for an examination. The latter produces a shut door, a stop, made apparent in the clipped syntax of the phrases "Here I'm learned," "this I understand," and "I am never caught at fault or doubt." When Aurora's father sends "the schools to school," he teaches her to question the centuries-old intellectual traditions at Oxbridge. By constantly reassessing what one learns, Barrett Browning implies, one can avoid becoming too self-congratulatory. Her father encourages Aurora to read inquisitively instead of reading to master, laying the groundwork for the alternative educational approach she seeks later in life.[9]

A Girl's Education Like "Water-Torture"

After her father's death, Aurora encounters the education he critiques when she goes to live with her aunt in England. Her aunt tries to educate the 13-year-old Aurora using the curriculum prevalent at girls' schools and in conduct manuals of the period. Founded on gendered notions of knowledge, a typical girls' school curriculum focused on the acquisition of facts and so-called accomplishments and skills aimed to help girls entertain future husbands rather than develop intellectually and morally, much like the model Austen critiques.[10] Schools encouraged girls to concentrate on drawing, dance, and needlework.[11] The Schools Inquiry Commission reported in the 1860s that establishments for girls were characterized by "want of thoroughness and foundation, want of system; slovenliness and showy superficiality; inattention to rudiments [and] undue time given to accomplishments" (De Bellaigue 11). The education offered by mid-century girls' schools resembles that of Austen's Bertram sisters and Mary Crawford.

Barrett Browning satirizes the girls' school model by means of Aurora's aunt, who "liked accomplishments in girls" and prescribes a constricted pedagogy in contrast to the education advocated by Aurora's father (I.426). Matching form to content, Aurora lists the facts and skills her aunt wants her to learn:

> I learnt a little algebra, a little
> Of the mathematics,—brushed with extreme flounce
> The circle of the sciences, because
> She misliked women who are frivolous.
> I learnt the royal genealogies
> Of Oviedo, the internal laws
> Of the Burmese empire,—by how many feet
> Mount Chimborazo outsoars Teneriffe,
> What navigable river joins itself
> To Lara, and what census of the year five

> Was taken at Klagenfurt,—because she liked
> A general insight into useful facts. (I.403–14)

In her satire of a nineteenth-century girls' school curriculum, Barrett Browning stresses that Aurora's aunt "misliked women who are frivolous," but the language Aurora uses to describe this education ironically suggests a superficially ordered method to learning. These lines stress the incoherence inherent in her aunt's educational model; Aurora learns "a *little* algebra, a *little* / of the mathematics." She does not even use the verb "to learn" to describe her experience with "The circle of the sciences," which she "brushed with extreme flounce." Her aunt's curriculum encourages Aurora to view people of other cultures only in terms of trivial textbook facts instead of trying to understand how they lived. Aurora's aunt's supposedly utilitarian education, intended to be useful to Aurora when she embraces her role as a wife, appears most ridiculous when Aurora calls these geographical facts "useful."

Using Alice Jenkins's study of what she calls the "spatial imagination" in the nineteenth century, we could also think about how Barrett Browning views education in terms of conceptual space (1). When Aurora explains, "I learnt the royal genealogies / Of Oviedo," for example, we hear Aurora, prompted by her aunt, speaking from a space that is conceptually distant from the people she studies. Barrett Browning critiques the predominant educational models because they cannot break down the distance between students and the world they learn about in books.

Barrett Browning criticizes both the girls' school model and the types of informal education often available to women. Aurora recounts reading "a score of books on womanhood / To prove, if women do not think at all, / They may teach thinking, (to a maiden-aunt / Or else the author)" (I.427–30). Here Aurora rejects traditional conduct-manual training in "books on womanhood."[12] Although, as scholars have noted, conduct books and women's periodicals offered an informal education for women outside of institutions—something that, seemingly, Barrett Browning would have supported—this brand of informal education espouses the dangerously authoritative approach against which Aurora's father warns her.[13] Conduct books teach feminine conformity and submissiveness, helping women to "boldly assert / Their right of comprehending husband's talk / When not too deep" (I.430–32). Ultimately, Aurora equates her aunt's training to an education in repression, which, far from stretching the mind, offers only the experience of drowning. "In looking down" her past education, she says, "I wonder if Brinvilliers suffered more / In the water-torture . . . [author's ellipsis] flood succeeding flood / To drench the incapable throat and split the veins . . . [author's ellipsis] / Than I did" (I.467–70). Invoking images of terror, she describes her aunt's educational method in terms of constriction.

Despite receiving a torturous education, Aurora manages to maintain a lively intellectual life deep within herself. She mitigates the harmful effects of her aunt's teaching:

> I kept the life thrust on me, on the outside
> Of the inner life with all its ample room
> For heart and lungs, for will and intellect,
> Inviolable by conventions. (I.477–80)

This education proves instructive but not in the way that her aunt intends. Aurora realizes her need for an intellectual life. As Virginia Woolf writes in her essay on *Aurora Leigh*, Aurora was able to escape the tortures of her aunt's education because "Aurora herself was blessed with a little room.... There she retired; there she read" ("Aurora Leigh" 441). But it was *how* Aurora read that mattered most to Barrett Browning. Aurora desires learning in order to cultivate an "inner life" instead of pursuing an education that manifests itself in accomplishments deemed valuable in the marriage market. Barrett Browning distinguishes Aurora's desire to cultivate an inner life from conduct books encouraging women's reading in order to develop their interiority. Instead of an education that fosters her emotional intelligence to fulfill her socially scripted roles as wife and mother, Aurora yearns for an education that will inspire her as a writer and reformer.

Escaping the education that Aurora's aunt prescribes for her requires more than simply obtaining a room of her own. She transcends her aunt's oppressive pedagogy by shifting from an education in facts to an experiential education. The headlong reading at the heart of her learning approach encourages her to develop emotional intelligence: she says, "But, after I had read for memory, / I read for hope" (I.729–30). Instead of reading to memorize "formal universals" (III.747) as Romney does, Aurora reads to acquire a capacity for empathy along with intellectual depth. She rejects the curricula that Romney and her aunt follow because they have not gained any emotional insight. In opposing ways, her aunt's "score of books on womanhood" and the books that Aurora's father uses to show her the ignorance of men help her to break free from the constraints imposed upon her as a woman and to become, ultimately, a poet.

In the first book of her "novel-poem," Barrett Browning teaches us to be headlong readers of her text. We receive our own education as readers along with Aurora; just as Aurora needs to consciously work against the education she receives from her aunt, Barrett Browning unteaches us as readers, encouraging us to let go of our trained habits of reading. Before Aurora begins to describe her headlong reading, she interrupts herself, saying, "Mark, there" (I.702). These two words stand visibly apart from the lines of verse surrounding them. Aurora's interjection acknowledges the reader of the book and encourages attention to the act of reading. Here Barrett Browning begins to teach us to read like Aurora. After this interruption, Aurora's description of reading shifts from the first person singular, "I . . . read my books," to the inclusive plural in her call for headlong reading: "It is rather when / We gloriously forget ourselves and plunge / Soul-forward, headlong" into books that we benefit from them (I.698–700, 705–7). In the didactic passage that follows this interruption, the plural pronouns draw readers into the lesson and guide them toward a different mode of reading. Barrett Browning urges us to read her text not through the conventional methods used by Romney or Aurora's aunt but precisely through Aurora's experience of resistance to these approaches. Barrett Browning teaches us an engaged—even empathic—reading that can break down the barriers of class and gender reinforced by institutional models. She urges us to feel her poetry and therefore become involved in the reform she proposes.

Aurora's Experiential Learning and Headlong Reading

Rejecting the approach to learning that she sees in Romney and her aunt, Aurora turns to an approach to texts that depends on the reader to bring them alive. If, as Herbert Tucker suggests, we can consider *Aurora Leigh* as a spasmodic epic, we might also consider how spasmodic tropes allow us, as readers, to experience first-hand Barrett Browning's model of experiential education. Tucker discusses Barrett Browning's use of "shudder, pulsation, outburst, and spasm" as "tropes of creative power" in the context of spasmodic poetry (378). Spasmody, as Tucker establishes, calls attention to the reader's experience of reading poetry, and Barrett Browning relies on spasmodic images to involve her reader in her project of educational reform. Aurora rejects reading texts in a way that distances the reader:

> We get no good
> By being ungenerous, even to a book,
> And calculating profits,—so much help
> By so much reading. (I.702–5)

A "calculating" reading stands in contrast to headlong reading, which allows for an element of unpredictability. Education, for Aurora, works not in strictly cerebral terms—in calculations or balanced equations, with "so much reading" giving "so much help." She tells us it is when we "plunge" "into a book's profound" and become "impassioned" for a book's "beauty and salt of truth— / 'Tis then we get the right good from a book" (I.706–9). Aurora's headlong reading opposes the "passivity" of female reading often encouraged in the nineteenth century, as Kate Flint discusses in *The Woman Reader 1837–1913*, and the metaphor of plunging into water stands in direct opposition to the image of Aurora drowning in her aunt's pedagogy (330).

Aurora experiences a strong bodily engagement with texts as a result of her headlong reading. She feels the text even before she begins reading, explaining how she "felt it beat / Under my pillow, In the morning's dark, / An hour before the sun would let me read! / My books!" (I.841–4).[14] "At last because the time was ripe," Aurora "chanced upon the poets" (I.844–5); the word "chance" reminds us that she refuses to follow a prescribed curriculum. The books' palpable heartbeat gives them a human element and invites an intimate reading. Aurora's living, beating books require the reader to feel their meter, to register their spasmodic pulse. Instead of regarding book learning in opposition to experiential learning as Wordsworth does in "The Tables Turned" (1798) when his speaker cries, "Up! up! my Friend, and quit your books" (1), Aurora enacts an experiential reading of poetry—a headlong reading—that moves her and changes her. "As the earth / Plunges in fury, when the internal fires / Have reached and pricked her heart," her soul, she explains, "At poetry's divine first finger-touch / Let go conventions and sprang up surprised" (I.845–7, 851–2).[15] This forceful, energy-infused diction makes it clear that reading not only affects her intellectually but also affects her physically; texts cause her to spring up, they prick her heart, and they set it beating with its own rhythms. Aurora's reading results in embodied knowledge, achieving permanence unlike the memorized theories that Romney takes in only to regurgitate on examinations. Embodied knowledge, Barrett Browning suggests, can be especially important for women reformers who seek to overturn existing systems.

Barrett Browning compares the effect of the reader on the text to that of the wind sweeping through trees, setting them in motion:

> But the sun was high
> When first I felt my pulses set themselves
> For concord; when the rhythmic turbulence
> Of blood and brain swept outward upon words,
> As wind upon the alders, blanching them
> By turning up their under-natures till
> They trembled in dilation. (I.895–901)

The act of reading becomes a reciprocal engagement between reader and text. Barrett Browning draws our attention to "the rhythmic turbulence / Of blood and brain swept outward upon words." The words need to be read in order to come alive. The reader must "blanch" the words, "turning up their under-natures till / They trembled in dilation." Aurora feels the power of herself as a reader akin to the wind that disrupts the stillness of trees. Headlong readers participate in their own self-directed, active, trembling, turbulent, and exciting education. Education, for Barrett Browning, is a hands-on project. She underscores both the intellectual and moral benefits of her ideal pedagogy: readers can make intellectual meaning as they read, and their openness to texts can translate to an empathy for other people, as shown in Aurora's friendship with Marian.

Marian's Education through "Stray Odd Volumes"

The emotional intelligence Aurora gains from her empathic education allows her to narrate the unconventional pedagogical experiences of working-class Marian. Aurora meets Marian because Romney initially intends to marry her as part of his socialist project, informed by the theories he gleaned from his university education. In Romney, we see a precursor to the character of Egremont who proposes an idealistic educational plan for the working classes in Gissing's *Thyrza*. In contrast to Romney, who only understands Marian on the level of "universals," Aurora empathizes with Marian's intense desire to learn. Barrett Browning stresses that Aurora's understanding of Marian, enabled by her education, distinguishes her friendship with Marian from an act of charity. Isobel Armstrong notes that "Aurora and Marian are united in a truly democratic way which transcends class through their capacity for imaginative passion and outgoing love, particularly the love of children, for the poem is an intense defence of the expressive, emotional, affective life allied with passionate intelligence" (369). Reading *Aurora Leigh* in the context of Barrett Browning's educational ideas allows us to understand their friendship as a result of the experiential education each woman embraces.[16]

Though mostly self-educated, Marian very briefly attends a formal school. Here Barrett Browning critiques another type of utilitarian educational institution—the elementary school formed as part of the mass education movement in the nineteenth century, which promoted learning through rote memorization. "A lady" sends Marian to "Sunday-school," so that Marian can "learn books / And sit upon a long bench in a row / With other children" (III.901–4). Instead of actually learning from books, however, the students "laugh and laugh and maul their texts" (III.905). The Sunday School teaches reading to Marian in a way that sparks no intellectual excitement; this school produces an environment where texts are ridiculed and "mauled." Sunday School students form a physical relationship with texts but it is an unproductive one, unlike Aurora's headlong reading.

Bourgeois educational reformers, like the organizers of Marian's Sunday School, encouraged working-class readers to passively read a controlled set of predetermined texts. But readers from the working classes often chose to read beyond what was deemed appropriate for them. Many read the works of well-known authors such as Milton and Shakespeare and responded in writing to what they read. They valued their own role as individual readers who make texts come alive. As their autobiographical writings show, the kinds of reading done by the working classes often served to undermine a bourgeois cultural hegemony instead of satisfying it.[17] In this way, working-class readers departed dramatically from the projected plan of mass education. As Altick discusses, once working-class readers could be identified as a large group, bourgeois politicians initiated a campaign to preserve the status quo and prevent them from gaining too much power; this campaign, shown to have been unsuccessful by Jonathan Rose's research, promoted the kind of utilitarian reading that Sunday School requires of Marian (Altick 140). Unlike Barrett Browning, who encouraged headlong reading of her own text, some authors expressed anxiety about this mass readership, attempting to control potential interpretations of their work by employing strategies such as the direct address.[18]

Education for the working classes, dependent on rote memorization, often echoed the monotony of children's lives in factories. In her earlier poem "The Cry of the Children" (1843), Barrett Browning emphasizes what children cannot know as a result of "driv[ing] the wheels of iron / In the factories, round and round" (75–6). In her rhythmic lines that mimic the turning of machines' wheels—"All are turning, all the day, and we with all"—she reminds us that child laborers have become accustomed to the "droning" and "turning" of the "wheels" at the expense of knowing the world outside of the factory (84, 77). As a result, they cannot grasp the difference between flowers and weeds: "Are your cowslips of the meadows / Like our weeds anear the mine?" (61–2). When they observe the sky, they see the clouds only in terms of factory images; the clouds are "wheel-like, turning" (130). I suggest that we consider Marian's education in *Aurora Leigh* as evidence of Barrett Browning's continued exploration of what an education for a working-class child might look like—an education that defies the monotony of factory work and the models of rote learning for the working classes.

Marian yearns for knowledge beyond the material she learns in Sunday School. Through her experiential learning, she discovers that she can define her own role as a reader instead of accepting a position predetermined by a patriarchal and class-based hierarchy. Barrett Browning experiments with the possibility that an experiential approach can help someone transcend gender and class biases. When Aurora analyzes Marian's self-education, she begins to notice ways in which Marian resembles a woman of a higher class. Aurora deems Marian "capable / Of catching from the fringes of the wind / Some fragmentary phrases, here and there, / Of that fine music" (III.1003–6). These fragments not only reach her mind but are also "carried in / To her soul," which implies an education that affects Marian deeply, much as Aurora's "Soul-forward," headlong reading allows her to inhabit a book (III.1006–7, I.707). We learn that Marian's education "had reproduced itself afresh / In finer motions of the lips and lids" (III.1007–8). Like Aurora's headlong reading, Marian's reading manifests itself permanently in her body, giving her face a delicate, virtuous appearance that links Marian to Aurora. By underscoring their similarities, Barrett Browning sets up the possibility that these two women from vastly different classes can share an approach to reading. Their pedagogical methods can potentially break down class barriers.

Aurora tells us what Marian reads in terms that Barrett Browning's nineteenth-century readers would have understood. She assumes an audience that has read Milton and Shakespeare and can understand these references. Unlike Aurora, who receives early guidance from her father and can read his books, Marian lacks educated parents and has little access to literature. Even though Marian tries to educate herself by going "To hear a lecture at an institute," she grows "To no book-learning,—she was ignorant / Of authors" (III.997, 998–1000). Marian attends a local evening school for working men and women, which provides education for the lower classes, but the "lecture" format proves unsuccessful in providing a meaningful education for her.

The education Marian cobbles together on the street while her parents "tramped" proves more valuable to her than the one she receives at Sunday School or through lectures (III.948). She learns by mixing fragments of books:

> Often too
> The pedlar stopped, and tapped her on the head
> With absolute forefinger, brown and ringed,
> And asked if peradventure she could read. (III.968–71)

Aurora recognizes how much of Marian's learning depends on chance—on the whim of the peddler. Marian, who otherwise might have continued "mauling" texts like her classmates, needs to piece together what she gathers from snippets of books the peddler "toss[es]" her: "A Thomson's Seasons, mulcted of the Spring, / Or half a play of Shakspeare's [*sic*] torn across" (III.974–5). Outside of an institutional setting, Marian must fill in the blanks between the fragments of books she receives. Unlike Mill and Newman—and Gissing's character Egremont in *Thyrza*—who describe accidentally reading texts, Marian enacts an "accidental" reading by necessity. The texts that Marian obtains require her to become a writerly reader:

> (She had to guess the bottom of a page
> By just the top sometimes,—as difficult,
> As, sitting on the moon, to guess the earth!)
> Or else a sheaf of leaves (for that small Ruth's
> Small gleanings) torn out from the heart of books,
> From Churchyard Elegies and Edens Lost,
> From Burns, and Bunyan, Selkirk, and Tom Jones (III.976–82)

Like Aurora's texts that depend on the reader, the pieces of books that Marian receives require her to pull them together. Marian's headlong reading thus challenges educational reformers' reading plan for the masses because she not only reads texts by Milton and Shakespeare, which are associated with the more powerful classes, but also involves herself in the stories and crafts her own endings. She encounters them, creating her own versions of each text piece by piece instead of memorizing them whole. The figure of the self-taught student piecing together an education reappears in Hardy's Jude, who conjures up a way to read while driving a cart selling baked goods.

Connecting with texts on an individual, emotional level lets Marian "weed out / Her book-leaves" (III.987). She "threw away the leaves that hurt" (III.988). Her use of the word "hurt" implies Marian's deep emotional connection to what she reads: she allows texts to affect her to the extent that they can hurt her. Through her piecemeal version of headlong reading, Marian experiences these texts on her own terms, writing herself out of a gendered and classed reading.

Despite showing some of its benefits, Barrett Browning resists romanticizing Marian's education completely. In addition to recognizing the writerly qualities of Marian's reading, Aurora acknowledges the challenges Marian confronts in learning without any formal intellectual context:

> 'Twas somewhat hard to keep the things distinct,
> And oft the jangling influence jarred the child
> Like looking at a sunset full of grace
> Through a pothouse window while the drunken oaths
> Went on behind her. (III.983–7)

Aurora's narration stresses the hurdles Marian faces in learning outside of a formal educational context, without the privileges of a family library. It is "as difficult, / As, sitting on the moon, to guess the earth!" (III.977–8). Despite the exciting possibilities inherent in her learning approach, Marian's education cannot allow her to transcend her own social position completely. Barrett Browning unveils the possibility of a pedagogical alternative for working-class students and for women, but this approach needs more social support in order to truly empower marginalized students. Marian's fate is undeniably tragic: society ostracizes her when she bears a child after being raped. In Marian, Barrett Browning shows us the potential for a learning approach that can capitalize on the creativity in new groups of readers, but reminds us—urgently—in Marian's tragic fate how much work still needs to be done.

56 *Radical Education in* Aurora Leigh

Barrett Browning affirms the importance of supporting a framework for Marian's experiential education and making such frameworks accessible to everyone. She remains aware of the challenge that this undertaking will involve, especially because it will require inventing new forms of education rather than transferring existing models to a wider population. Merely teaching new groups of students with old pedagogies will not be productive, she realizes. New forms of learning need to capitalize on headlong reading. Marian's learning is a step in the right direction, reminding us that an intellectual framework need not take the shape of an institution, as she reiterates throughout *Aurora Leigh* in her examples of learning outside of schools.[19]

Ultimately Barrett Browning asks nineteenth-century readers to change the course of their thinking about educational reform. Can we provide Marian with an educational context in which to understand her fragments of knowledge without losing the positive aspects of her experiential approach? Barrett Browning's accounts of Aurora's and Marian's experiential educations invite us to become headlong readers of Barrett Browning's text and, in so doing, to become involved in educational reform. The questions that Barrett Browning raises about teaching nontraditional students like Marian remain unanswered for much of the nineteenth century. Thomas Hardy grapples with them in his novels, as will be discussed in Chapter 4.

Barrett Browning urges us to continue thinking in new ways about educational reform for all kinds of students including Marians, Auroras, and Romneys. If we adopt the main principles of her vision of education, we resist reading her book—or any book—in search of one neatly defined, authoritative answer to the questions she raises about education. Through our headlong reading of *Aurora Leigh*, we learn to imaginatively pull ideas together, forming the roots of our own reform.

Notes

1 See Dalley for a discussion of both writers in the context of Barrett Browning's politics (538–9). The educational reformer Alice Woods mentions *Aurora Leigh* in her book *Educational Experiments in England* (15); Stone discusses *Aurora Leigh*'s influence on Woods in her biography of Barrett Browning (192–3).
2 Some scholars have briefly discussed women's education in *Aurora Leigh* in relation to Tennyson's *The Princess*, and others have noted Barrett Browning's attraction to Romantic ideas about education. See especially work by Beverly Taylor and Marjorie Stone on education in *The Princess* and *Aurora Leigh*. Several scholars have studied *Aurora Leigh*'s resonances with the Romantic tradition. See Kathleen Blake ("Elizabeth Barrett Browning and Wordsworth: The Romantic Poet as a Woman"), Linda K. Hughes ("Elizabeth Barrett Browning, *Aurora Leigh*"), Linda Peterson ("'For My Better Self': Auto/biographies of the Poetess, the *Prelude* of the Poet Laureate, and Elizabeth Barrett Browning's *Aurora Leigh*"), Marjorie Stone (*Elizabeth Barrett Browning*), Beverly Taylor ("Elizabeth Barrett Browning and the Politics of Childhood"), and John Woolford ("Elizabeth Barrett and the Wordsworthian Sublime"). Aurora's model of learning resonates with ideas about education expressed by Romantic poets and philosophers, particularly Wordsworth's distaste for relying solely on book learning; Rousseau's emphasis on individualistic, experiential learning; and Locke's emphasis on self-knowledge. As Beverly Taylor has helpfully noted, Barrett Browning aligns herself

with Rousseau, especially in her childrearing practices, particularly her "insistence on the importance of play and refusal to set her son Pen to organized study of reading and math" ("Elizabeth Barrett Browning and the Politics of Childhood" 406).

3   My argument about Barrett Browning as both poet and reformer through her educational vision speaks to a more general ongoing conversation in Barrett Browning criticism. In his 2007 article, "An Ebbigrammar of Motives; or, Ba for Short," Herbert Tucker lists the various roles to which critics have assigned Barrett Browning before offering his own reading: "The EBB whom I mean to praise is the EBB who meant to be above all, not a reformer or woman writer or evangelist or polemicist or lover but a poet, a maker of verbal art—in which capacity, to be sure, those other roles may be included and their several aims made good, nay better, in poetry's gift" (445). For a detailed study of the critical, social, and cultural context of *Aurora Leigh*, see Michele Martinez's *Elizabeth Barrett Browning's* Aurora Leigh: *A Reader's Guide*.

4   Barrett Browning's ideas about looking within oneself as the first step of reform were most likely influenced by Thomas Carlyle, who concludes his "Signs of the Times" with the statement: "To reform a world, to reform a nation, no wise man will undertake; and all but foolish men know, that the only solid, though a far slower reformation, is what each begins and perfects on *himself*" (49).

5   Anticipating our contemporary understanding of "experiential education," she proposes an experiential approach through which students engage in the learning process physically and emotionally, as opposed to simply memorizing facts and repeating directed lessons assigned by a teacher. Her experiential model encourages students to make meaning of their experiences, transforming what they learn into knowledge that they can draw upon to understand others. Writers, educators, and philosophers began to use the term "experiential" in the nineteenth century to describe knowledge based on experience or observation (*OED*) and "experiential education" became a common term in educational discourse starting in the twentieth century (Association for Experiential Education).

6   As I will discuss later on, Herbert Tucker has pointed out the ways in which *Aurora Leigh* can be considered a spasmodic epic (377–84). It will also be helpful to keep in mind, as Rachel Ablow has noted, "in the mid- to late- nineteenth century, reading was commonly regarded as at least as valuable as an affective experience as it was as a way to convey information or increase understanding" (2).

7   For detailed accounts of the expansion of education in the nineteenth century, see Richard D. Altick, *The English Common Reader: A Social History of the Mass Reading Public, 1800–1900*, 2nd ed., and David Vincent, *Literacy and Popular Culture: England 1750–1914*.

8   See Mermin (19–20). Christina De Bellaigue discusses the broader prevailing notion that the study of Greek and Latin was considered inappropriate for women (see especially 177).

9   Aurora starts to use alternative pedagogies that enable this experiential education as early as when she gazes at her mother's portrait (I.128–73). While Sandra M. Gilbert and Susan Gubar suggest this passage depicts Aurora observing the scripted roles available to her as a young woman, restricted by past depictions of women in myth and literature (18–19, 25) and Beverly Taylor claims that Aurora finds "only confusion in the ambiguous portrait and the silence of her dead mother" ("School-Miss Alfred" 17), my interpretation of this scene is more in line with Carrie Preston's reading: "For Aurora, they represent the 'incoherencies' of life and how types are 'mixed and merged,' rather than static, bounded categories of being" (45).

10 Several scholars have noted Barrett Browning's satire of the typical girls' school education of accomplishments. See Armstrong (319), Gilbert & Gubar (560–61), and Beverly Taylor ("'School-Miss Alfred' and 'Materfamilias': Female Sexuality and Poetic Voice in *The Princess* and *Aurora Leigh*" 17). I argue that the girls' school model of education that Aurora receives gives her knowledge of ignorance and propels her toward her alternative experiential education.

11 De Bellaigue's discussion of "accomplishments" provides helpful context for Barrett Browning's use of this vague word: "For all the criticism of 'accomplishments,' precisely what they consisted in varied, although prospectuses and educational treatises usually suggest that they included music, drawing, dance, and needlework. A study of the curriculum in twenty-nine private boarding-schools for girls does suggest that these subjects did account for a considerable proportion of what was taught in girls' schools" (173).

12 As Dalley points out, the language of Aurora's description of the lessons she learns from "a score of books on womanhood" (1.427) "offers a direct rebuke to the 'Angel in the House' figure lauded by many of her contemporaries such as Patmore" (531).

13 See especially Kate Flint's *The Woman Reader, 1837–1914* and Jennifer Phegley's *Educating the Proper Woman Reader*. Flint's extensive research on women's reading reveals the informal education women received outside of schools, especially from conduct books. She summarizes the conflicted views on women's reading and sentimentality; some believed that women should read texts in order to cultivate their capacity for sympathy while others thought that women's susceptibility to emotion and sensation should be closely monitored (91–2). In her discussion of how *Cornhill* emphasized its educative role for women, Phegley reminds us that periodicals also played a role in women's informal education (76–80).

14 Aurora feels the physical presence of her book before she reads it. See Leah Price's *How to Do Things with Books in Victorian Britain* for a study of books' physical presence as part of the social context for reading practices.

15 Rudy comments on the powerful physical imagery in this passage, noting that it is "nearly masturbatory in its suggestion—the soul 'sprang up surprised' at being touched so by poetry's finger—the image insists on a spiritual dynamic but relies for its power on the physiological . . ." (180).

16 In my reading of Marian's and Aurora's similar educational approach and understanding of each other, I depart from Daniel Karlin's who claims that "even though Aurora herself goes out into the social world, she portrays herself as alien to it, always on the edge of a conversation or reluctantly drawn in to the circuit of gossip, keener to observe than to take part" (117).

17 See in particular Jonathan Rose's work on the autobiographies of working-class readers (*The Intellectual Life of the British Working Classes*).

18 Patrick Brantlinger's *The Reading Lesson: The Threat of Mass Literacy in Nineteenth-Century British Fiction* and Garrett Stewart's *Dear Reader: The Conscripted Audience in Nineteenth-Century British Fiction* both discuss nineteenth-century British writers' anxiety about how their novels will be perceived and read by the newly forming mass readership.

19 Whereas Barrett Browning experiments with an experiential education that emphasizes reading outside of one's prescribed lessons—outside of an educational institution—George Eliot, writing *Mill on the Floss* (1860) just a few years after *Aurora Leigh* is published, analyzes the limits of independent reading in Maggie Tulliver. In a different way from Barrett Browning, Eliot critiques the institutional education given to women, showing in Maggie a woman who cannot successfully educate herself because her upbringing proves to be too limiting.

4 "I Will Do without Cambridge"
Thomas Hardy's Autodidacts

Writing at a time when more first-generation college students than ever before sought higher education in England, Thomas Hardy recognizes that universities were missing out on the chance to benefit from students' originality. Hardy's fictional autodidacts approach their studies with unbounded curiosity. They seek ways to connect the lessons they learn with their experiences in the real world. The eponymous hero in *Jude the Obscure* (1895), for example, conjures up a way to study the dictionary while driving a cart selling baked goods; he would "ingeniously fix open, by means of a strap attached to the tilt, the volume he was reading, [and] spread the dictionary on his knees" (28).[1] For Jude, whose education takes place in the world outside of an Oxford classroom, learning is an essential part of human experience.

By the time Hardy was writing, the Education Act of 1870 had paved the way to more widespread elementary education for the masses. The working classes could pursue higher education at schools such as the Working Men's College or through the university extension. Meanwhile, the first colleges for women at Cambridge and Oxford had opened their doors, and more avenues existed for working-class men to attend these universities. Recognizing this progress but not enthusiastically applauding it, Hardy noticed that much educational reform served to reinforce class distinctions instead of allowing students to climb the social ladder.

For Hardy, it was not enough for schools like Oxford and Cambridge to become more accessible to students from less traditional backgrounds; he challenges these centuries-old institutions to reassess their pedagogies. The largely self-taught Hardy critiques both old and new schools for not valuing the qualities he sees in autodidacts, and he fears that a largely self-taught student will lose his energy for learning as a result of adopting institutional pedagogies. Hardy's fear is historically grounded because this is precisely what happens to many students who enter educational programs for the working classes. Instead of capitalizing on the initiative that Hardy identifies in self-taught intellectuals, school administrators often decided that their working-class students needed a pedagogical model based on lectures and memorization. The classism inherent in these schools led instructors to assume that the lower classes were unable to think creatively; but, in fact, teachers were destroying that very capacity. These same schools then faulted students for not thinking independently. One university extension examiner remarks of the responses to Latin exam questions: "In the unprepared translation, the majority of the candidates signally failed, apparently because they had not been taught to think out clearly translations for themselves."[2] A report on the Botany examination notes: "There was a marked deficiency" by "Seniors" and "Juniors" "in the answers to those questions which required thought rather than mere memory, and the almost universal failure of the attempts to describe plants from the actual specimens seems to shew that this part of the subject has scarcely been taught at all" (299). Students were taught to memorize but not to think critically about what they had absorbed. Despite these dissatisfied examiners' reports, however, the movement proceeded largely unchanged. It was not until the twentieth century that leaders of the university extension such as Professor M.E. Sadler, writing in the 1908 University Extension report *Oxford and Working-class Education*, criticized these lectures for being too disjointed and ineffective (38). Decades before Sadler's report, Hardy anticipates his critique, faulting institutions for failing to recognize learning techniques that less traditional students might bring to college.

In his depictions of autodidacts, Hardy stresses the qualities that institutions rarely value. Like Jude, who feels an "impulsive emotion" to learn, Stephen Smith, the son of a mason in *A Pair of Blue Eyes* (1873), has learned everything from Latin to chess on his own, developing approaches that work well for him (29). When he visits the home of Reverend Swancourt and his daughter, Elfride, Stephen finally has the opportunity to play chess with a "living opponent," Elfride (83); he moves the chess pieces with an "indescribable oddness" (83–4), the narrator tells us, playing "by thought" instead of "by rote" (85). Stephen uses engaged thinking instead of relying passively on memorized repetitions of moves as his opponent does. What is unfortunate about Stephen and Jude, Hardy suggests, is not that Oxbridge excludes them; rather it is that the institutional education to which they aspire prevents them from valuing their own strategies. Both men strive desperately to "hob and nob" (96), as Stephen says, with the men "of letters" found at Oxbridge (331). They do not realize what Hardy, also an outsider of Oxford and Cambridge, stresses throughout his novels: that an Oxbridgean education sometimes closes students' minds more than it opens them.

Although he draws our attention to the assets of an autodidact's education, Hardy resists adopting a celebratory tone characteristic of nineteenth-century stories about self-taught men. He rewrites the narrative of the self-made man often recounted in *The Popular Educator*, a publication that Hardy read when he was young, which encouraged autodidacts to take advantage of the freedom afforded by a self-education. It offered ambitious teach-yourself courses ranging from Latin to Physics to Poetry as well as accounts of other self-taught men. The short tales in this publication of working-class men rising rapidly to success are characterized by a formulaic, simplistic plot. A young man desperately wants to rise above his humble origins; he works hard to do so by teaching himself; and his self-education results in financial success, immeasurable happiness, and respect from people of all classes. Departing from these narratives, Hardy takes advantage of the novel's length to weigh the positives and negatives of learning on one's own. He identifies the deprivation of social literacy as a substantial negative of an autodidact's education.

In order to investigate autodidacticism as part of a broader educational debate, Hardy often puts the narrative of the autodidact in tension with the story of the university-educated man. Hardy's novels do not just critique the elitism of established schools; they also call into question the limiting model of learning offered within those institutions. Echoing Austen and Barrett Browning, Hardy points out that universities reserved for the upper classes often hinder students' thinking. He sets up a contrast repeatedly in his novels between autodidacts who espouse active learning versus Oxbridge men who depend on memorized, received ideas. In *A Pair of Blue Eyes*, for instance, Stephen's Oxford-educated mentor Henry Knight has "abstract" knowledge and "could pack [words] into sentences like a workman, but practically was nowhere" (199). Hardy further challenges common ideas about class and education by associating rote learning, usually linked to the working classes, with Knight, a gentleman. Highlighting the rote learning in elite schools and the energetic learning done by self-taught men, Hardy calls into question the labels we ascribe to people based on their education. He challenges the category of "autodidact" itself. Although the autodidact in the nineteenth century was usually conceived as a man from humble origins, Hardy reverses this assumption in the character of the privileged-class Angel in *Tess of the D'Urbervilles* (1891) who declares "I will do without Cambridge," deciding instead to become a self-taught farmer (115). In order to connect with the farmers he meets on a personal level, he needs to "obliterate" the information about farmers he read in books (116).

This chapter examines Hardy's exploration of autodidacticism as a significant contribution to nineteenth-century educational discourse that has remained largely overlooked by Hardy scholarship.[3] By studying Hardy's ideas about pedagogy in the context of the educational debates of his time, I consider Hardy's depiction of self-education in his novels not only as a personal investigation of his own educational experience; I suggest we also view it as an exploration of an alternative to education reform that focused almost exclusively on replicating existing institutional models. The number of new colleges and universities that enlisted Hardy for his support—rather ironically, given his general resistance to educational institutions, but tellingly, nonetheless—attests to his far-reaching influence in the world of education.[4] Although he never attended college, he received honorary degrees from the Universities of Aberdeen, Oxford, and Cambridge. When he received the honorary degree from Cambridge in 1913, his sister Mary recalled how he had considered applying to study there in the 1860s: "Now you have accomplished it all with greater honour than if you had gone along the road you saw before you."[5] This message—that there is honor and value in learning on one's own—appears repeatedly in the novels to be discussed. While Hardy's self-education was undoubtedly labor intensive and at times a lonely endeavor, as other critics have noted, nevertheless his approach was not a hindrance but rather an intellectually stimulating method of learning that linked him to a large community of other autodidacts.[6] Hardy was part of a long tradition of male autodidacticism in Britain, particularly in the nineteenth century, which included well-known authors such as Charles Dickens and public figures such as Francis Place. The autobiographies that Jonathan Rose studies resonate particularly with Hardy's self-education in London (409–11). Whereas Barrett Browning emphasizes the possibility of reform from within individual female characters, Hardy sees the potential for reform in an entire community of autodidacts.

Even as he imagines autodidacticism as a realistic substitute for schools, what remains problematic for Hardy is society's fantasy of Oxbridge, associated with masculinity, power, and personal fulfillment. The patriarchal foundation of Oxbridgean pedagogy troubles Hardy's characters, especially in their relations with women. As Laura Green notes, "if Hardy, despite the frequent misogyny of his narrative voice and the punitive outcomes of his plots, remains a compelling figure for feminist criticism, it is precisely because of his recognition of the Pyrrhic quality, and frequent failure, of patriarchal resolutions" (107). "At the same time," she acknowledges, "he remains unable fully to imagine the emancipation toward which both his heroines and his heroes strive" (107). Whereas Green's helpful study of male and female characters illuminates what she sees as Hardy's exploration of an androgynous intellectual ambition, this chapter focuses on the figure of the *male* autodidact because this is where Hardy registers most clearly the failure of patriarchal educational systems. Hardy champions a self-directed education that can counteract the reinforced class biases of existing institutions, but he acknowledges how difficult it will be to implement, given broader society's adherence to male-dominated models.

This chapter first looks at Hardy's self-education, examining its benefits. Next, it turns to analyzing the receptivity and intellectual hunger of Stephen, in *A Pair of Blue Eyes*, and Jude, in *Jude the Obscure*, who cannot value these qualities in themselves. As part of the discussion of these two novels, the chapter also examines *The Woodlanders*. In the concluding segment, it considers how Angel's choice to become a self-taught farmer in *Tess of the D'Urbervilles* enables him to abandon class biases but does not let him escape the misogyny promoted by a society preoccupied with Oxbridge masculinity. Ultimately Hardy's tales of autodidacts unteach readers who might come to his texts with classist views of those who are self-taught.

Hardy as Autodidact

Mowbray Morris, one of Hardy's contemporary reviewers, criticizes him for writing like "a man 'who has been at a great feast of languages and stole the scraps,' or, in plain English, of making experiments in a form of language which he does not seem clearly to understand, and in a style for which he was assuredly not born" (Morris 220).[7] Morris attributes what he perceives to be shortcomings in Hardy's writing to his autodidacticism, connecting Hardy's self-education with his lack of what Pierre Bourdieu and John Guillory call cultural capital.[8] Raymond Williams resists this trend in the critical reception of Hardy, describing Hardy's depiction of "the educated world" as "sober and just observation":

> What Hardy sees and feels about the educated world of his day, locked in its deep social prejudices and in its consequent human alienation, is so clearly

true that the only surprise is that critics now should still feel sufficiently identified with that world—the world which coarsely and coldly dismissed Jude and millions of other men—to be willing to perform the literary equivalent of that stalest of political tactics: the transfer of bitterness, of a merely class way of thinking, from those who exclude to those who protest.

(206)

Williams urges us to take heed of Hardy's observations about elite education's effects, urging us not to dismiss them as bitter reflections from an excluded student. He reminds us of our own tendency as readers to evaluate self-taught writers through the lens of their educational background; by doing so, he suggests, we limit our reading of texts. Although it is possible, as Millgate suggests, that Hardy "never quite lost the sense of inferiority and resentment stemming from the incompleteness of his schooling," this chapter focuses on how he productively took his education into his own hands as a young boy and set out on a rigorous course of learning that he would continue for the rest of his life (*Biography Revisited* 56).

We know that from a young age Hardy sought education outside of formal schooling, encouraged by his parents and early teachers, and that he accomplished a considerable amount of reading on his own.[9] Hardy, like Austen and Barrett Browning, read extensively, devouring works such as Dryden's Virgil, Samuel Neil's *The Art of Reasoning: A Popular Exposition of the Principles of Logic*, John Ramsay McCulloch's *Principles of Political Economy*, and much of Shakespeare, purchasing his own 10-volume edition (Hardy and Hardy 16; Millgate, *Biography Revisited* 83). He studied Latin and Greek and at age 12 he bought his own copy of *An Introduction to the Latin Tongue*, learning the genders of Latin nouns "by colouring the nouns in three tints" (Hardy and Hardy 22).[10]

In his notebooks we see Hardy taking advantage of the freedom his self-directed education allowed. He studies the language of Wordsworth and Shakespeare (another autodidact) in his *'Studies, Specimens &c.'* notebook. For example, he underlines phrases from Shakespeare such as "soil the fact" and "two days' shine," and makes notations about specific words from Wordsworth (*'Studies, Specimens &c.' Notebook* 3). He plays with Wordsworth's language, writing: "its faint undersong / flapping / jibe / rancour / tarn = mere = lake" (*'Studies, Specimens &c.' Notebook* 3). In their introduction to the *Notebook*, Pamela Dalziel and Michael Millgate repeatedly call our attention to the difficult labor the notebook shows. But these notes also exhibit the liberating aspects of Hardy's self-education, which he would later scrutinize in his novels. Hardy's study of Shakespeare and Wordsworth does not follow a prescribed pattern. He is not performing an exercise or memorizing lines of poetry. Unlike his counterparts at Eton or Oxford in 1865, he can devote considerable time to studying the language of British authors instead of spending most—if not all—of his time mastering Latin and Greek. He can choose which texts to study and how to approach them.

Hardy's self-directed study of the works of Shakespeare and Wordsworth echoes the vitality for learning encouraged by *The Popular Educator*. Anna Henchman discusses how Hardy first learned about astronomy from this publication, and biographers of Hardy mention that he used *The Popular Educator*'s language instruction to teach himself German (Henchman 21; F.E. Hardy 25; Millgate, *Biography Revisited* 54; Tomalin 41).[11] But biographers have not fully considered the implications of its effect on Hardy as a writer and educational thinker, shaping his ideas about his own pursuit of education. *The Popular Educator* exposed Hardy to a culture of autodidacts, influencing his later retelling of the self-taught man's story.

John Cassell first published *The Popular Educator* in 1852 for people wishing to educate themselves on a variety of topics. Cassell, an advocate of the teetotal cause, believed in publishing self-improvement books to keep the working classes away from the public house (Feather 104). Published in many parts, it was widely popular; by the early 1860s it was selling between 25,000 and 30,000 copies a year (Roebuck 44). In addition to the extensive range of rigorous self-guided courses, it provided an illustrated history of England as well as an illustrated family Bible. A quick glance at a page from Volume 6, for example, reveals the end of an intensive lesson on "Electrical Machines" and a study in "Moral Science" titled "The Kind of Indifference which Has Been Considered Essential to Free Agency."

The Popular Educator urged autodidacts to love learning and to take their education seriously. It encourages readers to question and engage with ideas about various subjects ranging from Physics to "Moral Science." A quotation from Locke on the title page urges readers not to focus on memorizing facts but to think critically about what they read: "Reading furnishes the mind only with materials of knowledge" (*Popular Educator* Volume 6). Reading can only do so much: "it is thinking makes what we read ours. We are of the ruminating kind, and it is not enough to cram ourselves with a great load of collections; unless we chew them over and over again, they will not give us strength and nourishment" (*Popular Educator* Volume 6). In contrast to the Oxbridge and university extension model of memorizing and "cramming" for exams, Locke's passage reminds autodidacts to be engaged learners and to think for themselves. The reward comes not in the form of degrees, prestige, or social literacy but in the form of "strength and nourishment" for oneself.

The sense of community fostered by *The Popular Educator* aims to motivate readers, in much the way that the "marginal readings" in Jude's textbook do for Jude; he feels connected to the past readers of his book, using them "as he would have used a comrade or tutor who should have happened to be passing by" (28). From reading *The Popular Educator*, Hardy would have learned about other self-taught men such as John Harrison, a carpenter who taught himself mathematics from "a manuscript copy of Professor Saunderson's lectures" and invented "the first chronometer maker" (I.362).[12] George Stephenson, another autodidact, overcame his "unpromising beginning" by educating himself and patenting a locomotive engine, becoming "an extensive locomotive manufacturer at Newcastle, a railway contractor, and a great colliery and ironwork owner" (I.75–6). *The Popular Educator* quotes Stephenson: "I've dined with princes, peers, and commoners—with persons of all classes, from the humblest to the highest. . . . I've seen mankind in all its phases, and the conclusion I have arrived at is this, that if we were all

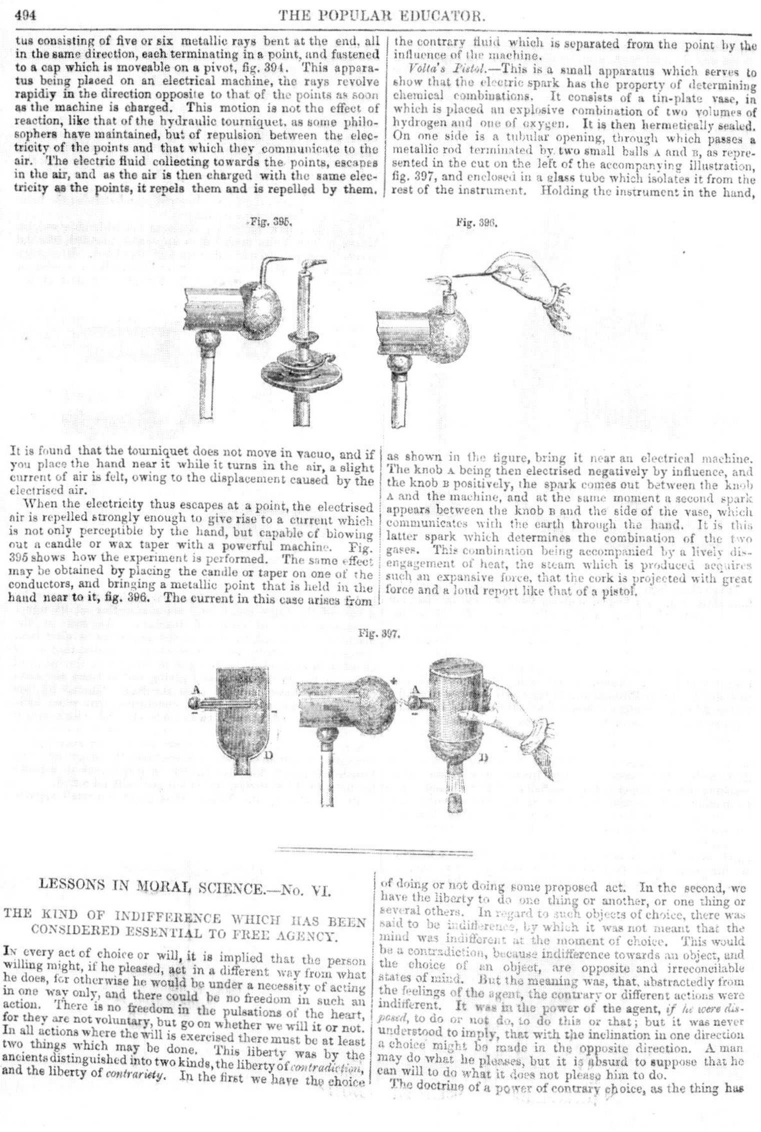

Figure 4.1 Page from *The Popular Educator* (1855)

Source: The Bodleian Libraries, The University of Oxford (OC) 260 h.8 (vols 5–6), p. 494.

stripped there is not much difference!" (76). These stories of autodidacts, written in a motivational tone, pass quickly over the details of the education the men provided for themselves and dwell exuberantly on the individuals' successes. In the article "The Education of the People," the editors celebrate the class equality Stephenson suggests and emphasize the publication's appeal to all classes: "it is

66 "*I Will Do without Cambridge*"

not only among the humbler classes that our work is read and appreciated, but many among the affluent welcome its appearance" (I.97). They cite an appreciative member of the House of Commons: "I find it invaluable; indeed, I have commenced my education over again" (I.97). Although *The Popular Educator* tries conspicuously to make its effort transcend class, the fact remains that most of its readers craved the knowledge on its pages because they were not of a higher class and could not attend elite universities. Hardy contests claims of easy class mobility in his exploration of the role that education plays in providing social literacy.

The Popular Educator's promotion of education as a collaborative effort across classes contrasts with the ideas perpetuated by the institutional communities of Oxford and Cambridge. This publication reminds us of the less publicized but very present culture of learning on one's own that persisted despite widespread educational rhetoric that focused only on institutions. Multiple resources existed for those seeking an education outside of schools. The following excerpt from the National Home Reading Union shows another example of the initiative of the autodidact community. The brochure announces "The Second Summer Assembly" held at Blackpool, Lancashire, from 15–25 July 1890.

There is much choice in terms of format, and attendees can choose between a weeklong course or individual lectures. The "Assembly" offers an eclectic list

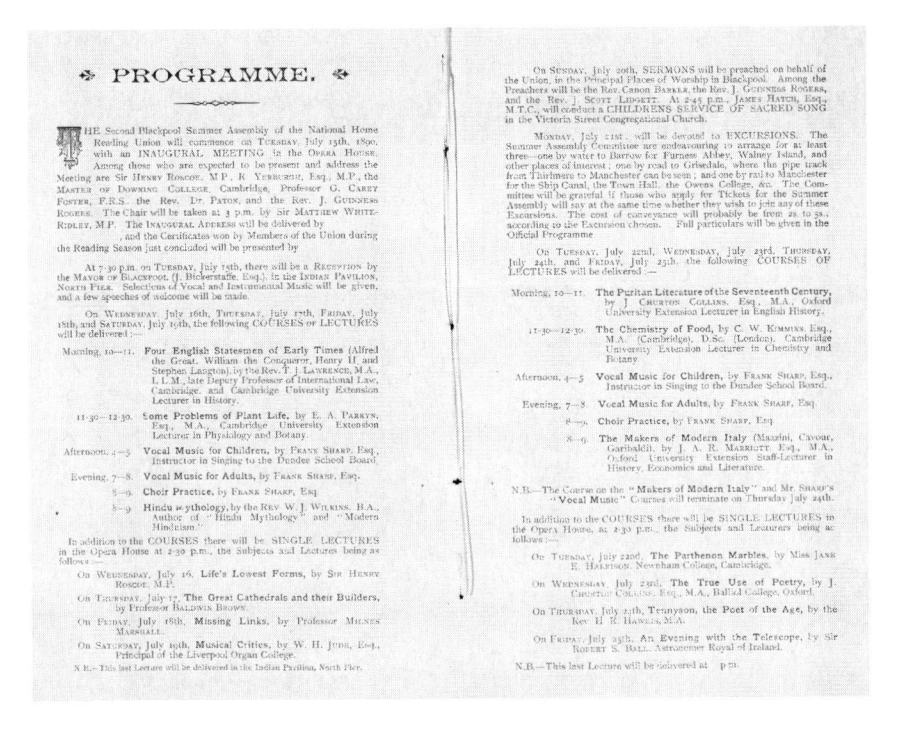

Figure 4.2 National Home Reading Union Program (1890); see Appendix 3 for a larger reproduction

Source: The Bodleian Libraries, The University of Oxford 26271 e.3, pp. 1–2.

of subjects, and the formats include lectures, science presentations emphasizing hands-on learning, and "Excursions" by boat, land, or rail. The National Home Reading Union reminds us that autodidacts had opportunities to gather with other self-taught students.

Whereas *The Popular Educator* and the National Home Reading Union aim to cultivate the autodidact's intellectual curiosity, other resources for the self-taught working-class student were not as genuine in this effort. In *The Reason Why? A Careful Collection of Some Hundreds of Reasons for Things Which, Though Generally Known, Are Imperfectly Understood* (1856), available for only twopence, readers can peruse answers to an extremely broad range of questions such as:

103. What is life?
Life is a state of existence endowed with certain faculties of sensation, and depending upon various conditions or laws, by which the living creature is brought into relation to the various objects surrounding him.

134. Would it not be better to drink beer than water?
Not so. Most beer is more impure than water on account of adulteration. Besides which the constant use of beer is expensive, and is liable to induce habits of intemperance.

171. Why is the elephant's neck so short?
Because the weight of a head so heavy could not have been supported at the end of a longer lever. To a form, therefore, in some respects necessary, but in some respects also inadequate to the occasion of the animal, a supplement is added, which exactly makes up the deficiency under which he laboured.

The range of subjects exhibits autodidacts' desire to gain information, attesting to the market for such a work. But the question-and-answer format resembles the rote learning promoted in many working-class schools. The rhetoric itself suggests a didactic attempt to promote acceptable behaviors amongst the working classes. In the question regarding water versus beer, the answer—veiled as a scientific explanation of beer's impurity because of its "adulteration"—guides the reader to temperance. Beer is "liable to induce habits of intemperance," the answer warns. Although we see in this particular publication more evidence for the widespread autodidact culture, we also hear echoes of the classist university examiners who encourage students to pursue intellectual study but do not design their pedagogy to make this possible.

In his novels, Hardy suggests that if this energetic community of self-taught independent thinkers could value their approach to learning as much as they value that of Oxbridge, they could challenge the class and gender biases of traditional educational frameworks. Beginning as early as his 1873 novel *A Pair of Blue Eyes*, Hardy analyzes the appetite for learning noticeable in self-taught men. In the character of Stephen Smith, we see a man who resembles in many ways the autodidacts whose stories appear in *The Popular Educator*. Unlike the nonfiction accounts of self-educated men, however, Hardy presents the character Stephen in a way that cautions us from accepting his tale as a simple celebration with a simplistic message. Hardy takes into consideration the social literacy that Stephen sacrifices by not attending an elite university; in his novel, he recovers this piece of the autodidact's story that *The Popular Educator* glosses over in its motivational rhetoric.

Hob Nob with Oxbridge in *A Pair of Blue Eyes*

In *A Pair of Blue Eyes*, Hardy displays the tension between the intellectual curiosity encouraged by Stephen's autodidact approach and what Hardy sees as the limitations of Oxbridge pedagogies, manifested in Henry Knight as well as Reverend Swancourt and his daughter. Stephen, an architectural clerk, comes to Reverend Swancourt's parish to restore the church. Swancourt and Elfride assume he is from their educated class until a game of chess—itself a metaphor for social climbing—and a recitation of Latin—a trademark of a traditional education—reveal Stephen's lack of elite training. Elfride, who has absorbed many of her father's ideas, appears perplexed by Stephen's chess playing, eventually asking, "who taught you to play?" (83). Stephen replies: "Nobody, Miss Swancourt. . . . I learnt from a book lent me by my friend Mr. Knight, the noblest man in the world" (83). He tells her that he has "worked out many games from books, and studied the reasons of the different moves" but he has never played a real game (83). Hardy highlights their different playing styles in one succinct sentence: "Elfride played by rote; Stephen by thought" (85). Unlike Elfride, who relies on memorized moves, Stephen depends on his own engaged thinking because his education has required him to learn chess actively on his own. Early in the novel, the narrator clearly differentiates the two modes of learning, weighing what Stephen has gained from his self-education—capacity for original thinking—and what he has lost—the social literacy that accompanies Elfride's knowledge of chess moves.

Swancourt initially recognizes Stephen to be "a scholar" because he can recite a Latin quotation by memory (83). As Stephen continues reciting Latin, however, Swancourt notes his "most peculiar" pronunciation (84). Stephen's "accents and quantities have a grotesque sound" to Swancourt's ears (84). "It is not so strange when I explain," Stephen tells Swancourt:

> It was done in this way—by letter. I sent him exercises and construing twice a week, and twice a week he sent them back to me corrected, with marginal notes of instruction. That is how I learnt my Latin and Greek, such as it is. He is not responsible for my scanning. He has never heard me scan a line.
>
> (84)

Stephen's self-directed education, through correspondence with his mentor Henry Knight, has required much initiative. For a brief moment, the Swancourts become fascinated by Stephen's motivation. Swancourt exclaims that Stephen's education is "a novel case, and a singular instance of patience!" (84).

Elfride's fascination soon turns into skepticism, however, because she notices Stephen's lack of an Oxbridge education. Elfride associates Oxbridge closely with an attractive masculinity, and as a result Stephen's lack of an elite university education eventually makes her think less of Stephen as a man. She begins to notice the absences in his inventory of conventional knowledge: "'What is so unusual in you,' she said, in a didactic tone justifiable in a horsewoman's address to a benighted walker, 'is that your knowledge of certain things should be combined with your ignorance of certain other things'" (88–9). Stephen justifies his lack of riding skills by "lifting his eyes earnestly to hers" and saying:

> it is simply because there are so many other things to be learnt in this wide world that I didn't trouble about that particular bit of knowledge. I thought it would be useless to me; but I don't think so now. I will learn riding, and all connected with it, because then you would like me better. Do you like me much less for this?
>
> (89)

Stephen views education as an adventure in a "wide world" full of possibility. Hungry to learn as much as possible, he has refused to limit his learning to "bits" of knowledge others deem fashionable. Stephen places importance on the value that education will have in his own life versus learning to acquire cultural capital for display. Hardy stresses that Stephen chooses what to learn, unlike Barrett Browning's Marian, who is also self-educated but reads whichever books the peddler tosses to her. In deciding his course of study, Stephen eschews a typical course for working-class men that teaches them only facts and skills, often disconnected from their reality; instead he selects what to study based on how he can connect it to his own experiences.

Unfortunately for Stephen, however, Elfride does indeed end up liking him "much less" for his lack of social literacy (89). Instead of responding to his question, Elfride starts reciting lines from "La Belle Dame Sans Merci" (89).[13] Elfride has been trained to emulate the kind of scholarly approach her father values, characterized by regurgitating memorized phrases, and she begins to look for these qualities in her suitors. For her, being educated means that one has acquired cultural capital. In the process of trying to replicate this approach, Stephen ultimately devalues his own worth as a suitor.

Even though Stephen assures Elfride that his "feeling" of admiration for his mentor "is different quite" from his romantic love for her, we get the sense throughout the novel that the feeling is *not* entirely different (96). These characters can never completely separate their love of Oxbridge from romantic love because the characters link the self-worth of men to educational pedigree. When Elfride meets Knight—a scathing reviewer of her novel—after Stephen has left for India to try to become successful in her eyes, she begins to compare the two: "By the side of the instructive and piquant snubbings she received from Knight, Stephen's general agreeableness seemed watery; by the side of Knight's spare love-making, Stephen's continual outflow seemed lackadaisical. She had begun to sigh for somebody further on in manhood. Stephen was hardly enough of a man" (279). Ultimately, "the perception of [Stephen's] littleness beside Knight grew upon her alarmingly" (280). After spending time with the more conventionally educated Knight, Stephen's effusions of love seem childish to Elfride.

Knight's Oxbridge masculinity attracts Elfride and inspires Stephen. But Hardy emphasizes how Knight's education has shut down his imagination. The intellectual confidence he has gained from his education blinds him to Stephen's merits. Like Elfride, Knight places considerable stock in the cultural capital one gains from formal education. In contrast to Stephen's freer expression of emotions for Knight and for Elfride, Knight has learned to form theories about his feelings. Knight adopts a more rational, "abstract" knowledge, even of women (199). He tries to rationalize his love for Elfride by asking a series of questions: "Had he begun to love her when she met his eye after her mishap on the tower? He had simply thought her weak. Had he grown to love her while she stood on the lawn brightened all over by the evening sun? He had thought her complexion good: no more" (215). These questions lead him nowhere, and the narrator concludes, "it may be that Knight loved philosophically rather than romantically" (216). Desperate for answers, Knight rereads his own "theories on the subject of love" to no avail (216). Hardy emphasizes that Knight's education has taught him to think in "maxims" and "epigrams" versus thinking in a more liberating way like Stephen, who has pursued his own pedagogical path (216). Instead of feeling an intense energy to continue seeking knowledge, Knight's education leaves him bewildered about what he has learned. His education has proved regenerative—in his teaching of Stephen from afar—but he has passed on only his rote learning. He remains confused about how he can apply his knowledge to an understanding of his own life. Unlike Stephen, who actively decides what to learn based on the connections he can forge between his lessons and real-world experiences, Knight's education has given him no opportunity to reflect on what he has learned or why he has learned it. As readers who confront both narratives of Stephen and Knight's pedagogies, we weigh the positives and negatives of each, checking our own assumptions about class and education.

In a novel that mixes feelings about education with feelings about people, Knight cannot make sense of his own love or Stephen's love for Elfride; his "theories" and "epigrams" get him nowhere (216). Despite Stephen's success—we learn by the end of the novel that Stephen was "a richer man than heretofore, standing on his own bottom"—Knight views Stephen only as "the country lad whom he had patronized and tended" (386, 285). Stephen never wins the respect of Knight; neither Knight nor Stephen marries Elfride; and Elfride dies soon after marrying a man not for love but for money. Stephen never truly "hob nobs" with Oxbridge, and the energy he brings to learning goes unrecognized by society. Even worse, Hardy stresses, Stephen never appreciates his own educational approach and projects this onto a lack of self-worth as a suitor and as a man.

We see Hardy experimenting with similar ideas in *The Woodlanders* (1887) with a triangular romantic situation involving the university-educated Edred Fitzpiers, the working-class Giles Winterborne, and Grace Melbury, who has received schooling beyond that of most of her neighbors. From the very beginning of the novel, Hardy makes the flaws of Fitzpiers obvious to us as readers just as he does with Knight's shortcomings. Fitzpiers is a dilettante, unable to focus on one area of study, yet not curious in the manner of the autodidacts like Stephen Smith. In the discrepancy between Grace's perception of Fitzpiers and the narrator's description of his personality, we are reminded of Elfride's idealization of the university-educated man. "But, as need hardly be said," the narrator notes, "Miss Melbury's view of the doctor as a merciless, unwavering, irresistible scientist was not quite in accordance with fact" (111). The narrator proceeds to give us a fuller account of Fitzpiers:

> The real Doctor Fitzpiers was a man of too many hobbies to show likelihood of rising to any great eminence in the profession he had chosen. . . . one month he would be immersed in alchemy, another in poesy; one month in the Twins of Astrology and Astronomy; then in the Crab of German literature and metaphysics.
>
> (111)

In the narrator's description of Fitzpiers's intellectual pursuits as "hobbies," the tone is not one of admiration but of dismissal; the narrator dismisses Fitzpiers's frivolity. Fitzpiers's fickleness in learning relates to his fickleness with women; early on we learn of his affair with Suke Damson, which is one of a number of infidelities he tries to conceal from Grace throughout the novel.

Grace, like Elfride, is attracted to the veneer of learning Fitzpiers exhibits. When trying to find out if Grace has an admirer, Fitzpiers supposes that "he has all the cardinal virtues," to which Grace responds, "perhaps—though I don't know them precisely" (128). Fitzpiers continues, spouting out the textbook qualities a good admirer must possess and noting that Grace exhibits these: "According to Schleiermacher they are Self-control, Perseverance, Wisdom, and Love; and his is the best list that I know" (128). Grace begins to contemplate these values, noticing how Winterborne possesses most of them, but then stops herself.[14]

Winterborne, who has lived in Hintock all his life and has not received an extensive education, notices the "discourse" in which Grace and Fitzpiers engage (106). He feels excluded from it: "what he had been struck with was the curious parallelism between Mr. Fitzpiers's manner and Grace's, as shown by the fact of both of them straying into a subject of discourse so engrossing to themselves that it made them forget it was foreign to him" (106). Instead of recognizing it as pedantry, however, Winterborne feels excluded from the "discourse" and dwells on his own lack of education.

In *Jude the Obscure* and *Tess of the D'Urbervilles*, Hardy paints even gloomier portraits of societies that worship institutions perpetuating class and gender biases. He emphasizes that it is not only Stephen's or Winterborne's or Jude's loss for never attending Oxbridge; the institutions lose out because they do not benefit from the intellectual hunger of these men. He continues to pay very close attention to an autodidact's learning approaches with a level of detail not included in celebratory narratives about self-taught men. In doing so, he gives his readers access to a form of education not often documented in the midst of reform's focus on institutions.

Jude as Autodidact

By the time Hardy wrote *Jude the Obscure*, a novel "concerned first with the labours of a poor student to get a University degree," a man of the same class as Stephen Smith or Jude had several options for pursuing his studies beyond elementary education.[15] A Stephen or a Jude could participate in a Working Men's Club; he could attend one of the colleges that had been established for men of his class; he could, if he were a rare case, be given a scholarship to an Oxbridge college; he could study as part of the university extension program; or he could continue his education on his own.

Although undoubtedly aware of this range of opportunities, in his later novels Hardy continued to explore the barriers that still existed and in some cases were exacerbated by recent education reform. Even though by the end of the nineteenth century traditional schools had expanded access to a broader range of students, these institutions, Hardy suggests, fail to recognize the receptivity of someone like Jude. Jude's intelligence goes unacknowledged, contributing to his self-loathing and sense of failure.[16] In *Jude the Obscure*, even more than in *A Pair of Blue Eyes*, *The Woodlanders*, or *Tess of the D'Urbervilles*, Hardy painstakingly lays out the techniques that a self-taught student uses to teach himself, almost as if to give us this information so that we can evaluate it ourselves and judge what direction education reform should take.

For his entire life, Jude remains an outsider of Christminster and the elite intellectual culture it fosters; he is deprived but so is Christminster, which never benefits from his intellectual curiosity.[17] In contrast to Jude's receptivity, Hardy emphasizes Christminster's impenetrability with its plethora of walls and barriers. As a young boy, Jude gazes from afar at Christminster, the "gorgeous city—the fancied place he had likened to the new Jerusalem," spotting it "through the solid barrier of cold cretaceous upland to the northward" (20). As the novel progresses, we learn that no amount of learning can help Jude break through this "solid barrier" into elite intellectual circles. When he finally arrives in Christminster, Jude finds himself locked outside of college walls: "When the gates were shut, and he could no longer get into the quadrangles, he rambled under the walls and doorways, feeling with his fingers the contours of their mouldings and carving" (64). Christminster remains shut, but he walks along and touches the walls, craving the history in them. Hardy emphasizes how excluded Jude feels, but what Jude does not see is that his self-education has given him a broadened ability to understand the world. Jude can "read, naturally" "the numberless architectural pages around him" (68). He is blind to the value of his own education, but he proves more perceptive about the systems of the world because of this approach to learning. Unlike Christminster's scholars, Jude is not blind to the inequity of the educational system that reinforces the walls keeping him out.

Jude's education has made him more open to knowing the world around him, but he sees only the walls in front of him shutting him out of Christminster. From a distance, Christminster's physical buildings not only seem impenetrable but so do its pedagogies. These approaches to learning, Hardy emphasizes, remain inaccessible to less traditional students. As the young Jude gazes longingly towards Christminster, he is told by the "carter" passing by—who notices Jude's book—that he would "have to get [his] head screwed on t'other way before [he] could read what they read there.... [They] never look at anything that folks like we can understand" (21). The carter characterizes learning at Christminster as foreign, outmoded, and irrelevant, but also inaccessible for people like Jude: "on'y foreign tongues used in the days of the Tower of Babel, when no two families spoke alike" (21). Yet students at Christminster, the carter explains, have access to this ancient learning, reading "that sort of thing" almost as if by second nature, "as fast as a night-hawk will whirl" (21). The carter suggests that it is just as impossible to understand Christminster study habits as it is to trace a "night-hawk" whirling with exceptional speed in the dark. Jude lacks what Bourdieu calls "ease"; no matter how much he tries, Jude cannot replicate the social literacy that privileged students bring with them to their Oxbridge studies (Bourdieu 21). Hardy addresses the difficulty of separating education from social literacy—a fact that accounts of autodidacts often leave out.

While it may seem unfortunate that Jude cannot penetrate Christminster's walls of learning and that, as Andrew Cooper notes, his self-education is laborious, Hardy suggests that the more pervasive tragedy is the misguiding of his educational goals from the very beginning (396). Jude's craving for a Christminster education echoes the heartfelt pleas from Working Men's Clubs and Mechanics' Institutes for access to Oxbridge learning through the university extension movement. An 1872 letter from the Council of the Crewe Mechanics' Institution addressed to Cambridge officials exemplifies these appeals.[18] After expressing dissatisfaction with their current system, comprised of "evening classes" and "occasional lectures," they request a more institutional approach:

> We desire then to see established systematic courses of Lectures which, while stimulating and interesting in tone, shall be scientific in method, and above all, CONTINUOUS throughout some months and followed up by more individual and detailed teaching in evening classes by the Lecturer himself. We believe that personal intercourse with a man capable of undertaking such a course of teaching would be of the very greatest possible value to our members and would more surely and more permanently than any other method enable them to distinguish between the merely technical knowledge of details which can be immediately applied to practice and turned into money, and the higher comprehension of great principles by which alone detailed knowledge can be made of use as a means of Education.
>
> (142–3)

The largely self-educated writers of this letter long to be taught by a "Lecturer" and desire "personal intercourse" with him. Hardy emphasizes in his novels, however, that these students, like Jude, do not understand that the lectures they desire— "scientific in method"—are impersonal. The lectures may be less effective in helping them to achieve "higher comprehension" of "great principles" than their own learning methods. What they do not realize, along with Jude, is that they may be better off without an education with a capital "E" if it resembles Oxbridgean lectures and rewards what Bourdieu labels as "ease" (21).

Jude cannot see any positive alternatives to Oxbridge, never realizing that his self-education actually cultivates his own intense engagement with texts:

> His mind had become so impregnated with the poem that, in a moment of the same impulsive emotion which years before had caused him to kneel on the ladder, he stopped the horse, alighted, and glancing round to see that nobody was in sight, knelt down on the roadside bank with open book.
> (29)

Poetry "impregnates" Jude's mind, affecting him so deeply that he must stop everything in order to read. Jude becomes part of the world of the text, making it come alive for himself. He is receptive to texts and to the potential they have to affect him, unlike the Oxbridge-educated Knight, who takes a more rote approach to reading.

Like Barrett Browning's "Mark, there," which calls attention to the act of reading, Hardy's detailed passages describing Jude's reading allow us to experience learning without any guidance; we read these passages without having access to what lies in Jude's texts (I.702). Although as we see in Stephen, Hardy esteems the element of choice that autodidacts have in pursuing their own course of education, here he values the inevitable possibility of venturing off a prescribed course when learning without any guidance. Hardy appreciates the possibility for the kind of accidental reading that Newman and Mill describe, even though it might go unappreciated by a working-class character like Jude.

Jude thinks of learning as a process of "divining" rather than "beholding"; for him, learning proves to be an exciting exchange (28). We are told that Jude works his way through texts with "an expenditure of labour that would have made a tender-hearted pedagogue shed tears; yet somehow getting at the meaning of what he read, and divining rather than beholding the spirit of the original, which often to his mind was something else than that which he was taught to look for" (28). Jude does not just "behold" straightforwardly what lies in front of him. He accidentally perceives "something else" other than what the institution—or what he imagines to be the institution—teaches him; he sees beyond the text in front of him, coming to these texts with an open, imaginative mind.

Jude brings this excitement to learning languages, expecting to learn Ancient Greek by a process of "transmutation" (26). He thinks there must be a code to understanding ancient languages, never guessing that he must learn Ancient Greek letter by letter: "Ever since his first ecstasy or vision of Christminster and its possibilities, Jude had meditated much and curiously on the probable sort of process that was involved in turning the expressions of one language into those of another" (26). He concludes that "a grammar of the required tongue would contain, primarily, a rule, prescription, or clue of the nature of a secret cipher, which, once known, would enable him, by merely applying it, to change at will all words of his own speech into those of the foreign one" (26). Jude understands reading to be an active process; once the reader cracks the "secret cipher," he possesses agency over what he reads. The "words of the required language were always to be found somewhere latent in the words of the given language," available to "those who had the art to uncover them, such art being furnished by the books aforesaid" (26). The books must be "uncovered" by the reader who possesses the art to do so, the art one can learn at Christminster or through Christminster's learning methods. Jude's boyhood wish to find an easier way to learn a language may be naïve but it reminds us that Jude at a young age thinks about how best to learn in an adventurous way; he tries to solve intellectual puzzles on his own using original thinking, unlike Knight, who does not reflect on what he learns.

Realizing no such code exists—that his active reading and original thinking will not crack any code—he almost gives up his project of self-education completely. "He could scarcely believe his eyes" when he first looked at "the Latin grammar" that Phillotson sent him (26). "For the first time" he realized "that there was no law of transmutation, as in his innocence he had supposed (there was, in some degree, but the grammarian did not recognize it), but that every word in both Latin and Greek was to be individually committed to memory at the cost of years of plodding" (26). Instead of imagining himself as an energetic reader with control over the text, he envisions himself taking part in a "labour like that of Israel in Egypt," referring to Exodus (27). He relinquishes the possibility of discovering an exciting way to memorize words of a new language.

Hardy critiques the Christminster model of learning, yet he critiques it through Jude's own ignorance; Jude himself does not realize that he relinquishes intellectual adventure for academic drudgery. As he tries to adopt the Christminster model of "plodding," the task of learning languages starts to look like a "mountain-weight of material under which the ideas lay in those dusty volumes called the classics" (26, 27). This material "piqued him into a dogged, mouselike subtlety of attempt to move it piecemeal" (27). When Jude emulates Christminster's educational approach, learning begins to look like an insurmountable mountain. But even though he attempts to move mountains of knowledge piecemeal, he retains some of his energy for learning in an unsystematic way—moving forward "doggedly" and halting "mouselike." We see Jude setting himself up for failure, however, because these two modes of learning (autodidact, Christminster) remain incompatible. Jude sadly feels he does the wrong reading: "Ultimately he decided that in his sheer love of reading he had taken up a wrong emotion for a Christian young man" (30).[19] He concludes that "it was next to impossible that a man reading on his own system, however widely and thoroughly, even over the prolonged period of ten years, should be able to compete with those who had passed their lives under trained teachers and had worked to ordained lines" (93). Jude's technique goes unrecognized by Christminster, and his awareness of institutional learning actually gets in the way of his self-education.

Jude fails as an autodidact because he does not recognize the inherent worth of his own learning. This, for Hardy, is far worse than not gaining access to Christminster—Jude misses out on what he has developed on his own. Unlike

Jude, Angel Clare in *Tess of the D'Urbervilles* chooses his autodidacticism. In the character of Angel, Hardy imagines a new type of English gentleman that requires an education outside of schools. He reverses the typical autodidact tale from a self-taught working-class man who longs for Oxbridge to a man from a Cambridge-educated family who opts for autodidacticism.

"Doing without Cambridge" in *Tess of the D'Urbervilles*

In *Tess of the D'Urbervilles* Hardy sketches out the "uncribbed" and "uncabined" benefits of the autodidacticism Angel chooses; he breaks with the language and ideas of class that are characteristic of narratives about autodidacts (10). Angel sees Cambridge not as a vibrant place of intellectual exchange, as Jude imagines Christminster to be, but rather as a place that produces industrial-strength conformity at the expense of encouraging individuality. The younger Angel rejects his Cambridge-educated brothers' limited worldview that prevents them from interacting with less educated people. In his description of Angel's brothers as "well-educated, hall-marked young men" who are "correct to their remotest fibre," Hardy satirizes the idea that education should produce a generically manufactured "correctness" (156).

As a result of their institutional education, Angel's brothers are "somewhat short-sighted," prone to trends in fashion as well as intellect: "when it was the custom to wear a single eyeglass and string they wore a single eyeglass and string; when it was the custom to wear a double glass they wore a double glass; when it was the custom to wear spectacles they wore spectacles straightway" (156). They remain more concerned with appearing to be fashionable than with having correct vision, following trends "without reference to the particular variety of defect in their own vision" (156). Angel's brothers view the world around them with a short-sightedness of mind-set as well as vision. Just as their choice of eyewear depends on the latest trend in fashion, their literary taste corresponds with the literature considered fashionable at the time: "when Wordsworth was enthroned they carried pocket copies; and when Shelley was belittled they allowed him to grow dusty on their shelves" (156). This exhibition of fake intellectual curiosity extends to their study of art: "when Correggio's Holy Families were admired, they admired Correggio's Holy Families; when he was decried in favour of Velasquez, they sedulously followed suit without any personal objection" (156). Angel's brothers depend on others to tell them what to read and admire instead of remaining open to unconventional ideas. They neither choose what to study nor reflect on what they learn, as Stephen and Jude do.

In addition to narrowing their reading of texts, their institutional training has limited their connection with less educated people, discouraging them from engaging with "persons who were neither University men nor churchmen" (156). They "candidly recognized that there were a few unimportant score of millions of outsiders in civilized society" (156). But their engagement with people of other classes stops there, as they conclude that these people "were to be tolerated rather than reckoned with and respected" (156). When Angel wants to dance with country girls in one of the novel's earliest scenes, his oldest brother discourages him, insisting that they "get through another chapter of *A Counterblast to Agnosticism*" (11). He expresses concern about "dancing in public with a troop of country hoydens—suppose we should be seen!" (10–11). The eldest brother's institutional associations dictate his decisions, and he cannot be persuaded to interact with people—particularly women—of a lower class.

In contrast to his brothers, Angel embodies an Englishman who chooses not to follow a prescribed plan. Angel splits with the conventions of a privileged-class man, and the narrator struggles to break from literary conventions in order to find a new way to tell his story. His "entry into the ranks of the agriculturalists and breeders was a step in the young man's career which had been anticipated neither by himself nor by others" (112). Whereas the narrator conveys information about Angel's brothers using stereotypes of the time, he finds no reference point to describe Angel. The narrator lists the eldest brother's attire in a matter-of-fact way, "white tie, high waistcoat, and thin-brimmed hat," concluding that these elements of his garb are "of the regulation curate" (10). The second eldest brother is simply "the normal undergraduate," implying that the characteristics of a university student are recognizable to the point that they need no description (10). It is only Angel who cannot be labeled. The narrator tells us, "the appearance of the third and youngest would hardly have been sufficient to characterize him; there was an uncribbed, uncabined aspect in his eyes and attire, implying that he had hardly as yet found the entrance to his professional groove" (10). The other brothers exhibit easily recognizable institutional associations, but the third brother remains uncategorized. Here Hardy uses the word "uncribbed" to suggest that there does not even exist a word to describe this "desultory tentative student of something."[20] Hardy brings to the surface the limited categories such as "the normal undergraduate" that have come into use when thinking about class and education, urging his readers to push beyond these classifications.

Hardy suggests that Angel, a new type of Englishman, can benefit from adopting the qualities of autodidacticism rather than relying on institutional models. In contrast to his brothers, who feel obligated to read *A Counterblast to Agnosticism*, Angel orders a book that contains a "system of philosophy" (113). His father struggles to understand why Angel must read this book instead of preparing to attend Cambridge and to take orders:

> It had never occurred to the straightforward and simple-minded Vicar that one of his own flesh and blood could come to this! He was stultified, shocked, paralyzed. And if Angel were not going to enter the Church, what was the use of sending him to Cambridge? The University as a step to anything but ordination seemed, to this man of fixed ideas, a preface without a volume.
>
> (114)[21]

Angel's "straightforward and simple-minded" father adheres to "fixed," conventional ideas about education and religion; he cannot fathom any form of secular education. For Angel, we get the sense that even a secular, institutional education would be undesirable; Hardy critiques more than Cambridge's ties to religion. Angel decides that the intellectual freedom he craves cannot be found at Cambridge. Farming, on the other hand, "was a vocation which would probably afford an independence without the sacrifice of what he valued even more than a competency—intellectual liberty" (115). Once he has rejected an institutional education, Angel can read more freely in his "immense attic" room as a "boarder at the dairyman's" (115). He can finally pursue his own course of reading: "for the first time of late years he could read as his musings inclined him, without any eye to cramming for a profession, since the few farming handbooks which he deemed it desirable to master occupied him but little time" (117).

The autodidactism Angel chooses enables him to judge the individuals he meets on their own terms instead of relying on what he has learned from biased books referring to farmers as indistinct members of a lower class.[22] After initially spending most of his time reading by himself in the farmhouse attic, soon he "preferred to read human nature by taking his meals downstairs in the general dining-kitchen, with the dairyman and his wife, and the maids and men, who all together formed a lively assembly" (116). In order to do this, Angel must "obliterate" what he has read about the "conventional farm-folk of his imagination—personified by the pitiable dummy known as Hodge" (116). Initially, when Angel's "intelligence was fresh from a contrasting society," he thought "these friends with whom he now hobnobbed seemed a little strange" and "sitting down as a level member of the dairyman's household seemed at the outset an undignified proceeding" (116). To Angel, "the ideas, the modes, the surroundings, appeared retrogressive and unmeaning" (116). The narrator describes Angel's change of mind-set after living there for a while: "the acute sojourner became conscious of a new aspect in the spectacle. Without any objective change whatever, variety had taken the place of monotonous. His host and his host's household, his men and his maids, as they became intimately known to Clare, began to differentiate themselves in a chemical process" (116). Angel must dismantle the prejudices of his own class, which have been reinforced by what he has read in books about the farming class. He acquires a new kind of literacy, an expanded idea of what things he can read and study, like Jude reading Christminster's "architectural pages" (68); unlike Jude, however, Angel celebrates this new literacy. Here the narrator's language emphasizes Angel's radical transition, initially describing the farm as a "spectacle" and then underscoring the "intimacy" Angel forms with the people he meets (116). Eventually, Angel's self-education displaces the preexisting class biases inculcated in him by his father and his earlier reading. His "years and years in desultory studies, undertakings, and meditations" result in his beginning "to evince considerable indifference to social forms and observances. The material distinctions of rank and wealth he increasingly despised" (115). Hardy's Angel echoes Gissing's character of Egremont, who turns to Walt Whitman's poetry, which has the effect of prompting him to discard the biases he has learned from books, as will be discussed in the next chapter.

Hardy encourages us to "obliterate" the prejudices that we bring to bear on our own thinking about class and education (116). Throughout the novels discussed, he draws us into thinking about what it means to learn entirely on one's own. The detailed information about Stephen's, Jude's, and Angel's learning tactics encourages us to get involved in thinking about broader educational reform. By developing a character like Angel that defies stereotypes of nineteenth-century autodidacts because of his privileged class, Hardy calls into question the label of "autodidact" itself.

Although Angel's mode of learning allows him to "obliterate" some of his class prejudices, Hardy suggests that society's deeply rooted respect for Oxbridgean masculinity makes it difficult for Angel to release his patriarchal authority (116). At the end of the novel, he can only watch the flag that indicates Tess's hanging for her crime of murdering the man who raped her. Even though Angel's relinquishing of Cambridge pedagogy allows him to overcome class bias, he never escapes his own misogyny. It is acceptable for Angel to live among people of a lower class, but no amount of learning can enable him to view Tess above the category of "fallen woman."

On the one hand, Hardy shows the great value of Angel rejecting Cambridge and embracing a self-directed education. But on the other hand, part of his broader social critique suggests that as much as one person can reject Cambridge's model for himself, society as a whole needs to reject it on a larger scale. Angel's decision is a step in the right direction, but the novel's dismal ending suggests that a broader overhauling of the educational system needs to happen before Stephen and Jude can let go of their Oxbridge fantasies and before society will accept Angel's autodidacticism, paving the way for reform from the autodidact community. The shortcomings within Jude, Stephen, and Angel reflect British society's intolerance of their educational path. Hardy's self-education helped him question from an outsider's perspective pedagogical practices that went unchallenged by many educational reformers. At a crucial moment in the history of education in Britain, he explores what it would mean for British society to "do without Cambridge." In Gissing's work, we shall see how the binary between insiders and outsiders of educational institutions that bears itself so clearly in Hardy's writing starts to loosen its grip on British society by the end of the century.

Notes

1 Jude's reading while driving a cart exemplifies what Howard Eiland discusses in Walter Benjamin's *The Arcades Project* as "reception in distraction" involving the "whole sensorium" (63). Jude's learning style, full of distractions from the outside world, encourages an openness to knowledge not just from books but from the world around him and in this way encourages an engaged approach to education.
2 See "Sixteenth Annual Report of the Local Examinations Syndicate" in the *Cambridge University Reporter* (March 31, 1874), 297. These reports were published as part of an ongoing study about the inclusion of women and the middle and working classes into Oxbridge universities.
3 Several critics have discussed education in Hardy's work, but no full study exists of autodidacticism in his life and work. For general discussions of education in Hardy, see Raymond Williams, *The Country and the City*, 197–214; Philip Collins, "Hardy and Education," 41–75; and Jane Mattison, *Knowledge and Survival in the Novels*

of Thomas Hardy. Laura Green's more specific study in *Educating Women: Cultural Conflict and Victorian Literature*, which also points out that traditional educational institutions reinforce systems of class and gender oppression, discusses what she sees as Hardy's androgynous intellectual ambition in *Jude the Obscure* and in *A Pair of Blue Eyes*. Andrew Cooper studies the labor of Jude's learning as part of his larger study of Hardy's language. Matthew Potolsky discusses Hardy's short story "Barbara of the House of Grebe" in the context of Victorian debates about aesthetic education.

4   We have significant evidence that suggests Hardy influenced Britain's educational landscape. When the Reverend Albert A. Cock, Professor of Education and Philosophy at University College, Southampton, proposed transforming the College from a satellite of the University of London to a self-governing University of Wessex, he sought out Hardy's support, sending him details of his proposal, also mentioning that he envisaged the creation of a Thomas Hardy Chair of English Literature (see Hardy's 14 Jan. 1921 letter to Cock, *Collected Letters* 6:321–2). The *Times Educational Supplement* (18 Oct. 1917) lists Hardy as a member of 'the Provisional Committee to further University Education in the South-West' (400), and the *Journal of Education* lists Hardy as a supporter of art in National schools (see his 11 Apr. 1883 letter to Mary Christie, *Collected Letters* 1:116–17).

5   Cited in Tomalin (328).

6   Millgate describes Hardy's self-education as "sterile labour" (*Biography Revisited* 56). Tomalin observes, "he felt his solitary situation. For him there was none of the support that sustained other young aspirant writers and artists, nurtured by educated families, public school and university, so that they had an established body of knowledge, a critical audience and a network of friends before they were in their twenties" (74).

7   Andrew Cooper helpfully links Millgate's discussion of Hardy as an autodidact to Mowbray's critique (391).

8   Philip Collins agrees with Millgate's characterization of Hardy's autodidacticism. Collins's study of education in Hardy's novels does not focus on the novels' persistent theme of autodidacticism; he claims that Hardy "is much more interested in the consequences than in the process of education" (51, 48).

9   As Tomalin notes, his mother was a voracious reader and his father was an avid musician; both recognized Hardy's intellectual talents (6, 11). With the exception of a brief experience at what he called a "Squeers" model of schooling promoting rote learning (28), Hardy's early formal schooling was a positive experience, encouraged especially by the landlord's wife, who helped out at the Church of England school on the estate where Hardy's family lived (Tomalin 26, 29). Outside of school, he met regularly with one of his friends in the fields to study classics and continued to read extensively on his own; when he moved to London, he continued to learn music and poetry (Hardy and Hardy 32; Tomalin 68).

10 As Millgate points out, Hardy would later write about Jude's attempt to teach himself Latin (*Biography Revisited* 63). In addition, his parents paid for private Latin lessons with his school's principal outside of regular schooling (Tomalin 38).

11 "At fifteen . . . he began the study of German from a periodical in which he had become deeply interested, entitled *The Popular Educator*, published by that genius in home-education, John Cassell. Hardy's mother had begun to buy the publications of that firm for her son, and he himself continued their purchase whenever he had any pocket-money" (Hardy and Hardy 25).

12 Although *The Popular Educator* includes biographies of accomplished women, the accounts of autodidacts are almost all of men.

13 In this scene Hardy casts Elfride in a position of intellectual power; Elfride rides a horse, talking "in a didactic tone" and literally down to Stephen, who walks beside her because he does not know how to ride (88). Here Hardy associates her with an Oxbridgean learning approach linked to a higher class. But when she meets Knight, Elfride differentiates his knowledge from hers and Stephen's, and in the presence of this Oxford-educated

man, Elfride associates herself more with the working-class Stephen. See Laura Green for a fuller discussion of this association between middle-class women and working-class men in terms of their intellectual position.

14 Laura Green aptly notes that in Hardy, "linguistic pedantry occurs with remarkable frequency in moments of flirtation or jockeying for position between male and female characters" (118). In her discussion of this scene, she observes, "the intention of the lovers seems to be merely to impress each other with their cultivation; but such exchanges can be more sinister" (118).

15 Hardy writes this in a 10 Nov. 1895 letter to Sir Edmund Gosse. He begins this section by saying, "it is curious that some of the papers should look upon the novel as a manifesto on 'the marriage question' (although of course, it involves it)" (*Collected Letters* 2:93).

16 As Green points out, Hardy also depicts Sue's thwarted intellectual ambition as an outsider of Christminster. This chapter focuses primarily on Jude because it is in him that Hardy most pointedly registers the tragedy associated with the Oxbridgean system's preclusion of autodidact learning methods.

17 As biographers have noted, Jude's exclusion resonates with Hardy's own exclusion from Oxbridge. From a relatively young age and during the approximate years that *Jude the Obscure* depicts, Hardy had developed ties to Cambridge mostly through his friendship with Horace Moule and his Cambridge-educated brothers and father (Tomalin 49). Although Moule initially encouraged Hardy's education and spoke to the Dorchester Working Men's Mutual Improvement Society about how recent changes would make the university more accessible to the middle classes, he discouraged Hardy from pursuing a university degree when Hardy told him of his university aspirations (Tomalin 53, 56).

18 *Cambridge University Reporter* (31 Jan. 1872), 142–3.

19 His engagement with books becomes sacrilegious in the context of his Christminster one; he does not consider that in order to get a good education, he may need to reject some of the ideas he has received about religion.

20 Hardy's description of the liberated Angel inverts the line from *Macbeth*; Macbeth, who declares he can no longer think clearly, says he feels "cribbed, cabined, and confined" (Shakespeare, III.4). I appreciate Andrew Christensen bringing this to my attention.

21 Other writers have linked the rational Oxbridgean model to a loss of faith; Matthew Arnold, for example, criticizes a rationalist mode of education that purges him of his faith. Here one of the reasons Angel gives his father for not going to Cambridge is his lack of interest in becoming a clergyman.

22 As Millgate has noted, Hardy undoubtedly had his earlier 1883 essay titled "The Dorsetshire Labourer" in mind when writing *Tess of the d'Urbervilles* (Introduction, *Public Voice* 37–8). In this essay Hardy hypothesizes about what would happen if an outside visitor from middle- or upper-class London came upon a working-class Dorsetshire village and "by some accident. . . . were obliged to go home with this man, take potluck with him and his, as one of the family" (*Public Voice* 39). Hardy suggests that the visitor would begin to see members of the working class more as individuals (39–40).

5 Neither Inside nor Outside in George Gissing

The tradition this study has been tracing begins in the early nineteenth century with Jane Austen's skepticism of institutions; Gissing's work shows how it shifts by the end of the 1800s. Like the writers studied earlier in this book, Gissing uses his extensive knowledge of elite universities to critique them while exploring alternative educational ideas in his writing. Gissing's work, however, departs from the emphasis on the binary between those who can easily be identified as insiders of educational institutions and those who are clearly outsiders. Whereas other authors' depictions of pedagogy were shaped by their reinforcement of this binary, Gissing portrays intellectuals who are neither inside nor outside of educational systems as a result of the democratization of education.

Gissing writes at a time when the power of Oxford and Cambridge in shaping Britain's intellectual life was becoming less hegemonic. Prominent scientists of his time often received their education in Scottish universities and new English universities—or they were self-taught.[1] At the same time, English literature became institutionalized, earning a place in the curriculum of Oxford and Cambridge. Someone who did not attend one of these established universities could now read the same literature as an Oxbridge student, whereas before this would have been impossible unless one read Latin or Greek. It was taken for granted that someone like Hardy's Jude would receive some early formal schooling and could pursue higher education in the form of lectures at institutes, working men's colleges, or new universities. Furthermore, an expanding book and periodical marketplace made it more common for lower-middle-class and middle-class writers—like many of the characters in *New Grub Street* (1891)—to become producers of English literature.

Gissing does not attempt to give us a unified vision for education. Instead, he captures the complex landscape of those trying to pursue individualized approaches to education in order to supplement the increasingly standardized learning at various types of schools. In *Thyrza* (1887), the Oxford-educated Walter Egremont lectures to working-class men; Thyrza, who works in a factory, receives an education through the upper-class Mrs. Ormonde as well as through her own reading and the tutoring she seeks for herself; the working-class Gilbert Grail reads extensively on his own in addition to attending Egremont's lectures; Annabel Newthorpe receives tutelage in the classics from her father; and Mrs. Ormonde educates working-class children from London in her country home, improving them "physically and morally" (102).

Despite this myriad of learning approaches and mingling of classes, Gissing's characters remain starkly aware of the constraints associated with their positions in society. Even if one pursues education, it is unclear that there will be a space for one to inhabit as an intellectual. In spite of considerable education reform, education was still largely about enforcing class boundaries (Bourne Taylor 67). Like Hardy, Gissing is cautious about the potential leaps and bounds that can result from getting a formal education. To an even greater extent in Gissing's novels than in Hardy's, we encounter characters who are very much attuned to—and accepting of—the limitations of their formal education.[2] In Gissing's early work, we start to see how intellectuals accepting of the confines of their schooling begin to form a recognizable group in society, whereas in the world of Hardy they were just solitary figures to be found here or there.

In addition to reflecting the diversity of educational approaches available by the end of the nineteenth century, Gissing draws on his own varied experiences as student and educator. He tutored many students and taught briefly at an American high school. Many of his fictional characters reflect different kinds of educators. In *Demos* (1886), Richard Mutimer lectures at socialist meetings. Mary Barfoot teaches women to lead useful lives in *The Odd Women* (1893). In *The Whirlpool* (1897), Harvey Rolfe develops his own plan of education. Much of this chapter focuses on *Thyrza* and on Gissing's depiction of Egremont, who experiments with teaching working-class men and who, by reading Walt Whitman's poetry, eventually unlearns the habits and theories he was taught at Oxford. In scholarship on Gissing, this novel is often studied in the context of explaining other novels such as *Demos* or *New Grub Street*.[3] Here it receives extensive attention because of its emphasis on intellectuals from a range of classes who are neither insiders nor outsiders.

Despite interest in Gissing's portrayal of intellectuals, surprisingly little sustained attention has been paid to Gissing's treatment of education in the context of nineteenth-century educational ideas and in relation to other nineteenth-century authors who engaged with educational debates of the time.[4] As Pierre Coustillas states, we see a shift in English fiction "up to about 1870" from a focus on the self-made man who successfully rises in social class to "another type of hero, many variants of which appear in Gissing's works—the lower-class young man with frustrated intellectual aspirations" (Coustillas, *Diary* 3).

A current that has run through Gissing criticism for several decades focuses on Gissing's exploration of the figure of the intellectual who has no distinct place in a particular class or intellectual tradition. Fredric Jameson writes of *Demos* and *Thyrza*, "the protagonists of these early 'experimental' novels, Richard Mutimer, Egremont, and even Gilbert Grail, are all in one way or another figures for that alienated intellectual" (200). Jameson distinguishes Gissing's figure of the alienated intellectual from Romantic notions of this figure or from a Mallarmé-inspired figure—linking his fictional depictions to "Gissing's own personal 'wound'"—and states that "alienation here designates class alienation and the 'objective treason' of intellectuals perpetually suspended between two social worlds and two sets of class values and obligations" (200). Labeling this class of people as "displaced intellectuals," Greenslade discusses how Gissing carved out a niche for himself by writing fiction depicting marginal groups, laying "claim to a distinctive fictional world—the territory of marginality, assigned to the 'unclassed' poor, the aspiring lower-middle class, displaced intellectuals, or unintegrated 'odd' women" (509–10). Lelchuk argues that the impact of an emerging new culture on the lives of intellectuals is not only a central theme in Gissing's best work but also a subject that "places Gissing as the major link in the English novel between the world of George Eliot and that of D.H. Lawrence" (374).[5] Building upon this scholarship that investigates the figure of the intellectual in Gissing, this chapter examines Gissing's preoccupation with the unclassed in the context of education. It also considers how Gissing explores how the breakdown of the binary between insiders and outsiders of educational institutions extends to the middle and upper classes as well as the working class.

Gissing's Education

Gissing's social vision encompasses educational models for a range of classes as part of his study of the intellectual who exists as neither an insider nor outsider of educational institutions. This vision is informed by his own diverse experiences in relation to education. His familiarity with education on many levels undoubtedly contributed to his ability to portray a broad spectrum of pedagogies in his fiction. Gissing's father was involved in a local institute; Gissing himself became a stellar student for a while, which opened doors for him; he was taken in and mentored by a schoolmaster; he taught in an American school and was exposed to the American system; he tutored both male and female students in England from the middle and upper classes; and he was aware of debates over mass education programs. Even though he did not attend Oxford or Cambridge, he would have been familiar with them because he had close acquaintances—like William Summers—who followed a traditional path to Oxbridge (Coustillas, *Alderley Edge* 13–14). Whereas other scholars, as discussed above, have focused largely on the male characters in Gissing's fiction that resemble his own social class, I pay particular attention to the character of Egremont in *Thyrza*, who occupies a privileged position in the upper-middle class but feels unclassed.[6]

Although Gissing wrote about Oxford and Cambridge as someone who never attended these universities, like the other writers studied in this book, he is a unique case. Unlike the other authors, he was actually on an academic path to enroll in one of these universities, and even, perhaps, to become a professor. The goal of joining an established university was more palpably in reach for Gissing than for Hardy or any of the other authors studied here. However, he was aware that he relied on scholarships. He realized that his Oxbridge fate was not guaranteed. For Gissing, like many of his characters, one's rise in social class due to education seemed unpredictable and tenuous. Even though he received extensive education in school, he identified with largely self-taught individuals. He writes in his diary of an early meeting with H.G. Wells: "In afternoon went to see H.G. Wells at his house at Worcester Park, and stayed till 11 at night. . . . Liked the fellow much. He tells me he began life by two years' apprenticeship to drapering. Astonishing, his self-education. Great talent" (Coustillas, *Diary* 429). Gissing admires the way Wells has educated himself. He, like Wells, was not born into a privileged class, yet he himself thrived for a time in the institutional educational system.

The young Gissing excelled in a model based on examinations—something that he and the other writers in this book critique. At Lindow Grove school, run by his mother's acquaintance James Wood, he experienced a strict routine—including drilling by a Crimean War veteran—and spent much time "cramming" for exams (Delany 8). At age 14 he took the Oxford Junior Local Examination and scored the highest in the Manchester region, which earned him a scholarship to Owens College in Manchester; Gissing continued to perform well on examinations and won a number of awards at Owens College, including the English poem prize in 1873 and the Shakespeare scholarship in 1875 (Coustillas *Dictionary of National Biography [DNB]*, Delany 8). Even though Gissing did attend college—unlike the other writers in this book—it is important to keep in mind how different Owens College was from the established Oxbridge universities. It was a newer university; it offered degrees to Nonconformists, unlike Oxford and Cambridge; and it shifted the academic focus from the humanities to the sciences.[7] He also did well on nationwide examinations, scoring the highest in both English and Latin on the University of London's intermediate BA examination (Coustillas *DNB*).

What is so striking in studying Gissing's life, however, is that the formal education in which he excelled seems to have left him with little guidance about his personal life. When he decides to live on his own while a student at Owens College, he becomes embroiled in criminal accusations and begins a relationship with Nell, a prostitute who became his first wife; he was expelled from school and sent to jail when caught stealing money to support Nell (Coustillas, *The Heroic Life of George Gissing* 81–97). Gissing's academic and professional success often contrasts with much of his personal unhappiness. His own life story hints at the consequences of what earlier authors, beginning with Austen, warn: if one relies too heavily on an educational institution for one's education, one will miss learning how to develop one's own judgment. Gissing—in his life and in his fiction—later stresses the importance of reading beyond one's prescribed, class-based education, much as he praised H.G. Wells for doing.

Gissing as Educator

Gissing's work as a teacher and tutor most likely influenced his ideas about education.[8] After being expelled from Owens College, he went to the United States where he found work as a teacher at Waltham High School in Massachusetts for two months (Delany 21–2). In a 22 January 1877 letter to his brother Algernon, Gissing explains, "I have classes in German, French & English, (Salary $800) & all are very orderly, attentive & interesting" (*Collected Letters* 55–6). He was impressed by the co-educational, public American system. Gissing describes the three kinds of American public schools: "Primary, Grammar & High Schools" and writes, "I am first assistant teacher in one of the last. All the schools are free, & boys & girls attend the same classes. The perfect order that prevails, & the respect with which the masters are treated is delightful; I never saw anything like it in England" (*Collected Letters* 56).[9]

Gissing describes a particular experience outside of the classroom that suggests a positive, personal relationship between American teachers and students:

> The other night we formed a sleigh-party at the school, & had a real good time. All the teachers went & about thirty scholars. We started at half past seven in the evening; went to a town called Brighton, where we dismounted & played games &c. in a large hotel; then came back again & got home at half past twelve. You have nothing of that kind in England. You know it couldn't be done with a lot of English school-boys, but here you always treat your scholars like gentlemen & they respect you.
>
> (*Collected Letters* 56–7)

Gissing again emphasizes the unique nature of the American system, noting the mutual respect between teachers and students. He seems genuinely impressed by the interactions outside of the classroom between pupil and teacher that resemble people of equal worth. In describing the esteem in which teachers in the American schools are held, he notes: "When I first came here I had the newspaper reporters come to see know [sic], wanting to know where I came from & where I had studied. A High-School teacher is an important piece here" (*Collected Letters* 57). This is the first time Gissing experienced being on the faculty instead of being a student, and there is a note of idealism in his writing. It is interesting to keep in mind as we read accounts of education in his fiction that he had an American perspective on education at a time when England's educational system was changing rapidly. Gissing's experience with American education encouraged a personal approach to learning—one that promoted some degree of equity between teachers and students. These are qualities with which he later experiments in his fiction. His account of the greater respect American students in Waltham had for their teachers contrasts with Dickens's description in *David Copperfield* (1850) of the way that David's class persecutes Mr. Mell—whom they know to be poor—"mimicking him behind his back and before his eyes; mimicking his poverty, his boots, his coat, his mother, everything belonging to him that they should have had consideration for" (96).

Since Gissing seemed impressed by the American educational system, it might seem surprising that he did not spend more time in America. Gissing's reason for leaving Waltham High School to venture to Chicago and eventually back to England was most likely related to a romantic attachment he formed to Martha McCullough Barnes, one of his students, although it is not clear from the *Waltham Free Press* notice regarding his departure whether she rejected him or whether he was disciplined by authorities at the school.[10] In the notice, the *Waltham Free Press* merely states, "his departure is a great loss for he was a man of rare scholarship and his high toned character and the interesting general manner of conducting the lessons of his classes won the affection and respect of his pupils" (quoted in Delany 22).

Like Gissing himself, several of his male characters in later novels make trips to America: Whelpdale in *New Grub Street* has spent time in Chicago and New York—places Gissing also visited—and, most notably, the character of Egremont in *Thyrza* makes an influential voyage to America (Coustillas *DNB*). No doubt drawing upon his own American experience, Gissing uses the plot detail of Egremont's trip to America to emphasize how Egremont can view his own training, profession, and class position from an outsider's perspective.

The idea of a personal approach to teaching dependent on a close association between teacher and student is something that Gissing cultivated in his many tutoring jobs after he returned to England and while writing his novels. When he writes, "what tutor so enviable as *Cornelius Fronto*, whose pupil was Marcus Aurelius," we encounter Gissing's voice as a teacher who respects his students and enjoys working with talented young pupils (*Commonplace Book* 66). Some of his students wrote about their experience with Gissing as a tutor. Walter Grahame remembers Gissing as "a wonderful teacher. . . . He was always equally patient, helpful and interested, and always ready to be carried away by his enthusiasm for the glorious literature of Greece and Rome" (quoted in Coustillas, *The Heroic Life of George Gissing* 300). Accounts of Gissing as a tutor paint the portrait of him as an enthusiastic, somewhat unconventional educator. Gissing's tutelage of Grahame was one example of the ways in which his pupils brought him closer to Oxbridge life; he went to Oxford, for instance, to meet with Grahame's future tutor there (Coustillas, *The Heroic Life of George Gissing* 301).

Through his students, Gissing often gained more insight into the privileged class and the elite universities, which some of his students later attended. In his *Commonplace Book*, Gissing takes care to write a list of his aristocratic students:

> Whilst I am yet able to remember them, let me put down a list of the young aristocrats whom I have had for pupils in days gone by.
>
> Son of Lady Albert Gower.
> Grandson of Sir Stafford Northcote.
> Eldest son of Sir Henry Le Marchant.
> Sons of the Bishop of Hereford.
> Sons of Montague Cookson Q.C.
> Son of George Pepys.
> Daughters of Vernon Lushington.
>
> (*Commonplace Book* 57)

This list underscores his proximity to the elite class; he is never too far from thinking about class and education. We are reminded again of how Gissing the novelist has much material to draw upon in his fictional models of education for a range of classes. The spectrum of educational models he depicts surpasses the scope of learning approaches in all the other writings studied in this book.

Attuned to institutional education through the students he tutors, Gissing the educator expresses opinions about the curricula of universities and schools. In his *Commonplace Book*, for example, he writes: "Dist. Between the school uses of Latin & Greek. Latin is to train boys in general grammar, & in exercise of logical faculties; finally, to give knowledge of Roman civilization. Greek should be learnt (at school) only for its literature. Begin Greek, always, with the Odyssey" (*Commonplace Book* 65). We hear Gissing the educator stressing that students should learn Greek to appreciate the literature—not just as a means to an end to perform well on examinations.

As a tutor delivering personalized lessons and as someone who needed to pursue further education on his own after being expelled from Owens College, Gissing champions the need to preserve individualized learning beyond one's required lessons in school. In this regard, he echoes other writers studied here. Gissing alludes to the ambivalence he feels about institutional education: "What *may* result from education. Think of all that was at stake when that brave father of Horace— macro pauper ajello—decided not to be content with the School of Flavius at Venusia, but to send the boy to Rome!" (*Commonplace Book* 66). Gissing commends a father of a genius student for not granting a school the sole responsibility for his son's education and for sending him out to experience the city of Rome. We hear echoes of Austen cautioning us against relying wholly on a school to provide an all-inclusive education. Perhaps here we see resonances with Gissing's own life outside of educational institutions; his expulsion led him to pursue higher education by experiential learning rather than by further university training.

Whereas the educational path for his privileged students was fairly clear, Gissing continued to grapple with the effect formal education would have on students of the lower-middle and working classes. From studying his *Commonplace Book*, we know that Gissing considered the ambiguity about where students will find themselves after they have climbed the ladder to higher learning. This is something that Gissing grapples with in his fiction. He was drawn to a quotation by Grant Duff, who had much experience thinking about colonial education:

> I am all in favor of making ladders by which gifted youths may climb from obscurity to the high places of learning; but quite opposed to making inclined planes, by which youths, not gifted above their fellows, may easily proceed a little way up, only to look round in a bewildered way, asking "Why have we come here, & what shall we do next?" Grant Duff's Biog Essays. 1903.
> (*Commonplace Book* 54)

Duff acknowledges the opportunities that should be made available to a select few but reflects on how it might be problematic if extended to the masses. Like many characters in his fiction, Gissing felt like he "hung between two grades of society" (*Commonplace Book* 24). Gissing repeatedly tries to capture this state of being between classes in his fiction. *Thyrza*'s Gilbert Grail, for instance, feels torn between his old life and a new opportunity as library director. With trepidation, Grail attempts to navigate his old associations with co-workers and his new friendship with his well-educated teacher. Even Egremont, of a more privileged class than many of Gissing's other male protagonists, feels like he does not belong in one clear social class. An education might dislodge a working-class student from his or her original social class, and the expanded notion of what it means to be an intellectual might alter the worldview of an Oxford-educated man like Egremont. For Gissing, the educational opportunities available later in the century exacerbate a sense of not belonging to a specific class.

Educational Ideas in *Thyrza*

Many of Gissing's characters express awareness of the limitations of their class position at a time when expanded educational opportunities sometimes purported to guarantee a climb up the social ladder. From the beginning of *Thyrza*, the narrator suggests that even the university-educated Walter Egremont is aware of how fragile his own privilege is. Although Egremont attended Oxford, where he befriended the established Newthorpe family, his class privilege is precarious and accidental. He could have easily been born a member of a lower class: "He was the only son of a man who had made a fortune by the manufacture of oil-cloth. His father began life as a house-painter, then became an oil merchant in a small way, and at length married a tradesman's daughter . . ." (35). The narrator reflects Egremont's awareness of how he is only one generation away from being of a lower class and of not having the opportunity to attend elite schools. He echoes this reflection later in the novel: "What if in strictness he belonged to neither sphere?" (105). He understands his own position as "a mediator between two sections of society" (105). Even though in the works of earlier authors a male character of Egremont's social standing would have been labeled an insider because of his attendance at Oxford, Gissing explores the possibility that he is neither an insider nor an outsider.

Gissing's own sense of not quite belonging in elite intellectual circles with Oxbridge-educated men—and yet remaining somewhat distant from the working-class men he often depicts in his novels—shapes his exploration of the emerging class of displaced intellectuals. Gissing wrote, "the pathetic parts of my own stories affect me deeply when I open the book to revive my memory of them. The tears always come when I read parts of 'Thyrza'" (*Commonplace Book* 29). Although the published version of the book carries the title *Thyrza* and one of the main plots centers on the eponymous character, we know that Gissing considered calling it "The Idealist" (Coustillas, Introduction, *Thyrza* 9). The narrator informs us that "somebody had called [Egremont] 'the Idealist,' and the name adhered to him" (35).[11]

Thyrza centers on Egremont's plan to educate working-class men and to found a library for them. He intends to hire his leading student Gilbert Grail to run the library. Along the way, Egremont captures the affection of Thyrza, who is engaged to Grail. Coustillas remarks that the original title of *Thyrza* (*The Idealist*) "invited the reader to focus attention on the hero's half-baked educational project and, in our eyes, read like a criticism of the kind of education that was commonly given in some higher education establishments like Owens College in Manchester and probably Mason College in Birmingham" (Introduction, *Thyrza* 9). Coustillas is right that Gissing critiques the unsatisfactory education often given to working-class and middle-class men and women, but this chapter focuses on what is often overlooked in scholarship on *Thyrza* and what links Gissing to the other writers in this study: Gissing's exploration of the idea of unteaching through literature in the upper-middle class character of Egremont.

Egremont's project in some ways resembles Romney's idealistic plan for educating the masses in *Aurora Leigh*; Egremont differs from Romney, however, in that he turns to literature, which prompts him to let go of his Oxford approach. It is not a privileged-class female outsider like Barrett Browning's Aurora who is doing the unlearning—nor a working-class character like Marian—but the Romney character. Earlier writers such as Austen and Barrett Browning are attempting to unteach their readers, and it is the characters who explicitly envision themselves outside of elite institutions—such as Aurora—that we see unlearning, through reading literature, what they have been taught. Later in the century, we observe writers like Gissing and Hardy depicting privileged men such as Egremont and Angel Clare trying to abandon what they have been taught as gentlemen.

Like the other authors studied in this book, Gissing analyzes dominant philosophies of education during his time. He criticizes the practical politician who capitalizes on education as a campaign topic; in James Dalmaine we hear echoes of the educational programs for the masses that aimed to educate students just enough to benefit the state but not enough to inspire intellectual curiosity. Yet Gissing critiques more extensively the teaching of working-class students that perpetuates the learning approaches validated by elite universities. An education that is too practical—the kind touted by politicians—is unsatisfactory, but equally bad is an education that remains detached from the students' reality. As readers of Gissing's novel, we are put in the position of judging these two philosophies of education for ourselves.

From early in the novel, we hear Egremont's idealistic plan of educating the lower classes by teaching them literature. Gissing creates a tension between Egremont's idealistic plan and that of Dalmaine, an aspiring politician who makes fact-based education a central issue on his political platform. Unlike in *Demos: A Novel of English Socialism*, as Sloan observes, "the real enemy of Egremont, the idealistic reformer, is not the working man, but the political careerist, Dalmaine" (69).[12] We hear the narrator's critical voice—reflecting Egremont's opinion of Dalmaine—describing how Dalmaine uses the platform of education to advance his own political goals. The narrator explains that Dalmaine turns "his attention to politics at the time when the question of popular education was to the front in British politics" because "it was an excellent opportunity for would-be legislators conscious of rhetorical gifts and only waiting for some safe, simple subject whereon to exercise them" (150). He critiques the rhetoric Dalmaine uses to construct arguments in support of education for the masses. Gissing pokes fun at politicians and their views on education as a "safe and simple" topic (150). For Dalmaine, education presents itself as a means to a political end; by joining debates about education, he can show off his talents as a speaker. Dalmaine's impersonal view of education as a political tool serves as a counterpoint to Egremont's idealistic plan for educating working-class men like Gilbert Grail, whom he befriends.

The ironic narrator also calls attention to the complexity of education as a subject. In Gissing's novel, we do get the sense, as the narrator says, that "it was impossible" for his characters from a range of classes "not to have views on education (have we not all been educated?)" (150). Again and again in his novel, Gissing shows us that education is anything but a "safe and simple subject," which is full of educational projects with false starts and pedagogies that frustrate more than enlighten (150).

Egremont tries to enact his somewhat utopian plan by putting his ideas about teaching working-class men into practice, but he does not encourage them to relate the content they learn to their own lives. We see one of these men, Grail, struggle to find any correlation between his life as a factory worker and his life as an intellectual. Egremont's plan for educating the working classes is idealistic because it is based on "theories" that Egremont learned in his own education (465). He sets out to teach students in a way that is removed from their reality. Egremont "had chosen the Elizabethan period" (108) and reads to his students from Sir Philip Sidney's *Apology for Poetry*: "He beginneth not with obscure definitions, which must blur the margent with interpretations and load the memory with doubtfulness: but he cometh to you with words set in delightful proportion . . ." (109). In this passage, which denounces obscurity, Egremont's students find little to which to relate. The narrator tries to convey to the educated reader the challenges that Egremont's students face in absorbing his lectures and engaging with Sidney's poetry: "What were *that* to you, save for the light of memory fed with incense of the poets? Save for innumerable dear associations, only possible to the instructed, which make the finer part of your intellectual being. Walter was attempting too much, and soon became painfully conscious of it" (109).

In Egremont, we see a character who has received the kind of education for which Jude longed. Egremont initially wants to be a regenerative learner, and the narrator praises Egremont's "capacity for teaching" (108). What he wants to pass on to his students cannot be appreciated without already knowing a good deal of poetry, however; his students cannot connect their lessons to their lives. As readers, we realize this problematic schism early on, while Egremont only notices it later. Even when Egremont attempts to teach a series of lectures titled "Thoughts for the Present," in the hope of teaching more relevant subjects, the narrator informs us of his "failure" (195). When discussing religion, he "started" with the "loveliness of the Christian legend" and "dealt with the New Testament very much as he had formerly dealt with the Elizabethan poets" (195–6). The details of the "Christian legend" and the subtleties of "Newspapers" did not engage the students when given in Egremont's "lecture" format (195–6, 108). These descriptions about Egremont's lectures make more palpable the contrast between learning and practice.

The narrator communicates this disconnect in the tactile details describing Egremont's classroom. Gissing allows us as readers to inhabit the space of Egremont's classroom, which was above "the workshop of a saddler" and had a "pervading odour of leather" (105). Gissing reminds readers that Egremont aims to teach working men. The description of the classroom reinforces the disjointed context of their learning and highlights Egremont's detachment from them. The smell of leather that permeates the room reminds us that his students are working-class laborers trying out intellectual work, and that the connection between their intellectual work and their daily lives remains unclear. The personal connection between teacher and students that Gissing describes in his letters about Waltham High School—and mentioned by the students he tutors—seems absent. It is only later in the novel that Egremont realizes this shortcoming.

Gissing presents Egremont's own plan of teaching in detail for us as readers to judge:

> He read at large from his authors; to expect the men to do this for themselves—even had the books been within their reach—would have been too much, and without such illustration the lectures were vain. This reading brought him face to face with his main difficulty: how to create in men a sense which they do not possess.
>
> (108)

The narrator—adopting Egremont's point of view here—refers to the works of literature as "his authors"; Egremont feels a proprietary sense of ownership of the canon. When the narrator notes that "even had the books been within their reach," we hear an acknowledgement that Egremont chooses books that are not very accessible to them. They need the "illustration," or someone who understands these texts to read to them. The language used to describe Egremont's educational plan emphasizes the passive model of learning he attempts to impart. "He," Egremont, does the "creating" instead of instilling or activating knowledge already within them. The fact that "they do not possess" a "sense" suggests that the students lack something innate, hinting at the classist part of his educational plan.

Egremont sees his role as trying to fabricate something from nothing; he tries to make do, the narrator suggests, with their lack of intellectual or literary sense. Blunt sentences remind readers of Egremont's awareness, to a certain extent, of the difficulties facing his students and himself as an educator in this plan: "The soil was there, but how much do we not owe to tillage!" (109). Egremont acknowledges—with a hint of classism—some of the challenges his students will face. Gissing suggests that because of Egremont's own limiting educational experience, he does not try to teach in a way that will allow his students to apply their lessons to their everyday lives.

Egremont and Unteaching

It is only through dismantling what he has been taught—including academic modes of reading and the limited perspective on the working classes—that Egremont can become a good teacher. He discovers the poetry of Walt Whitman in a similar way to the experience that Mill describes in discovering Wordsworth's poetry. Gissing suggests that Egremont finds this individualistic reading experience a refreshing break from his more systematized learning. He begins to shed his preconceived notions of what an upper-class English man *should* learn and *should* think.

Gissing suggests that Egremont gains a new perspective on England and his own learning style by going to America. We hear about this experience from Egremont directly through his letters to Mrs. Ormonde. Gissing uses Egremont's travel to America as not only an important part of the plot—Mrs. Ormonde encourages him to spend time away from Thyrza to test his feelings for her, which leads to their separation—but also as an explanation for his discovery of Whitman's poetry, which has the effect of unteaching him. Gissing, perhaps influenced by his own time there, uses the geographical distance to emphasize the break that Egremont makes from his old views. Gissing depicts Egremont as caught between the comfort of the old world—"I long constantly for the old world and the old moods"—and feeling out of place in that world: "I cannot imagine myself back into them" (464). He resists reading classics even if he longs for the familiarity of them: "I would give anything to lock my door at night, and take down my Euripides; if I get as far as the shelf, my hand drops" (464). Egremont almost falls back into his habit of studying Euripides; yet when he slips into the routine, something stops him from returning to his old academic habits.

Egremont later describes that in America he has realized, "I am not a practical man; I am not a philosopher" and that "the poet's faculty is denied to me" (465). Here he expresses his awareness of the intellectual limbo he experiences. Egremont, who reflects throughout the novel on his precarious class position, conveys his realization that he is not easily categorized into one way of being. As a result, he takes on a more personal learning style, interested in things as they relate to him concretely instead of studying things in the abstract, at a distance. "It only remains to me to study the word in its relations to my personality," he explains, intending to "avoid the absurdities to which I have such a deplorable leaning" (465). Gissing implies that the "absurdities" are what Egremont has been trained to do from his academic study. He is still recovering from the limiting effects of his university education.

Gissing explores the idea of unteaching through literature by suggesting that the poetry of Walt Whitman encourages Egremont to unlearn the "theories" he was taught at Oxford (465). Like Mill, who turns to the poetry of the individualistic writer Wordsworth, Egremont recognizes the benefits of reading Whitman. Whitman, an individualistic writer who encouraged the democratization of poetry, contrasts with the classic Greek and Latin writers representative of the intellectual tradition in which Egremont has been trained. This contrast, for Egremont, allows for an intellectual—and even sensual—awakening. Gissing suggests that this new model of learning might also be of use to the working classes. Teaching Whitman, Egremont realizes, might encourage a more personal approach to learning through an affective reading that would allow his student Gilbert Grail to "feel" the "words" (126).

Egremont writes to the upper-class philanthropist and educationist Mrs. Ormonde about reading Whitman's poetry, reminiscent of Gissing's writing in a letter to his brother William describing his reading and translation of Heinrich Heine's poetry (*Collected Letters* 47). He recommends Whitman to Mrs. Ormonde, writing about how he imagines teaching this text to working-class students precisely because it begs for a less academic reading. At first, Egremont does not know what to make of Whitman, echoing prose writers' accidental reading discussed in the first chapter of this book. "I suspect, indeed, that he will in the end come to mean much to me," he writes, and immediately we get a sense that Whitman challenges Egremont when he states, "but I cannot write of him yet; I am still struggling with him, struggling with myself as regards him" (464).

By reading Whitman, Egremont comes to recognize his own pedantry as an educator. Gissing writes in detail about how Egremont realizes he needs to obliterate his former modes of reading to see the world from a fresh perspective. Egremont writes to Mrs. Ormonde, "I have been learning something about the latter end of the nineteenth century, its civilisation, its possibilities, and the subject has a keen interest for me" (464). He continues, "I believe that for me the day of theories has gone by" (465). Referring to his previous travels to America and elsewhere, he describes them as shadowed by his trained way of perceiving the world and by his "pedantry" (465). He dismisses his earlier studies because they do not serve him as an individual thinker in the real world. Egremont experiences firsthand the disconnect between lessons and reality that he observes in his students.

The character of Egremont identifies the "pedantry" in *himself* that narrators in the other authors' works exposed satirically in their Oxbridge characters:

> All my so-called study of modern life in former days was the merest dilettantism, mere conceit and boyish pedantry. I travelled, and the fact that wherever I went I took a small classical library with me was symbolical of my state of mind. I saw everything through old-world spectacles.... I came then with theories in my head of what American civilisation must be, and everything that I saw I made fit in with my preconceptions.
>
> (465)

Here Gissing's Egremont anticipates Hardy's Angel, who realizes that he has been living based on theories learned from books. He has relied on preconceptions about people outside of his social class instead of forming his opinions based on interactions with them. Egremont dismisses his earlier studies because they do not serve him as an intellectual outside of a university setting. We hear more echoes of Mill's *Autobiography* when Egremont writes about his experience falling ill, which paves the way to his intellectual blank slate: "This time I came with my mind a blank. I was ill, and had not a theory left in me on any subject in the universe.... Getting back my health, I began to see with new eyes.... And I have still not a theory on any subject in the universe" (465). His physical illness accentuates his fresh start and realization that he needs to break free from his "old-world spectacles" in order to then arrive at a "blank" mind that he takes as his starting point. Like Mill, who encounters Marmontel "accidentally," which paves the way to his reading of Wordsworth, Egremont describes accidentally encountering Walt Whitman's poetry, which serves as the impetus for his reflection on how he must break free from a course of life dictated by his academic training (Mill 99).

Gissing analyzes Egremont's discovery of affective reading. We see Gissing attempting to unteach through literature by stressing in the character of Egremont that one needs to pursue a reading that combines "heart and brain" (467). "You have heart and brain," Egremont writes to Mrs. Ormonde, "therefore his significance for you will be profound" (467). This description shows Egremont moving towards a new form of reading, departing from his detached reading of classics. He writes about the "completeness of manhood implied" in Whitman's poetry, adding that "such an ideal of course is not a new-created thing for me, but I never *felt* it as in Whitman's work" (468). Throughout Egremont's description of Whitman, he emphasizes the emotions he registers from reading his poetry. He discovers an affective reading, "foreign" to his "own habits of thought": "These fifteen months of practical business life in America have swept my brain of much that was mere prejudice, even when I thought it worship" (468). Egremont emphasizes the *feeling* he gets from Whitman's poetry—echoing the affective reading Barrett Browning models—and again refers to his own "prejudice." When he writes, "even when I thought it worship," he refers again to the pedantry resulting from his elite schooling, which encouraged him to perceive what he learned as authoritative ideas to be worshipped. It is through going to America and through reading the work of this individualistic poet that he learns to expand his worldview.

Whitman helps Egremont personally. Like Mill, who describes how his accidental reading helps to alleviate his depression, Egremont emphasizes how the act of reading Whitman's poetry helps him: "I believe that he has helped me, and will help me, inestimably, in my endeavour to become a sound and mature man" (467). Gissing investigates what one should learn versus what can help one. Reading Whitman enables Egremont to realize the ways he has relied on standardized modes of thinking and teaching. In the midst of describing Whitman's poetry and its effect on him, Egremont stops himself, realizing his inclination towards pedantry: "Look you! I write a sort of essay, and in doing so prove that I am myself still. Were it not that I have mercy on you, I could preach on even as I used to do to my class in Lambeth" (468). After discussing poetry, Egremont draws our attention to a genre—the essay—he associates with the "preaching" he remembers doing to his students. He comes to the realization that instead of lecturing to them, he could have helped them to understand Whitman's poetry. In reflecting on his teaching, he realizes he could have selected something like Whitman that would invite an individualized understanding of the text. "Ha, if I had known Whitman then! I believe that by persuading those men to read him, and helping them to understand him," Egremont writes, would have allowed him to "have done an honest day's work" (468). Egremont shifts his focus from valuing texts that one *should learn* as part of a canon to valuing texts to which one can connect on a personal level and that can "help one": "There were some who could have relished his meaning, and whose lives he would have helped. For there it is; Whitman helps one; he is a tonic beyond all to be found in the druggist's shop" (468). Whereas Sir Philip Sidney's work assumes that the reader possesses a wealth of knowledge about poetry and literary traditions, Whitman's work invites the reader to reflect on herself as an individual.

Egremont is a university intellectual who experiments with the idea that the same kind of reading required to unlearn his Oxbridge education through reading literature can be applied to teaching the working classes. The reading that Egremont comes to adopt is akin to the modes of reading in all of the other authors' models of education treated in this study. It has taken different shapes but embodies a similar idea: instead of reading texts in ways that keep the reader detached from what one reads, the reader penetrates the surface, allowing the text to transform oneself. For Austen, this reading is central to her exploration of an education that enables one to develop one's judgment; it is not through making lists of books to read as Emma does or passively receiving an Oxbridge education as Austen's male characters in *Northanger Abbey* have done. In *Aurora Leigh*, Barrett Browning encourages a "headlong" reading, which she poses in opposition to Romney's reading (I.707). Hardy's Jude enacts a reading akin to Egremont's reading of "heart and brain," but what is disheartening for him, Hardy emphasizes, is that this reading proves incompatible with the academic reading to which he aspires (467).

Like Aurora's reading, which helps her develop empathy, and like Angel's reading, which allows him to let go of his book-learned prejudices, Gissing links Egremont's mode of reading with an ability to be open minded. In exploring the idea that literature can unteach the university-educated intellectual, Gissing also experiments with the idea that the same kind of reading required to unlearn an Oxbridge education can be applied to a model of education for the masses. Even though we do not see this plan come to fruition—we only see Egremont let go of his failed idealistic educational plan—Gissing raises this as a possibility. He considers what it would take to counteract the standardization in both elite universities and schools for the working classes.

Conclusion

Egremont's leading student Gilbert Grail is very different from Gissing's earlier ambitious working-class male characters such as Richard Mutimer in *Demos*. Mutimer has pursued a very limiting self-education, as exemplified by his books, which "belonged to that order of literature which, if studied exclusively and for its own sake,—as here it was,—brands a man indelibly, declaring at once the incompleteness of his education and the deficiency of his instincts" (71–2). In contrast, Gissing emphasizes Grail's openness to learning and his intellectual curiosity. For Grail, true learning involves *feeling*, as he explains to his mother about Egremont's lessons: "They don't understand him, Bower, and Bunce, and the others; they don't *feel* [original emphasis] his words as they ought to" (126). Grail "loved literature passionately, and hungered to know the history of man's mind through all the ages" (89). Grail instinctually enacts the kind of affective reading that Egremont eventually learns through reading Whitman's poetry.

Grail has read widely and continues the tradition of earlier writers' characters such as Austen's Fanny and Barrett Browning's Marian, who are invested in pursuing an education beyond the one prescribed to them by tutors or Sunday School. Grail is acutely aware of his position as an intellectual without a clearly defined class; he occupies a different space from his fellow workers who do not *feel* Egremont's intellectual lessons. Grail's job "at a large candle and soap factory" as well as the job offered by Egremont—that of director of the library for the working classes—emphasize how Grail is caught between two paths (89).[13]

Gissing's characters do not operate in a system that revolves as much around whether one goes to Oxbridge or not. Although Egremont's star student shares similarities with Hardy's Stephen Knight—including his intellectual hunger and his involvement in a romantic triangle with a woman and an Oxford-educated man—Grail does not aspire to attend Oxford or Cambridge. Gissing registers the power of Oxbridge but shows that intellectual life no longer pivots around it in the same way. We see Gissing exploring this shift further in his later works such as *New Grub Street*.

As Jameson argues, in *New Grub Street* Gissing resolves some of the tensions about the "alienated intellectual" that surface in *Thyrza* (204). Yet it becomes clear in the later novel that the concerns of the displaced intellectuals in *New Grub Street* are not only caused by the fact that characters such as Edwin Reardon and Harold Biffen cannot produce lucrative texts. Gissing points to the broader societal problem that there exists no outlet for lower-middle and middle-class students to be intellectuals. Outside of the market of capitalist literary production, in which Jasper Milvain profits with his "ideas that are convertible into coin of the realm," there exist few opportunities for working-class and middle-class students who have become intellectuals (70). Gissing does not suggest that characters like Reardon and Biffen fail as writers and scholars because of their reluctance to join the capitalist marketplace; it is the lack of an outlet for them that is problematic. Reardon says, "If I had had the means, I should have devoted myself to the life of a scholar. That, I quite believe, is my natural life; it's only the influence of recent circumstances that has made me a writer of novels" (73). He realizes he is not destined for a university career but also knows that he has no channel through which to conduct his intellectual work.

Reminiscent of Grant Duff's words, Gissing's writing highlights the frustrating consequences of an educational system that expands opportunities but never fully opens doors to elite cultural traditions or provides an established alternative. He begins to analyze this in *Thyrza* and explores it further in *New Grub Street*. Near the end of *New Grub Street*, Biffen acknowledges his misguided intellectual life: "Because I was conscious of brains, I thought that the only place for me was London. It's easy enough to understand this common delusion . . . we think of London as if it were still the one centre of intellectual life" (424). Although Biffen does not express his aspirations to attend an Oxbridge school, he views "London" the way Hardy's Jude views Christminster. Biffen envisions an intellectual community in which he could take part, but realizes that no such community exists in London. Gissing questions a system of education that sets people up for a life they cannot lead because there does not yet exist any means by which they can pursue their intellectualism. Even as society moves away from the insider/outsider binary in relation to educational institutions, there does not yet exist an appealing space to inhabit as an intellectual outside of schools. Gissing gestures towards the further complications this poses for women trying to find an intellectual outlet.[14]

In *New Grub Street*, Gissing further explores what institutional reform has created: many people on different levels of the social ladder who have been given access to an education—and sometimes an intellectually rigorous one—but who remain in limbo between classes. They are not completely insiders, yet they are not clear institutional outsiders. In *Thyrza*, then, Gissing anticipates his exploration of this in *New Grub Street*. Gissing registers a new class of intellectuals in characters like Grail, and we observe Egremont navigating how to interact with intellectual traditions outside of the curriculum learned at Oxbridge, including the ideas of working-class intellectuals in England and literature by American authors.

Ultimately, beginning in *Thyrza*, we start to see the figure of the institutional outsider—as it was featured in many nineteenth-century novels—disappearing. Some of the central ideas inherent in work by the other writers explored in this book live on, but the idea of the institutional outsider as a clearly recognizable entity has changed by the end of the nineteenth century, as Gissing shows. By the time Woolf is writing, her appeals for the institutional outsider seem like faded echoes from the nineteenth century. Her work reveals the contradictions inherent in her reliance on the notion of the institutional outsider as a figure that, as Gissing shows, has become much less clear by the end of the nineteenth century. The category of the institutional outsider is more difficult to easily define by the time we get to Woolf because there is an entire class of intellectuals that exists on the margins of Oxbridge.

Notes

1 Charles Darwin, for example, attended Edinburgh University (Desmond and Browne), and naturalist and evolutionary theorist Alfred Russel Wallace was largely self-educated (Smith). See Bernard Lightman's *Victorian Popularizers of Science: Designing Nature for New Audiences* for many accounts of the study of science outside of schools. Gissing reminds us how accessible the field of science is in his depiction of the amateur scientist Luke Ackroyd in *Thyrza*, who conducts experiments from his living room.
2 Sloan suggests, "unlike Hardy's Jude, who battles with the obstructive circumstances of a refusing society, Grail—and the novel itself—accepts those barriers as absolute" (73).
3 See, for example, Jameson and Sloan.
4 I agree with Coustillas that it is important to keep in mind the context of late nineteenth-century education reform at least in part because "the date of Gissing's birth made him an ideal observer of the enforcement of the 1870 Act since he belonged to the first generation that was to benefit from it" (Coustillas, *Diary* 3). Diana Maltz helpfully studies Gissing's engagement with aesthetic education, and Marisa Palacios Knox mentions the context of the development of higher education for women in her study of *The Odd Women* and *New Grub Street*. Bourne Taylor discusses the influence of Owens College on Gissing's fiction and his critiques of rote learning (67–9).
5 See Parrinder for a discussion of how Gissing's depiction of the alienated intellectual influenced twentieth-century works, especially ones that capture the experience of the college student who then becomes alienated from his home life.

6 See Martin H. Ryle, for instance, for an exploration of how Gissing's own social class is brought to bear on his narrative style (125).
7 See Delany, 9. Owens College, which later became Victoria University and is now the University of Manchester, was influenced by German universities. According to the college's history, the college underwent a transition in the 1860s that "stressed the creation of knowledge, not simply its transmission." See http://www.manchester.ac.uk/discover/history-heritage/history/victoria/. See Bourne Taylor for a study of Gissing's depiction of Owens College (68).
8 Gissing may have also been influenced by reading Huxley's *A Liberal Education and Where to Find it*, as Bourne Taylor has suggested (68).
9 Gissing touches upon important distinctions between American and British education at the time. Free schools were the norm (and compulsory) for American students, and these schools had long been co-educational.
10 See Delany (21–2) for a detailed account.
11 Parrinder notes that "any Gissing protagonist (like Egremont in *Thyrza*) who sets out with philanthropic ideas is headed for disillusionment and failure" (149).
12 Sloan explains the shift to an idealistic educational project in Egremont from Gissing's focus on Richard Mutimer in *Demos*, the self-made man who attempts to construct a socialist project after receiving a false inheritance meant for the upper-class Eldon (69).
13 Sloan remarks, "if in *Demos* the absence of English literature from Mutimer's library is used to measure the spiritual deficiency of working-class instincts, their presence in Grail's bookcase indicates the inevitable estrangement of the cultured workman from his life of necessary toil" (72).
14 Much attention has been paid to his complex and sometimes ambiguous portrayals of women, and Gissing has often recently been studied in the context of the New Woman tradition (see both Marisa Palacios Knox, "'The Valley of the Shadow of Books': George Gissing, New Women, and Morbid Literary Detachment" and Emma Liggins, *George Gissing, the Working Woman, and Urban Culture*). Liggins addresses Gissing's desire to expose limitations of the New Woman genre while showing us how Gissing's works appealed to feminists in 1800s in her study that puts novelists such as Gissing in dialogue with investigative writers.

Conclusion

Writing in the early twentieth century, Virginia Woolf echoes earlier writers' critiques of pedantic Oxbridge men. Throughout much of her work, she analyzes the comforts and self-congratulation that accompany the privilege of wearing black robes at Oxford or Cambridge. Professor von X in *A Room of One's Own* (1929), for instance, never supposes anyone would question his project of "*The Mental, Moral, and Physical Inferiority of the Female Sex*" (31). In *To the Lighthouse* (1927), Mr. Ramsay's conviction that "thought ran like an alphabet from A to Z" reminds us that elite institutions can train someone to believe that there exists only one correct way of studying and that there is only one intellectual tradition worth pursuing (179).

Woolf's writings also confirm that the tradition of "educational outliers" traced in this book changed dramatically—if not disappeared completely—by the early twentieth century. As Gissing's work shows, the breakdown of the binary between institutional insiders and outsiders at the end of the nineteenth century makes it much more difficult to clearly envision the figure of the institutional outsider—a figure that Woolf repeatedly attempts to reconstruct in her writing. In addition to the historical changes and significant education reform that separate Woolf from the other writers in this study, her intimate connections to insiders of Cambridge set her apart as well.[1] Woolf was an outsider in the sense that she never matriculated at Oxford or Cambridge as a degree student. But her close association with Bloomsbury as well as her enrollment in classes at King's College prevent her classification as an outsider in the same sense that it might be applied to an author like Hardy.

Woolf felt ambivalent about her exclusion from elite universities. Referring to her father, she said: "He spent perhaps 100 [pounds] on my education" (quoted in Lee 146). Addressing her brother Thoby at Cambridge, she writes: "I dont [*sic*] get anyone to argue with me now, and feel the want. I have to delve from books, painfully and all alone, what you get every evening sitting over your fire and smoking your pipe with Strachey etc. No wonder my knowledge is but scant. Theres [*sic*] nothing like talk as an educator I'm sure" (Lee 143). She feels left out of the intellectual community Thoby experiences but famously celebrates her position outside of institutions, especially in her proposal for an "Outsiders' Society" in *Three Guineas* (1938).

She writes in a 1932 letter to Harmon H. Goldstone: "Education and early reading. Partly from reasons of health I was never at any school or college. My father allowed me to read any book in his library when I was a girl; and it was a large library" (*Letters* 91).[2] Woolf's education at home resembled that of Austen and Barrett Browning. She benefitted from her father's extensive library and his guidance.[3] If Woolf's education at home resembled that of Austen and Barrett Browning, her education at King's College set her apart from them and put her more in line with Gissing and the limited college education he received. Woolf clings to the portrait of herself as entirely self-educated although she attended regular classes at King's College. As Emily Dalgarno has noted, many biographers themselves accept and perpetuate this portrait, even though it is not entirely accurate (2).[4] Kenyon-Jones and Snaith's recent study modifies previous biographers' accounts of Woolf's education, documenting her regular attendance at King's College from 1897 to 1901 (4).[5] She took courses in Continental and English History, Intermediate and Advanced Greek, Latin, and German; each class cost one guinea (Kenyon-Jones and Snaith 6–7). Even though she criticized women who took local university examinations, Woolf chose to take two optional exams during her time at King's College, receiving middle-pass grades (Kenyon-Jones and Snaith 28, 31).

In addition to her classes at King's College, her intimate association with Cambridge culture differentiates her from the earlier writers in this book. She was affiliated with Cambridge not just through her father and brothers but also through her cousin Katherine Stephen, Principal of Newnham College from 1911 to 1920; from Stephen, Woolf gained familiarity with the early women's colleges (Lee 63). Her involvement in the Bloomsbury Group, made up of many of her brother Thoby's college friends, shaped her position as an insider to this culture despite never having attended Cambridge. What began as a gathering of friends following their Cambridge graduation evolved into a more organized group of writers, philosophers, and artists who met frequently.[6] Although not an institution per se, the group was more formal than any community to which Austen, Barrett Browning, or Hardy belonged. The group was much more closely connected with Cambridge culture than any group or institution to which Gissing was associated. One wonders how much Woolf could have really set herself outside of Oxbridge culture given her interaction with this group. Whereas Gissing tries to capture the communities of intellectuals not defined by universities, Woolf clings to the idea that intellectual communities are still defined in institutional terms.

Despite historical changes that made it more difficult by the early twentieth century to inhabit the role of an intellectual defined by being an outsider of Oxbridge, she continues to explore the figure of the institutional outsider. Woolf imagines what this figure would look like inside Oxbridge colleges; she depicts characters that feel like outsiders from within universities. In the two texts by Woolf discussed here, the heroines have an insider's access to the universities that once excluded women, but they remain feeling like outsiders. Woolf's work connects in this way to the first women's college writers who write about how they feel like outsiders within universities. This conclusion traces the end of the tradition of the institutional outsider as defined by Austen, Barrett Browning, Hardy, and

Gissing, and a turn towards a new figure of the displaced intellectual within elite universities.

A Woman's College from Outside

Woolf's short story, "A Woman's College from Outside" (1926), narrated by someone situated literally outside of the college buildings, wandering the gardens at Newnham College and looking in on students' rooms, presents itself initially as a tale of education and class. The heroine Angela is a student at Cambridge who feels like an outsider because of her social class. She is up late, "pursing her lips over a black book and marking with her finger what surely could not be a firm grasp of the science of economics" (145). We learn in a detailed passage that "only Angela Williams was at Newnham for the purpose of earning her living, and could not forget even in moments of impassioned adoration the cheques of her father at Swansea; her mother washing in the scullery . . ." (145). In contrast to the brevity of this story—just a few pages long—the lengthy paragraph in which Woolf gives background information about Angela is exceptionally detailed.

Woolf sets out to write a story exploring class within the setting of a women's college, investigating what it might be like as an outsider within a university setting. An invitation Angela receives from "Alice Avery" to "Bamborough Castle" for a future visit disrupts the material reminders of her obligations to her family (147). Angela thinks, "that after the dark churning of myriad ages here was light at the end of the tunnel; life; the world. Beneath her it lay—all good; all lovable. Such was her discovery" (147). Her education will not only allow her to "earn her living"; it also opens doors to gain access to exclusive places like Bamborough Castle (145).

At the end of the story, however, Angela comes to the painful realization that the potential of education to change social structure is fleeting. Woolf begins the story by emphasizing Angela's realistic, material limitations, then explores the potential for her to rise above her class, and ultimately concludes with the suggestion that her education will not allow her to transcend her social position. With "the morning coming," she cries "as if in pain" (148). In this short story, Woolf sends an ambivalent message about class and education. It is not the straightforward critique of institutional education that we hear in *Three Guineas*, but it is an earlier working through of class and education that she would continue in *The Pargiters*. We see her working through the figure of the outsider within an educational institution through the lens of social class.

Experimentation in *The Pargiters*

As if to recover the nineteenth-century ideal of the outsider, Woolf sets the story of *The Pargiters* in the Victorian period. She focuses in part on the character of Kitty, who has grown up inside an Oxford college where her father teaches. Instead of wanting to attend one of the newly formed women's colleges, Kitty longs to interact with people outside of Oxford. In this unpublished "Essay-novel," written in the early 1930s, which was then adapted into her novel *The Years* (1937), we see Woolf experimenting with the idea of a woman from within Oxbridge culture trying to become an outsider (Woolf, *A Writer's Diary* 189). Yet she never fully captures Kitty's motives or the place Kitty occupies in society, and the work ultimately remained unpublished. It serves here as a helpful text to gain insight into the ways that Woolf tries to hold onto the idea of the nineteenth-century institutional outsider—rooted in class and gender—even when the tradition has faded.

When Woolf began *The Pargiters*, she writes in her diary, "I have never lived in such a race, such a dream, such a violent impulsion and compulsion—scarcely seeing anything but *The Pargiters* (*A Writer's Diary* 190).[7] She attempts to try "every kind of experiment" (220). We see Woolf testing out ideas of class and education, as well as genre. She aims to unhinge readers' conceptions of genre: "But *The Pargiters*. I think this will be a terrific affair. I must be bold and adventurous. I want to give the whole of the present society—nothing less: facts as well as the vision. And to combine them both" (197). She wants to capture fact and vision but fears sounding too "didactic"; she promises that there will be "no preaching" (194, 198). Woolf never published *The Pargiters* in the form she originally envisioned, however, and the experience of writing it proved very taxing.[8]

In *The Pargiters*, we see Woolf trying to gesture back to nineteenth-century writers, like Barrett Browning, Hardy, and Gissing, who capture interactions between various social classes in their stories about outsiders. She traces Kitty's growing awareness of her own social class in relation to that of others: "[Kitty] knew nothing of all those grades of society that lie between the working class and the upper class" (*The Pargiters* 151). Kitty runs through a catalogue of people she knows and the classes to which they belong: "Of the working class she only knew the Carters: of the upper class, only her own class, in the persons of some dons and professors, and the aristocracy, in the persons, for a time, of earls and a duke or two" (151). Kitty longs for an alternative to a life at Oxford entertaining undergraduates and helping her father compile a history of "every man who had been at Katharines [College] in the course of five hundred years" (93).

Reminiscent of Hardy's description of Angel, Woolf repeatedly affirms Kitty's own desire to become a farmer, transferring the Angel figure to a female character. Kitty "cherished a secret passion for becoming a farmer, which led her to underrate the advantages of the male society of Oxford, was at present very little concerned with the other sex" (*The Pargiters* 111). Kitty longs to become an outsider of Oxford culture: "Why should . . . she not become a farmer? That was her dream. She would have to marry, she supposed, in order to become a farmer—& her parents wd. never let her marry a farmer" (105). She desires to mingle with those far beyond the walls of Oxford colleges. When she studies the history of the "Angevin Kings" with her tutor Miss Craddock, her mind often wanders to Yorkshire: "That was what she saw . . . as she closed Bishop Stubbs vol 3" (104).

At the same time Woolf attempts to recover the figure of the institutional outsider, she tries to break away from the nineteenth-century marriage-plot novel. She underscores the unconventionality of Kitty's desired alternative path in 1880, using the essay portions for emphasis. Kitty's questioning of convention fuels her desire for a different life. The accompanying essays in the volume inform us that Kitty constantly poses questions unthinkable by women of her mother's generation: "And why can't I walk by myself in the country? . . . And why mayn't I play football if I want to? And why must I sit next old Chuffy at dinner?" (*The Pargiters* 118). These questions, the essay tells us, "had their share in making her conclude that she, at least, intended to be a farmer" (119). The essays signal Kitty's acceptance of her own role in undoing the marriage plot as well as her desire to be on the outside of Oxbridge culture.

The education that Kitty seeks is ultimately one that displaces her from her immediate Oxford world. When Kitty has tea with her friend Nell's family from Yorkshire, Woolf underscores the connections she forms with them instead of drawing out their differences. She highlights the upper-class Kitty's physical resemblance to a farmer. Kitty is equipped for farming: "her body though too big" is "flat between the shoulders" (*The Pargiters* 94). Her flat-chested, masculine physique renders her an undesirable heroine for the marriage plot; we are again reminded that Woolf attempts to step outside of the marriage-plot novel in *The Pargiters* while experimenting with ideas of class and education. Her physical appearance indicates to Mrs. Brook, Nell's mother, that she does not fit the conventions of a Don's daughter: "there was something in her height, & strength, in her broad cheekbones & honest . . . eyes, set too far apart as they were, that [*pleased*] <gave> Mrs. Brook [pleasure]. <She was thinking that if Kitty had been her own daughter, she could have made something of her>" (136–7).⁹ In Kitty's physique Nell's mother recognizes something familiar that surpasses their difference in social class. Kitty finds much in common with Mrs. Brook, who "reminded her, oddly enough, of the old Duchess of Newhaven" (142). They both often compare Oxford and Yorkshire, and "thus she & Kitty had a great deal in common" (143).

Kitty and the Brook family can converse openly and understand each other instinctively. When Mr. Brook points to a portrait of his mother on the wall and "ask[s] Kitty what she thought of that old woman?" we learn that Kitty "understood her"; she goes on to imagine that "she had [*worked in a mill; she had*] [*her husband had left her;*] her husband had drunk; & she had brought them all up" (*The Pargiters* 146). Kitty interprets Mr. Brook's great admiration for his mother "though Sam never said a word to that effect" (146). The narrator continues, "Kittys senses again told her, [*in*] undeniably, that he [*was*] respected & admired that old woman, [(*hence his attitude to Lucy Craddock; to his wife; to his daughter; to Kitty herself*)] & thought her [*worth all*] <more than> the Masters & Mistresses in Oxford . . ." (146). The characters in this scene understand each other without needing to speak. Kitty interprets the life of Mr. Brook's mother from her portrait, using her imagination to comprehend the woman in the painting.

Kitty begins to understand the values of the working-class people she meets. She does what Woolf does not always seem to do in real life: she relies on her imagination as a tool for empathy. In 1905, Woolf began teaching classes at Morley College, a school that provided evening instruction for women and men in London's Waterloo district.[10] The school had its origins in the Royal Victoria Coffee and Music Hall, which began hosting weekly "penny" lectures in 1882 by well-known scientists on a broad range of subjects (Morley College). These lectures proved to be so popular that starting in 1889, classes were offered officially through what became the Morley Memorial College for Working Men and Women (Morley College). The history of Morley reminds us of the ways in which British education had become more democratic in the late nineteenth and early twentieth centuries. Originally, Woolf was hired to teach composition, but her students requested to learn "English History from the beginning" (*Passionate Apprentice* 245; Lee 219).[11] She taught at Morley intermittently for approximately two years. Her "Report on Teaching at Morley College" expresses the skeptical views about educating the working classes that would shape her portrayal of class and education in her later fiction.[12]

The vague, strange language Woolf uses to describe her students suggests her uncertainty about whether the project of teaching them history will prove worthwhile:

> I do not know how many of the phantoms that passed through that dreary school room left any image of themselves upon the women; I used to ask myself how is it *possible* to make them feel the flesh & blood in these shadows? So thin is the present to them; must not the past remain a spectre always?
> (203)

Woolf dwells on the challenges facing these students. Her approach contrasts with that of Barrett Browning, for example, who celebrates the possibilities inherent in Marian's piecemeal learning and emphasizes the value in her personal educational approach. Woolf describes their learning in physiological terms, but unlike Barrett Browning, who draws on the universal quality of poetry's physiology, Woolf emphasizes that what separates these women from herself is their level of engagement with the physiological dimension of learning. They cannot feel "the flesh & blood" of history as Woolf does—or as Barrett Browning imagines that Marian Erle can and as Gissing imagines that Gilbert Grail can.

Woolf's writing elsewhere testifies to the unusual degree of experimentation with class and education that we see in *The Pargiters*. In *The Years*, we observe Woolf's retreat from this earlier experimentation.[13] Whereas she pushes the limits of formal conventions in novels such as *The Waves* (1931) and modifies the marriage plot in the character of Lily Briscoe in *To the Lighthouse*, Woolf pulls back from innovation in *The Years*.

In *The Years*, Woolf leaves out all of the essays originally included in *The Pargiters*, and she drops the detailed Kitty plot. She reverts to a more conventional novel form. We hear only fleetingly of Kitty's unusually tall physique and her desire to become a farmer. Instead of forging friendships with Nell's family when Kitty visits them, for instance, the parallel scene in *The Years* accentuates how alien she feels. Grace Radin interprets the scene in *The Years* in terms of Kitty as Alice in *Alice in Wonderland*, feeling giant and out of place (31–2). We do not hear of the connection Kitty makes with the Yorkshire family or of her desire to learn about a culture unlike her own. The scene ends with a formal, forced goodbye:

> 'Pleased to have made your acquaintance,' said Mrs Robson in her stately way.
>
> (*The Years* 53)

> Did they know how much she admired them? she wanted to say. Would they accept her in spite of her hat and her gloves? she wanted to ask. But they were all going off to their work. And I am going home to dress for dinner, she thought as she walked down the little front steps, pressing her pale kid gloves in her hands.
>
> (*The Years* 53)

Woolf concludes this scene in *The Years* with a series of unanswered questions. Although Kitty admires Nell's family, she cannot communicate openly with them. Woolf explains nothing early on in the novel about Kitty's yearning to become a farmer on the outside of Oxbridge culture. She only later reveals that Kitty has become Lady Lasswade. Kitty never lives on a farm; instead she marries a lord with a country estate. When she visits the country, she reflects: "Nothing of this belonged to her; her son would inherit; his wife would walk here after her" (203).

Woolf retreats from her more radical imagining of the character of Kitty, reverting to a traditional marriage plot. Instead of offering possibilities for a new future in this novel—as well as for the genre on the whole—Woolf only offers faint traces of the earlier writers' radicalism. The development of the Kitty plot in *The Pargiters* shows us how Woolf clings to an earlier tradition of innovative ideas about class and education in stories of institutional outsiders, but *The Years* signals how the tradition has changed by the twentieth century. If Woolf's work shows the disappearance of the figure of the institutional outsider as it existed in nineteenth-century fiction, her writing points to the emergence of a new kind of outsider: an outsider from within.

Early Women's College Writers

Even though Virginia Woolf maintained close associations with Cambridge and with King's College, she tried to preserve her position as an outsider of institutions, as discussed above. Her work serves as a starting point for thinking about how institutional insiders can preserve the positive qualities of outsiders. As we come to the end of this study, the remaining pages attempt an answer to this question: can institutions foster outsiders? In other words, can a historically excluded outsider—someone like Fanny Price, Aurora Leigh, Marian Erle, Jude Fawley, or Gilbert Grail—become a university student without losing the learning tactics that writers celebrate? How can he or she balance the demands of an institutional education without letting go of his or her appetite for learning?

I explore how one group negotiates its position within universities that had formerly excluded them: the first students at the Oxford and Cambridge women's colleges that opened in the late nineteenth century. Through their poetry, newspaper articles, and personal writing, these pioneering women's college students grapple with their position as outsiders within schools that do not fully embrace them. They offer insight into the difficulty that historically excluded groups face in entering institutions that fail to acknowledge their unique approaches to learning.

The students who attended the newly opened women's colleges at Oxford and Cambridge in the last few decades of the nineteenth century became the first female insiders of these centuries-old institutions. Their writings reveal, however, that they often remained outsiders. The physical separation of the women's colleges from the male colleges within the university contributed to students' feelings of isolation. Cambridge's Girton College, for example, was situated far from the center of town where Cambridge's male colleges were located. Girton student Anna Lloyd writes to her friend in 1869 that she wants "to see Cambridge very much, the place where our lecturers came from" (62).[14]

Women's college students' curiosity about the men's colleges often turned into distaste for the Oxbridge method of learning that was forced upon them. Their writing critiques institutions and it also shows their attempt to preserve some of their own attitudes towards learning. On one level, the writing of early women's college students might be dismissed as a collection of complaints about curricula focused on the classics. Most of them had not received the methodical preparation in Greek and Latin of their male counterparts but were held accountable in comparable assessments. But on a broader level, students register the detrimental effects of adopting learning modes that had gone unchallenged for decades—and even centuries. They use their outsiderness within these universities to critique them, turning the tables on the male administrators and students who mocked their academic pursuits. While earlier writers such as Arnold and Dodgson allude to the prevalence of cramming in Oxbridge schools, women's college writers probe its effects on themselves as individuals.

Girton student Anna Lloyd enters the widespread discussion of "cram" when she compares herself to a "Dorking fowl" (63), echoing Edward Caswall in his *Art of Pluck*. Women's college writers ultimately refuse to initiate themselves completely into an academic culture of cram. Girton students often expressed their discontent in *The Girton Review*, which was published each term by the college and contained a variety of student writing that reported on college events and attitudes about subjects studied. In "Girton's History Anticipated or The Savage and Triumphant Progress of the Classical Tripos over Two of her Loftiest Students," excerpted from the February 1875 issue of *The Girton Review*, Girton student Constance Louisa Maynard chronicles the "mysterious and progressive suffering" involved in pursuing the "Classical Tripos" at Girton.

Girton students' learning is not without its "deeply instructive," "honourably ambitious," and "inquisitionally-interrogative" elements. But Maynard underscores the influence of the other components of "The Classical Tripos" that promote rote learning and cramming: "a fiercely emulative Element," "a vainly-inflated Element," "a slavishly-copying Element," "a brain-racking frantic Element," "a malignantly-unjust Element," and "a tyrannically-cannibal Element." These elements come to life in the cartoon. In each image of the two Girton students taking exams, a don in cap and gown stands over the girls. In three of the pictures,

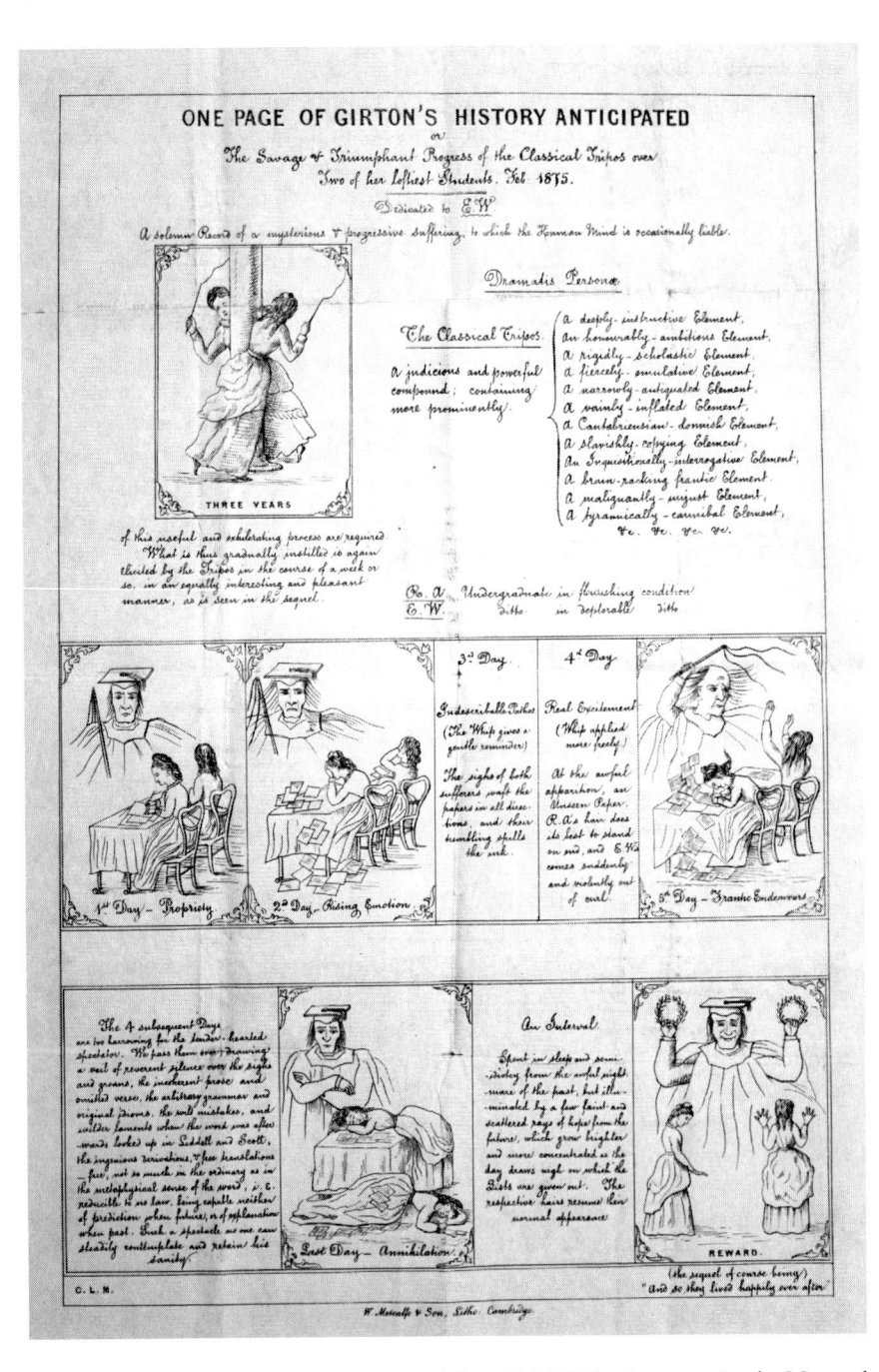

Figure 6.1 "One Page of Girton's History Anticipated" (1875) by Constance Louisa Maynard
Source: The Mistress and Fellows, Girton College, Cambridge.

he stands poised with a whip in his hand, presumably to carry on an education founded on punishments rather than rewards. This "anticipated history" plays upon the expectation that as bluestocking students at newly founded colleges they felt exuberant about making history. We see from this account, however, that students such as Maynard feel as though they are doing anything but making history.[15] They cram, they agonize over "arbitrary grammar," and then they try to sleep off "the awful nightmare of the past." They do not make new history as much as they feel pressured into a tradition of ritualized Greek and Latin examinations.

We might initially view this "history" as the testimony of a frustrated student and nothing more. But the "Anticipated History" also represents the broader culture of women's dissatisfaction with their inclusion in academic rituals in the late nineteenth and early twentieth centuries. Maynard highlights the difficulties of fostering creative thought in the midst of a degree of cramming that makes one's hair come "violently out of curl." Although she acknowledges an "inquisitionally-interrogative element" as part of the process, the "narrowly-antiquated element"—that rewards them for memorizing material—overshadows any active learning.

This *Girton Review* cartoon was one of many accounts of cramming and drudgery at the first Oxbridge women's colleges.[16] Elizabeth Macleod, another Girton student, describes an 1881 article titled "A Day at Girton," waking up early in the morning in her cold room to do Latin exercises: "A lot of work must be done before the post goes out at 10.0, and it is very dark and cold, and not at all the day one would choose for getting up at 6.30, to work for an hour in a cold study, ghastly with the remains of a revel (consisting of tea and cake) of the night before" (1).[17] Macleod provides an unromanticized glimpse into her daily life at Girton. The language she uses underscores the "dark and cold" learning environment in which she finds herself: "I seize the candle, and rush into my study, and after blowing on my cold fingers in vain to warm them I endeavour to compel my frozen brain to write a Latin prose" (Macleod 1). Her description has none of the intellectual excitement and sense of discovery in learning embodied in Barrett Browning's descriptions of Aurora's reading, for example. Macleod may have a room of her own, but this room in an institutional context represents her daily educational grind. Unlike Austen and Barrett Browning, she follows a prescribed curriculum; she is not free to pursue her own course of study. Education becomes not an intellectual adventure but a necessary means to pass examinations. She has the privilege of becoming a college student, but her college environment is far from inspiring.

In their autobiographical writings, early women's college students repeatedly resist institutional methods. Anna Lloyd recalls advice from her master who tells her, "you have not time to do more than remember a few rules," and she reflects on this dictum: "Unfortunately I cannot remember things in that way. Unless I can picture things in the imagination, I cannot recall them. I do not want to pretend to know more than I do, and I am very ignorant" (51). Even though she writes from within an Oxbridge college, she tries to unlearn the limiting institutional practices that the writers traced in this book expose. Like the authors outside of universities, she holds onto the imaginative, receptive modes of learning that she had developed before arriving at Girton. She resists rote memorization; she wants to not only take in facts and information but to mull over what she has learned. On her way "to London for the exam," she writes that cramming has only left her feeling "quite blank of knowledge" (51).

Lloyd and other students register that Oxbridge pedagogies do not simply present a problem on a personal level for students; they indicate a broader institutional flaw. Lloyd writes: "The object of the College in the minds of its promoters had been solely and entirely intellectual and they had not thought of the necessity of making any provision for relief from the continuous strain of work imposed upon its members" (61). The "strain" of work prevails over the potential excitement for learning. An 1883 letter to the administration, published in *The Girton Review* with the heading "Overwork," echoes Lloyd's concern for learning methods that emphasize cramming:

> Madam,—It is with growing concern that I have noticed for some time past a tendency on the part of some of our students to overwork, which, if it be allowed to prevail, will in the end have a most disastrous effect upon the College. It is, I think, partly due to the fact that the constant pressure of lectures (at which attendance is compulsory) consumes nearly the whole of our time in preparation, and so excludes almost all possibility of a wider range of reading. Another cause is, I fear, a growing anxiety about the place we shall take in our examinations, due partly to human nature, and partly to external pressure. . . .
> [I]t is lamentable to see the time wasted in "cramming" every detail of The Little Go subjects in order to get a good place, which would be much more profitably spent on the student's special work.

The writer of the letter not only notes the deleterious effects of overwork on students cramming for examinations; she also makes the argument that a pedagogy emphasizing rote memorization will negatively affect the college's learning environment.[18] Cramming not only influences students individually; these learning methods, as the students suggest, prove problematic on a more universal level.

Women's college students also resist the expectation to fake intellectual confidence. An 1897 poem titled "The Study of History," published in *The Fritillary*, Oxford's magazine written by women's college students and published by Somerville College, satirizes these expectations.

The poem pokes fun at the notion that students should put on a performance as part of their education, faking the part of an expert on history. The speaker describes an inquisitive student who would rather ask about different "views" of history than passively read Stubbs's history books, reminiscent of the young Austen who explores alternative versions of history. She is advised to fake original thinking instead of actually doing it: "Pretend it is original and write it down as such." One must "shew" to the listener that one is confident and intellectual, even in the face of ignorance.

In the voices of these writers, we recall Barrett Browning's letter to Mary Russell Mitford commenting on Tennyson's "The Princess," in which she warns against the idea of "transfer[ring]" the "worn-out plaything" of male colleges to

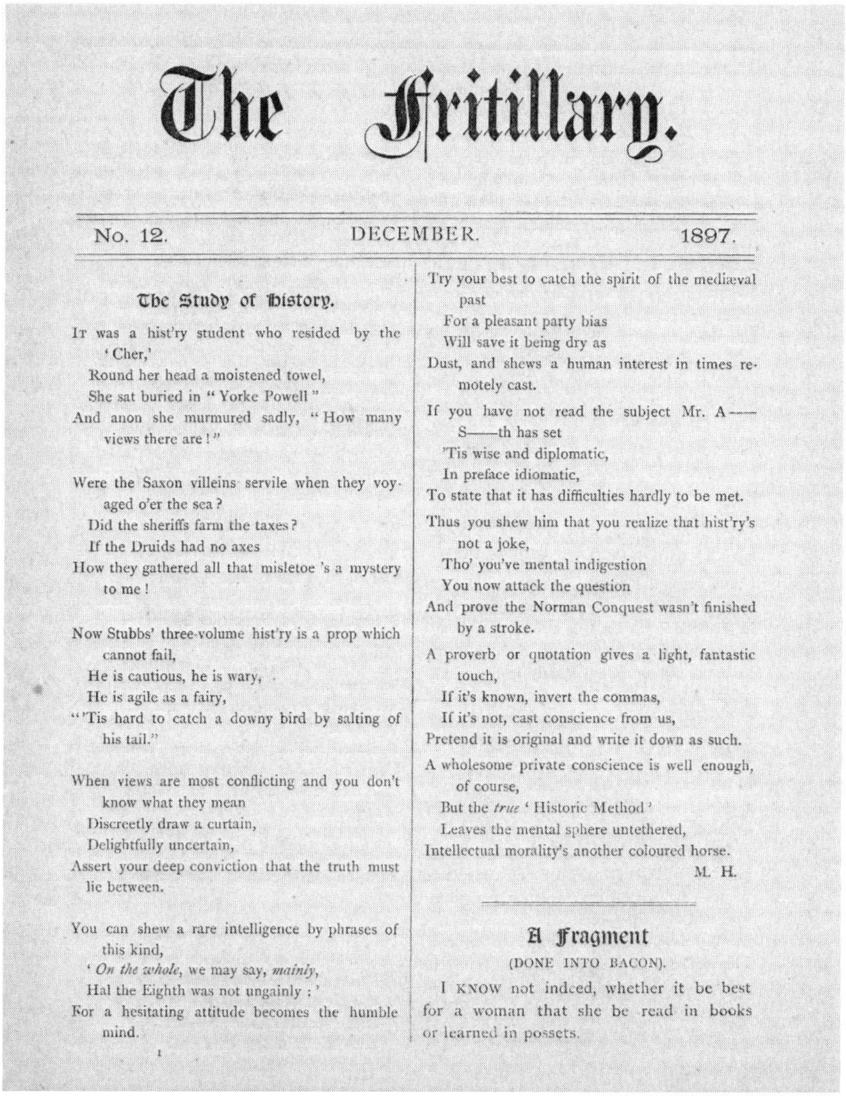

The Fritillary.

No. 12.   DECEMBER.   1897.

The Study of History.

It was a hist'ry student who resided by the
    'Cher,'
Round her head a moistened towel,
She sat buried in "Yorke Powell"
And anon she murmured sadly, "How many
    views there are!"

Were the Saxon villeins servile when they voy-
    aged o'er the sea?
Did the sheriffs farm the taxes?
If the Druids had no axes
How they gathered all that misletoe's a mystery
    to me!

Now Stubbs' three-volume hist'ry is a prop which
    cannot fail,
He is cautious, he is wary,
He is agile as a fairy,
"'Tis hard to catch a downy bird by salting of
    his tail."

When views are most conflicting and you don't
    know what they mean
Discreetly draw a curtain,
Delightfully uncertain,
Assert your deep conviction that the truth must
    lie between.

You can shew a rare intelligence by phrases of
    this kind,
'On the whole, we may say, *mainly*,'
Hal the Eighth was not ungainly:'
For a hesitating attitude becomes the humble
    mind.

Try your best to catch the spirit of the mediæval
    past
For a pleasant party bias
Will save it being dry as
Dust, and shews a human interest in times re-
    motely cast.

If you have not read the subject Mr. A——
    S——th has set
'Tis wise and diplomatic,
In preface idiomatic,
To state that it has difficulties hardly to be met.

Thus you shew him that you realize that hist'ry's
    not a joke,
Tho' you've mental indigestion
You now attack the question
And prove the Norman Conquest wasn't finished
    by a stroke.

A proverb or quotation gives a light, fantastic
    touch,
If it's known, invert the commas,
If it's not, cast conscience from us,
Pretend it is original and write it down as such.

A wholesome private conscience is well enough,
    of course,
But the *true* 'Historic Method'
Leaves the mental sphere untethered,
Intellectual morality's another coloured horse.

M. H.

A Fragment
(DONE INTO BACON).

I KNOW not indeed, whether it be best
for a woman that she be read in books
or learned in possets.

Figure 6.2 "The Study of History" from *The Fritillary* (1897)
Source: The Principal and Fellows of St. Hilda's College, The University of Oxford.

schools for women (*Letters to Mary Russell Mitford* 240). Barrett Browning anticipates what these women's college writers confirm: that entering into an established
university sometimes takes place at the cost of one's own innovation. Although
they attempt to preserve their curiosity and imagination, early women's college
students often succumb to the required institutional methods. Their writings reveal
that even once they have been admitted to elite universities, they often do not feel

completely like insiders and perhaps see the merit of remaining outsiders, even from within.

Modern Historically Excluded Insiders

Approximately a century after the first women's college writers documented their experiences, another historically excluded student arrives at British universities: the working-class woman studying through Open University. Willy Russell investigates the figure of the Open University student in his play *Educating Rita* (1980). The Open University was founded to provide expanded educational opportunities, particularly to less traditional students, and granted admission to every applicant (Open University). In his play, Russell explores what a working-class, nontraditional student like Rita gains and what she loses from learning inside of an institution. In the words of Rita trying to define "assonance," what does it mean to get "the rhyme wrong?" (287). What does it mean for someone like Frank, her professor, to be told, after all of these years, that what he has been doing is "gettin' the rhyme wrong?" (287). Students like Rita, whether women's college students in 1880s England, female hair stylists such as Rita in 1980, or first-generation college students in Britain and the United States today, have offered alternative ways of understanding things like "assonance" for a long time. It was not until relatively recently, however, that more teachers like Frank have tried to discover new ways of teaching nontraditional students. Russell's play looks back to an earlier, nineteenth-century period of expanded educational opportunities, and it also looks forward to the challenges that persist in universities today.

In the United States, the large endowments of many universities enable them to give substantial financial aid to a diverse population of students. Yet often universities still do not fully recognize what an underrepresented student can offer their academic communities once they arrive on campus. Economic pressures can prevent both students and professors from taking chances to explore challenging new materials and methods. Educators often place high priority on examinations that do not test the reaches of students' critical thinking skills. These examinations reward students for thinking concretely instead of imaginatively and reflectively. In order to get to college, a student must jump through hoop after hoop of standardized entrance examinations.

Students often garner praise for working "at the one or two lowest levels of cognitive demand: knowledge and comprehension" versus learning on the levels of "critical and creative thinking" and "inquiry and analysis" (Olson 61; Association of American Colleges and Universities). Despite research like Howard Gardner's on multiple intelligences and despite the recent movement toward varied modes of learning, many believe that college professors still tend to rely on the lecture format instead of more active methods of instruction (Gardner, Bok K11).[19]

But contemporary educators are slowly making progress. Professors increasingly draw upon pedagogies that validate students' prior experiences, allowing for class discussion, group projects, and reflective practice. Through assignments that encourage multimodal learning, we see the potential for educators to reward students who learn in different ways. We catch glimpses of the innovation nineteenth-century writers imagined in contemporary practices. At a time when highly competitive schools like Stanford recruit homeschooled students because of their "inquisitive, self-directed learning style—an educational model that often gets lost in the highly structured, problem-set oriented environment of traditional high school," writers like Jane Austen, Elizabeth Barrett Browning, Thomas Hardy, and George Gissing still have much to say about the kinds of learning that institutions do not cultivate (Olson 199).

This book has explored a story resembling our own that unfolded over 150 years ago across the Atlantic. With the advent of mass education in England came a "payment by results" system of testing that determined the funding allotted to each school (*Hansard*, House of Commons, 5 May 1862, column 1268). Meanwhile, students at Oxford and Cambridge crammed for examinations that formed the focal point of their undergraduate experience. A tension much like the one that exists today materialized in nineteenth-century Britain: outmoded systems of testing persisted while innovative new theories emerged. Insight came from a group of people, excluded from universities, who capitalized on their individualized education outside of schools. In their writing, they anticipate contemporary educational theory that values multiple learning styles and active learning. They encourage us to carve out our own education, never allowing it to be dictated completely by an institutional system.

Notes

1 From 1902 to 1914, national education was reorganized, and measures were made to improve school conditions (UK Parliament, "Further Reform"). The 1918 Act raised the age at which most students left school from 12 to 14 and "made provision for a system of part-time 'continuation day' classes for those in work aged 14–18" (UK Parliament, "Extension of Education").
2 Dalgarno quotes part of this passage in her insightful description of Woolf's education (2).
3 From an early age, Leslie Stephen read aloud to his children, exposing them to works ranging from *Tom Brown's Schooldays* to Carlyle's *French Revolution* to works by Austen, Hawthorne, and Shakespeare (Lee 111). Virginia Woolf herself read Victorian novels aloud while her sister Vanessa painted (Lee 42). On her own, with some advice from her father, she studied Macaulay, Lamb's *Essays of Elia*, Pepys, Montaigne, Carlyle, Gibbon, and Shelley, as well as a range of nineteenth-century novels such as *Felix Holt*, *John Halifax, Gentleman*, *North and South*, *Wives and Daughters*, *Barchester Towers*, *The Scarlet Letter*, *Shirley*, *Villette*, *Alton Locke*, and *Adam Bede* (Lee 140–41). She was tutored by her father in German and took Greek and Latin lessons with Clara Pater, sister of Walter Pater (Lee 141).
4 Hermione Lee's account about why Woolf received much of her education at home exemplifies the conflicted views Woolf's biographers express about her self-portrait (146).
5 Gordon, for example, never mentions King's College, and Lee, who mentions Woolf's Greek and Latin classes, emphasizes that Woolf did not take the exams (Lee 141).
6 See Christine Froula's *Virginia Woolf and the Bloomsbury Avante-garde: War, Civilization, Modernity*.
7 In 1977, Mitchell Leaska published "*The Pargiters*: The Novel-Essay Portion of *The Years*," which consists of the manuscript "1880" section of the "novel-essay" Woolf originally envisioned (*A Writer's Diary* 189).

8 Despite her initial excitement about the project, the ambitious plan proved incredibly difficult, and while writing *The Pargiters* she suffered a major breakdown. Her initial exuberance about the project turned into torment: "I wonder if anyone has ever suffered so much from a book as I have from *The Years*. Once out I will never look at it again. It's like a long childbirth" (*Writer's Diary* 273).

9 I have preserved Mitchell Leaska's system of notation from Woolf's manuscripts.

10 As Julia Prewitt Brown notes, Woolf participated in the service work that her mother and sister did; it is surprising that more scholars do not acknowledge what Woolf must have learned about social class from an early age, even before she began teaching at Morley College (106).

11 Lee gives a clear overview of Woolf's teaching at Morley; see especially 218–19.

12 Here I depart from Melba Cuddy-Keane, who argues as part of her case for Woolf's democratic views of education that the report "leaves a strong impression of the intellectual hunger of her students contrasted with the limitations of their circumstances" (82).

13 *The Years* is not the only novel from which Woolf eliminated earlier innovative ideas about working-class education. In an earlier draft of *Mrs. Dalloway*, Septimus reads classics and Miss Pole teaches at a Working Man's College (Lee 220).

14 The introduction to *Somerville for Women* characterizes Somerville as typical of the Oxbridge women's colleges, emphasizing how even when they were formed as part of the university, they were still set apart from it "by geography and life-style, by their mode of government, sources of finance, social composition, and style of architecture" (2).

15 I try to complicate the story of early women's college students as proud pioneers captured in works such as Jane Robinson's *Bluestockings: The Remarkable Story of the First Women to Fight for an Education*. I align my study more with the discussion of women's difficult integration into Oxford suggested by the *History of the University of Oxford*.

16 These accounts came in particularly large numbers from Girton, which emulated the curriculum of men's colleges, unlike Newnham College, which modified it.

17 She wrote this article for the Macleod Family Magazine *Motley*.

18 These accounts echo more widespread concerns about overworking female students in women's colleges, linked to an anxiety about femininity and overwork. Ruth F. Butler, a student of St. Anne's Society writes, "but it was slightly discouraging to hear, rather later, from one of our lecturers, Mr. Laing, of Corpus Christi College . . . that he saw all the evil effects of examination upon women and feared that our lectures had not improved them, for that there used to be feminine character and originality about their writing, and now they tried to be manly and were only the ordinary man!" (9–10).

19 In 2011, Derek Bok, former president of Harvard University, urged faculty to "lecture less and experiment with new, more active methods of instruction" (Bok).

Appendix 1

Excerpt from *The Loiterer*; facsimile of issue 8 (1789)

Source: The Bodleian Libraries, The University of Oxford. Hope 8° 582 (No. 8), pp. 1–11.

No. 8.

OF THE

LOITERER.

Speak of us as we are.

PRINTED FOR THE AUTHOR,

AND SOLD BY

C. S. RANN, OXFORD;

Messrs. EGERTONS, Whitehall, LONDON;

AND

Messrs. PEARSON and ROLLASON, BIRMINGHAM.

MDCCLXXXIX.

No. VIII.

OF THE

LOITERER.

SATURDAY, March 21, 1789.

Perlege quodcunque est—Quid epistola lecta nocebit?
Te quoque, in hâc aliquid quod juvat, esse potest.
                                                           OVID.

To the LOITERER.

SIR,

AS I understand that your design is, by a weekly distribution of wit and advice, to amuse and instruct the University, of which I was once a member; and as I have already perceived that you have resolution enough to expose the

vices

4 THE LOITERER.

vices and follies, which have sprung up in a soil so friendly to each, I hope that you will not despise the communications of one, who in a former part of his life has been a considerable sufferer from both.

I was the only child of honest, though not wealthy parents, who discovering in me early symptoms of very extraordinary abilities (a discovery which parents frequently make) could not prevail upon themselves to deprive the literary world of so promising a genius; and therefore, instead of breeding me up to assist my father in his shop, they were determined to make a scholar of me. To this end, at the age of nine I was sent to the free school of the town in which we resided, where, in the nine succeeding years, I compleated my classical education; that is, I could construe Latin pretty well with an *Ordo verborum*, and generally knew Greek when I saw it. At this juncture I had the good-fortune of being recommended by the Master of our School to the Head of ——— College, in Oxford, and soon after had the inexpressible pleasure of being elected to a scholarship worth at least 15*l. per annum.*

Language is not adequate to express the joy, which spread itself through my family at the news of

THE LOITERER.

of such an unlooked for acquisition of fortune; and I need not say, that both my father and mother thought it an indispensible duty, to accompany their common hope to the theatre of science, that they might see me take possession of my estate, and make my first entrance on the world. Generous friends! I blush to think how much good advice, and good furniture ye enriched me with, and how little I regarded either. The pleasing surprise which a new place, and new acquaintance always occasion in the mind of a young man, equally disposed to please, and to be pleased, had not altogether subsided, and I had scarcely convinced myself that it was not all enchantment, when on looking about me I concluded, from several reasons, that I was the happiest man alive. In the first place I was totally my own master, and might do what I pleased; that is, I might do nothing at all. Secondly, I was convinced that I had money enough to last for ever. And thirdly, I had already made several friends, who were willing to lay down their lives to oblige me. This latter opinion, indeed, I had very reasonably drawn from seeing with what ardour they proposed to me, and with what eagerness they joined in every species of pleasure, merely to amuse me. To be sure, it often came to my lot to be general paymaster, but this might be the effect rather of their thought-

lessness,

6   THE LOITERER.

lessness, than any intention to defraud, or any inability to disburse; and flushed, as I then was, with the enjoyment of present, and the schemes of future pleasure, I thought (if I thought at all) that the continuance of such friends was cheaply purchased by defraying some of their extravagancies.

To convince you, Mr. Loiterer, that my daily employments left not much time for study or reflection, I shall, without sending you a journal, briefly inform you, that the morning was dissipated in doing nothing, and the evening in doing what was worse; the first part wasted in idleness, the latter drowned in intemperance. As it would be tedious to relate in what various scenes I played the fool and the rake, or to describe the many different expedients, which I adopted to lessen my knowledge, my fortune, and my health: suffice it to say, that in about six years I had so far succeeded as to have very little left of any; and when I took my degree, I was as ignorant as emaciated, and as much in debt as the first peer of the realm. I had lost every thing which I ought to have preserved; I had acquired nothing but habits of expence, which long outlived the means of gratifying them, and a relish for indolence at a time when I had my bread to earn.

The

THE LOITERER.

The firſt thing which rouſed me from this dream of pleaſure, was the gradual departure of my College acquaintance, and the melancholy change which I ſaw take place in the fate of thoſe whom common pleaſures, and common extravagancies, had made in ſome degree dear to me. The Orators of the Coffee-houſe, the Jockies of Port-meadow, and the Champions of the High-ſtreet, were alike forced to relinquiſh the ſphere of their glory, and ſinking into Country Curates, grew old on fifty pounds a year. Such is the melancholy, but certain change, which vicious extravagance may depend upon experiencing. Such are the comforts in ſtore for their latter years! Age has ever its peculiar infirmities, but the weakneſſes of declining life impart double anguiſh, when attended by the recollection of paſt pleaſures, which our eagerneſs to enjoy cut ſhort in the enjoyment; and whilſt we ſee what we might, and what we ought to have been, we feel too late what we are.

I now gradually recovered from my mental intoxication, in exact proportion as the companions of it decreaſed; and I acquired a knowledge of my real ſituation, by the time that I remained the laſt ſolitary member of our once gay, and numerous party.

To

8 THE LOITERER.

To render my diftrefs more afflicting, I at this time loft a moft indulgent father, to whom I had looked up for prefent fupport, and who, though he died, as I then thought, much too foon, had lived long enough to fee his hopes and defigns, for my future fortune and reputation, defeated by my own imprudence. But till the very laft, he had been too liberal in fupporting the expences of a fon, whofe conduct he had long fince condemned; and though it required a much larger income than his had ever been to fatisfy my wifhes, yet I am too well affured, that he often deprived himfelf of innocent pleafures, and reafonable gratifications, to fupply the drain of a fon's prodigality. Notwithftanding that he had been many years in trade, and had purfued his bufinefs with uninterrupted application, yet the fmallnefs of his original capital, and fome fubfequent and inevitable loffes, left it in his power to die only not infolvent. My mother fpent the few remaining months of a widowhood, which grief and ficknefs foon cut fhort, in a moft œconomical retirement; and when fhe died, I found my real property to be rather under 100l. my debts above four times that fum, and my profpects of future fubfiftence very uncertain. Something was to be done, and quickly too. I immediately hit upon the wifeft action of my life. I left Oxford, and

I have

THE LOITERER.

I have been wife enough never to return. Having previously taken orders, I put myself and my portmanteau into one of the northern coaches, nor suffered myself to make any confiderable delay in my journey, till I arrived at York. Here, after having kept myself in privacy for a few days to fetch breath, after fo precipitate and feafonable an efcape from duns and deftruction, I waited on a Reverend Doctor, who was the rector of two livings, which lay about fifty miles farther to the North, and to whom I had letters of recommendation as a Curate. After a fhort interview, I obtained my appointment, with a ftipend of 35l. per ann. for which I was to undertake only three churches on a Sunday, conftant weekly duty, and the care of two large parifhes. As my Rector had been engaged near twenty years in a law-fuit with the Squire of the parifh, who was one of his patrons, he never went near the livings himfelf, but conftantly refided in this Northern Capital, where I had forgot to mention that he had alfo a prebend. After he had given me the direction to his villages, advifed me to cultivate the good opinion of my flock, and to avoid all difputes, we parted, I hope to our mutual fatisfaction. At leaft for myfelf I can fay, that the profpect of approaching tranquility appeared to me more and more pleafing each moment as I advanced,

When

10   THE LOITERER.

When I arrived at my cure, I found that the face of the country could be beautiful even at the distance of three hundred miles from London; and I soon felt no small degree of affection for my habitation, which, though small and unornamented, was perfectly neat.

In short, at the end of six years, I found that my partiality to my present situation was rather increased than diminished, and that by some good fortune or other, I had recommended myself so well as a companion to the Squire of the parish, and his only sister, that I gained at once their common consent to become the brother-in-law of the one, and the husband of the other. My wife was to be sure a few years older than myself. But though the good-natured world may therefore put an unfavourable opinion on the motives of her regard for me, I can only say that fifteen years of the tenderest attention and uninterrupted contentment on both sides convinced me too well, what a friend I lost at the end of them. A little while after my marriage, my Rector was obliged by some other preferment to resign the living, of which I was still Curate; and my brother-in-law unasked immediately presented me to it. It's value was upwards of Three Hundred Pounds a year. An income, which joined to my wife's fortune, enabled

us

us to enjoy all the comforts, and some of the luxuries of life: at least the luxuries of Yorkshire. But my first care was to discharge all my Oxford debts, which I gradually accomplished in four or five years, and long before I was a widower, had not a thought to trouble me on that head.

Forty years have passed away since I first entered my retreat, and during that time I have not been twenty miles distant from it. My patron has followed his sister to the grave, and though most of my first acquaintance have retired to the same home, that can give but little concern to one, who recollects that at sixty-five, he need not be afraid of living much longer.

Thus much of myself, Mr. Loiterer. If I have been tedious, remember that this is the last opportunity I have of talking to the world. To the rising age say something more. Tell them to look on me as a beacon, held up for their observance, but not a model for their imitation. Let them shun my footsteps as they would avoid that precipice on which I tottered: and let them be well assured, that the guilty pleasures of a few months will entail many years of shame and remorse. Nor shall they urge in their defence,
" that

THE LOITERER.

" that they only do as the rest do." This is the defence of the fool. Individuals make the community. Let every one begin the reformation at home; for, were there no imitators, there would soon be no examples.

I am, Sir, your's, &c.

H. HOMELY.

E.

Appendix 2
Excerpts from *The Popular Educator*; facsimile of 1.2 (1852)

Source: The Bodleian Libraries, The University of Oxford. (OC) 260 h.5 (v.1–2), 1.2, pp.19–29 (non-consecutive pages).

LESSONS IN PHYSIOLOGY.—No. I.
MAN.

We are about to enter on a most delightful study; and we want you to sit down and go through the same lessons. We shall need no text-book but our own bodies; and our aim will be to find out of what elements these bodies are made, how they are nourished, how preserved, and how in being built up, each stands out as a living temple for the living soul, than which there is nothing greater or grander but God himself.

The world of nature is divided into three kingdoms—the animal, the vegetable, and the mineral. All within these three kingdoms is again divided into either living bodies or dead matter. A mineral has neither life nor fixed arrangement. A vegetable has both. So also has an animal, and in a still higher degree. This distinction between animal and vegetable structures, and mineral substances—between living bodies and mere masses of dead matter, is, in some cases, not very easy to trace, and yet it is most fixed and certain. For a long time CORAL was thought to be nothing more than a mineral; but when on examination it was found to be a growth, it was then taken from the mineral into the vegetable kingdom, and having still more recently been discovered to be a congeries of animals, it has been removed from the vegetable into the animal kingdom.

It is with this animal kingdom we have now to do. I have a body. This body is made up of hard or solid parts, such as the bones; of soft parts, such as the muscles, the bowels, the brain, and similar portions of the frame; and of fluids, such as the blood. Now, of what are these soft, and hard, and fluid parts composed? It is said, that " God formed man out of the dust of the ground;" and, wonderful to say, that the little minute atoms of the earth's surface most perfectly correspond with the materials of which my body is made up. In no living body has any element been yet found which does not also exist in the very matter on which we tread. The earth was created first, and gradually fitted up as a dwelling-place for man; and when the time came for the creation of man, God took the matter which already existed, and out of that dead, motionless, inactive matter, he reared the wondrous structure of the human frame.

All matter is either organic or inorganic. We call those organic bodies which are made up of parts,—these parts, however diversified in themselves, being mutually adapted and mutually dependent, and each of them capable of performing a certain function or action. A wax flower has its various parts mutually adapted and mutually dependent, but neither in their individual nature nor in combination, can these parts perform any vital function. They have no principle of life, and without vitality there can be no organisation, since all organisation implies a living arrangement of inanimate elements. You may cut a block of marble into the form and fashion of a man; but when so fashioned, it is only inert matter in a more elegant form. In one word, wherever we find the living principle in connexion with matter, there we have organisation in vital arrangement. In the absence of this principle we have nothing but a dead and inert mass. To the question:—What is life? we can give back no answer. That there is such a thing as life or vital action, cannot be denied; and the only thing which we can say with certainty concerning it, is, that life is that which admits of development. We go into our garden with a pebble and a flower-seed in our hand. We commit them both to the soil, and thus subject them to the same agencies and influences. The seed will burst, and germinate, and develop itself in a beautiful and fragrant flower, while the pebble may lie there for years on years without undergoing the least change. This mysterious life-principle enters into all organised matter, and is found in its highest and most perfect form in the animal economy, and, among animals, first and pre-eminent in man.

The material structure which man possesses for the manifestation of this life, is made up of certain chemical compositions, and anatomical arrangements. There is no organic or animal substance in which hydrogen, nitrogen, and oxygen, are not essential to its very existence, while the addition of one or more of the fifty-five elements of all known matter is composed, in whatever proportion, will determine incidentally in what that substance differs from any other form of organic matter. It must, however, be kept in mind, that since the elements which compose all animate and inanimate matter are the same, we must look for the difference between these two classes of substances to the mode in which the elements are combined. For example:—The combination of oxygen and nitrogen, of which the atmosphere is formed, or of oxygen and hydrogen, as they enter into the composition of water, does not render either the atmosphere or the water an organic substance. But if we take a plant, which exhibits the simplest form of animate or organic existence, we shall find the three elements of carbon, hydrogen, and oxygen, while in the animal economy, we shall discover that oxygen, hydrogen, nitrogen, carbon, and sulphur are united. Is life then the result of chemical combination? That cannot be. In water, which is without life, we find combined oxygen and hydrogen. In a plant with life, we find the same elements with the addition of carbon. Is the carbon the cause of life? Impossible. The true theory is, that life in the plant requires those three elements to sustain and preserve it, and that were it deprived of any one of the three, it would soon wither and die.

What, then, do we mean by human physiology? The term physiology is derived from two Greek words, ΦΥΣΙΣ—nature, character, or constitution; and ΛΟΓΟΣ, a treatise or discourse; and when applied to man, includes those conditions, phenomena, and laws of life, which are common to the human body in a state of health. In fewer and simpler words, it is the science of healthy function. It is no common good to have a sound mind in a sound body; but if the play and force of the intellect depend more or less on the sound and healthy condition of the body, then no means should be slighted, by which it may be more effectually preserved from injury or disease. Nor must we forget that disease is present when any structure of the body is changed, or when any function becomes unnaturally active or torpid, or is altered in its character. Is it the perfectness of every structure, and the harmonious play of every function, to which we give the name of health; and health is very much in our own keeping. Our everyday habits and pursuits will determine the condition of the body; and the particular state or condition in which our body is at any given time, is that to which we give the name of health or disease. Every one, therefore, should make himself familiar with the science of physiology. He should study his own structure, and the laws by which that structure is governed, that he may know how to preserve the one, and obey the other, so as to prolong life, and render being happy that life while prolonged.

Let us begin with the bones. The existence of bone is the result of organisation or vital arrangement. All animal substance springs from a germ. This germ is a minute particle or molecule, which cannot be seen without a microscope of high power, and may vary in size from a minuteness which cannot be measured to the ten-thousandth part of an inch in diameter. It is rather round in form. As it gradually enlarges, its outer wall becomes transparent, through which the colour of its inward substance can be seen. This germ or molecule is formed of fatty or oily matter; or perhaps of particles of oil coated over with a substance, which is called albumen—a substance which resembles the white of an egg—and which the molecule takes from the fluid in which it floats. By drawing to itself certain elements or particles from the fluid which surrounds it, this germ becomes a cell which may include a number of other germs or molecules. These little bodies being set free by the bursting of the parent cell, give existence to a new generation of cells, and so the mysterious yet beautiful process goes on from generation to generation.

As the cell gradually enlarges in size, it becomes an interesting inquiry, as to how its growth is promoted. Where does it obtain the materials for its increase? And how do these materials become assimilated, so as to be taken up into the substance of the cells? The source of supply must be sought in the elements by which every individual cell is surrounded. For example:—All that a vegetable requires for its growth, is a supply of water and carbonic acid; because the acid being the product of carbon and oxygen, and the water of oxygen and hydrogen; the water and the acid supply the three elements—oxygen, hydrogen, and carbon—which enter into the composition of the plant. Surrounded by these elements, the cell has the power, by virtue of the principle of life, of

THE POPULAR EDUCATOR.

converting them into a new compound, whose properties adapt it to become part of the growing organised substance.

So in animal structure. So in the human body. We have selected the bones with which to begin. All bone is developed from a substance called CARTILAGE, which is a species of gristle. In its simpler form, this cartilage is composed entirely of cells, with a jelly-like substance between, called GELATINE. These cells are found in little clusters of two, three, and four; but as they begin to take on the character of bone, instead of these smaller clusters, we have groups made up of a much larger number. These groups are still separated by the jelly-like substance which comes between, and it is in this substance that the bony matter is first deposited. Gradually assuming the form of deep narrow cups of bone, it receives the ends of the cartilage cells, as these become arranged in long rows. Then, these cartilage cells become consolidated, and take on the hardness of bone. When the temporary cartilage is converted into bone, the bone has still to be enlarged in conformity with the increasing size of the surrounding parts. How is this enlargement insured? In two ways. All the new cartilage at the edges and on the surface of the bone, becomes ossified, and it is known that the growth of a long bone takes place chiefly towards its extremities, while the bony matter on its surface contributes to increase its thickness. This is one method. The other is by having a cavity in the bone itself. You know that in mechanics, when we want to get the greatest strength with a limited amount of material, we choose a hollow cylinder. Just so in the human body. The bones are designed for strength and support; and instead of being a solid mass, they most of them are hollow. The matter first deposited on the inner surface of these tubes or hollow bones, is pushed outwards by succeeding layers, and thus the bone gradually acquires an increased diameter.

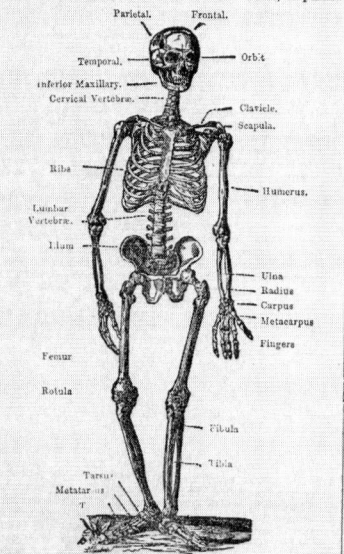

Having thus learned how bone is formed, and how it acquires increased strength and size, let us now see whether we can find out the number of bones in the human body, how they are held together, and what purpose they serve. Here is a skeleton which will help us to trace the connexion of the different parts of this wondrous structure, and show us how beautifully fitted it is for the ends designed by the great Creator. It includes one hundred and ninety-eight bones. These are exclusive of the teeth, of which there are sixteen inserted in each jaw, and also exclusive of a few small bones, which serve to lengthen and give additional strength to some others. We shall now arrange these one hundred and ninety-eight bones in the form of a table, that you may see more clearly and remember more easily their connexion:—

In the cranium or head	8
In the spine, called the vertebræ, including the sacrum and the coccyx, which are called false vertebræ, because they adhere to each other and do not move	26
In the face	14
A little bone which lies at the root of the tongue, called Os-hyoides, of this shape ∪	1
The ribs—and the breast-bone to which they are in part attached	25
In each superior extremity, including the shoulder, arm, fore-arm, and hand 32	64
In each lower extremity, including the pelvis, thigh, leg, and foot 30	60
Total	198

If we examine the composition of bone, we shall find that it contains the three essential elements, hydrogen, nitrogen, and oxygen; with a certain proportion of lime and phosphorus, or phosphate of lime. It is by the excess of this earthy matter in the bones of old people, that they are so easily and so frequently broken. We seldom if ever hear of a child breaking a bone, and yet how often do children fall, how sadly are they sometimes bruised.

The purpose of bone in the animal economy is purely mechanical. Not only do the bones serve as points of attachment to the muscles in the midst of which they are situated, but afford support and protection to the softer textures, and form inflexible levers, on which the muscles may act, and give motion to the different parts of the great fabric. The brain is a soft and delicate texture, and to preserve which uninjured, is essential to the play and activity of the mind. Now see how admirably this is insured by incasing it within the hard and bony substance of the cranium. So the heart and the lungs are defended by the ribs, and the spinal marrow by the vertebræ which compose the back bone. In all this, we behold the wise and benevolent arrangement of the Creator. If the brain had not been so defended, it would have been liable to constant injury, and in the proportion of the injury must the intellect have been impaired.

Or, suppose we break a bone, how disabled do we become? If it be in the leg, we have no longer the power of locomotion, or of moving from one place to another. If it be in the hand, we are no longer qualified to perform the every-day duties of life. But here again we see the goodness of God. While the bones are subject to manifold diseases and external injuries, there is no other structure of the same complex nature, which is capable of being so thoroughly repaired. There have been cases of the re-formation of nearly an entire bone, when the original one had been lost by disease. So in a fracture. Any portion of the shattered bone that remains connected with the surrounding membrane, and the vessels with which it is supplied, becomes the centre of a new formation, and the injury is repaired in a few weeks.

You know that the bones exhibit a great many joints, and that it is by these joints we are enabled to move our bodies in such a variety of ways. But for such an arrangement in the fingers, for example, and we could neither close our hands, nor grasp any object on which we wished to lay hold. Now if there be so many joints, how is it that the bones are preserved each in its place? This is done by ligaments and cartilages. Cartilage is a white elastic substance next to bone in solidity; ligament is a strong, whitish, flexible, fibrous substance; and both in some instances supply the place of bone; in other instances they fix the ends of the bones so as to confine the motions of the joint; sometimes they give origin to muscles, and sometimes they fix the bones almost immovably together. Between the joints there is a fluid called SYNOVIA, which is of a yellowish hue, like olive oil, and which like oil, serves to lubricate and render easy the motion of one bone upon another.

How beautiful and how gracious are these arrangements! How worthy of that wise and loving Creator, the purpose and end of all whose works is not less our happiness than his own glory! With what interest should we study His works, and how warm and grateful should be the praise of our hearts!

But we have gone far enough for one lesson. Let us now put the whole in the form of questions, and see how much you have learned, and how much you remember.

What are the three kingdoms into which the world of nature is divided?
Is the distinction between living bodies and dead matter to be always easily traced?
Give an example of this difficulty.
With which of these three kingdoms has human physiology to do?
Of what material is the human body made up?
Is there any difference between the particles of which the body is made up and the atoms of the earth's surface?
What do you mean by organised matter?
What are the essential elements in all organic or animal substance?
Does chemical combination produce life?
What do you mean by human physiology?
From what does all animal substance spring?
Of what is the germ formed?
Whence does it get materials for its nourishment and growth?
Give an example from the vegetable kingdom.
From what substance is bone developed?
How is cartilage formed?
In what substance does the bony matter first begin to form?
How is the growth of bone insured?
How many bones are there in the human skeleton?
Give the number in each part.
How many teeth are there in each jaw?
What purpose do the bones serve?
Give an example of the protection which they afford to some of the softer textures.
When a bone has suffered from disease, is it easily and ever thoroughly re-formed?
What holds the bones together?
What substance is found between the joints to make the bones move more easily the one upon the other?

LESSONS IN LATIN.—No. I.
By JOHN R. BEARD, D.D.
INTRODUCTORY.

BEING about to give you, reader, some lessons which may enable you to learn the Latin language, with no other resources than such as may be supplied by your own care and diligence, I take it for granted that you are desirous of acquiring the necessary skill, and am willing to bestow the necessary labour. If the study were not recommended as a good mental discipline; if it were not recommended as giving a key to some of the finest treasures of literature; if it were not recommended as a means of leading you into communion with such minds as those of Cicero, Virgil, Horace, Livy, and Tacitus, it would have a sufficient claim on your attention, as greatly conducing to a full and accurate acquaintance with your mother tongue—the English. The English language is, for the most part, made up of two elements: the Saxon element, the Latin element. Without a knowledge of both these elements, you cannot be said to know English. If you are familiar with both these elements, you possess means of knowing and writing English, superior to the means which are possessed by many who have received what is called a classical education, and have spent years in learned universities. In order to be in possession of both those elements, you must, for the Saxon element, study German, and for the Latin element, study the lessons which ensue.

In studying the ensuing lessons, you must implicitly follow my directions. I have been for many years engaged in teaching, and, from my experience, know that there is no obstacle to progress greater than that which scholars create for themselves, in giving preference to their own judgments and following their own fancies and opinions. In your practice, acknowledge and observe it as a first principle, that your instructor knows better than you. Take it for certain that he is right, until should it so happen—you have proved that he is wrong. At the same time, scrupulously follow my directions. Do not attempt to get before me; take care not to fall behind me. Do *what* I bid, do it *when* I bid it, do it *as* I bid it. The more rigid you are with yourself, in obeying these injunctions, the more certain and the more rapid will your progress be. As having myself gone through every thing that I am about to teach you, and as having for more than a quarter of a century been engaged in teaching these things to others, I know what difficulties are in the way, and I have learned how to diminish or remove them. On these grounds I claim your confidence; and if you are not willing to give me your confidence, you had better not enter on the study of the Latin language.

In the instructions which I am to give you, I shall suppose myself addressing a friend, who besides some general acquaintance with his mother tongue, has acquired from the English Lessons in the POPULAR EDUCATOR, or from some other source, a knowledge of the ordinary terms of English Grammar, such as singular, plural, noun, adjective, verb, adverb, &c. The meaning of such words I shall not explain. But everything peculiar as between the English and the Latin I shall explain. I shall also explain any grammatical term, which though used sometimes in English Grammar, you possibly may not understand. In my explanations I think it safer to err on the side of superfluity rather than on the side of deficiency. I have said that I shall suppose you to possess a general acquaintance with the English language. But I advise you to suspect yourself as being probably acquainted with it, but in a very imperfect manner. And this advice I give you in the hope that it may lead you to the constant use of a good English Dictionary. In every case in which you have the least doubt whether or not you know the exact meaning of any word I use, look out the word in your dictionary, and put it down in a note-book to be kept for the purpose. Having written it in the note-book, add the meaning. When you have, say a score of words thus entered in your note book, look them over again and again until their signification is impressed on your memory. If you listen to this suggestion, and continue to make progress with me, you will soon find numerous exemplifications of the assertion I made but now, namely, that a large proportion of the words in the English language are of Latin origin. Take, for instance, the last sentence. In that sentence alone the following words are derived from the Latin: I mean *suggestion, continue, progress, numerous, exemplification, assertion, proportion, language, Latin, origin.* Of the two-and-forty words of which the sentence consists, ten are from the Latin. Should you ever possess an acquaintance with the science of philology, or the science of languages, you will know that in the sentence there are other words which are found in the Latin as well as in other ancient languages. Independently of this, you now learn that about one-fourth of our English words have come to us from the people who spoke Latin, that is the Romans and other nations of Italy. In reality, the proportion of Latin words in the English is much greater, as in time you may know. Observe, too, that these Latin words in the sentence are the long and the hard words, are what perhaps you may call "Dictionary words." These are the very words which give you trouble when you read an English classic, or first-rate author. But they give me no trouble. With me, they are as easy to be understood as any common Saxon term, such as *father, house, tree.* The reason why they have long ceased to give me trouble, is, that I am familiar with their roots, or the elements of which they each consist. Having this familiarity, I have no occasion to consult the dictionary. There are thousands of English words of Latin origin, the meaning of which I know, though I have never looked them out in a dictionary. I wish to assist you in putting yourself into a similar position; and although you may have no aid but such as these pages afford you, I do not despair of success, if only you will strictly observe my requirements.

I shall, however, have little chance of carrying my wishes into effect, if you begin with a notion that the task is an easy one. Were it an easy task, it would not be worth your trouble. I tell you plainly that the task is hard; that it is a long task; that it will require on your part patience and diligence. If you commence the study under the delusion that it is mere play, you will do as very many have done before you,—in a short time you will grow weary, and give it up. But if, in a true manly spirit, you take up the task as a worthy task, as a useful though a difficult task, as a task in which whatever I may do for you, you must do far more for yourself, then you will not fail to make progress; your course will become easier as you go on; and you will have the delightful satisfaction that you are employing your time and your faculties so as to produce definite, important, and abiding results. If, however, it is not an easy thing to acquire an acquaintance with the principles of the Latin language, then you will at once see that it is not wise to be engaged at the same time in other difficult studies. Many persons, especially young persons, fail to give themselves a good education, because they attempt too much—because, indeed, they attempt what is impossible. I remember that when I began in earnest to study Latin, I was saved from this danger, by the judicious opinion of a learned and venerated friend, who advised me not to attempt more than one subject at a time. In part, my friend, I am like you, self-taught. In the ordinary phrase, indeed, I learnt Latin when a boy at school; but so wretched were the methods of teaching some forty years ago, that though I learnt Latin I knew nothing of Latin when I left school. Soon, however, I began the study in earnest; I began almost unaided. But an adviser came, and under his directions I for a time confined myself almost exclusively to my Latin studies. They were hard, very hard; much harder were they to me than they need be to you. But by giving my mind perseveringly to the task, I reaped success, and so in time became prepared for college. Let me be your adviser. Even in the treasures of the POPULAR EDUCATOR you may find a source of danger. If you engage in all the studies here offered, you will become proficient in none. Make a selection. If you wish to learn Latin, pursue the study wisely. But wisely you cannot pursue it, if you combine therewith several other subjects. For you, one language at a time is enough. Do not attempt more. If you want relief from this, which is a severe study, unite with it the Lessons in History which these pages supply. But do not attempt to learn French while you are learning Latin. When you know Latin, you will find French very easy. With a knowledge of Latin you would also have no difficulty at all in becoming, in a short time, acquainted with the Italian, the Spanish, and the Portuguese languages, which have Latin for their common parent. In the Latin, too, you will find great assistance should you wish to learn Greek, and so acquire the power of reading the scriptures of the New Testament in their original tongue.

You may practically regard the Latin alphabet as the same as the English. The English letters may be traced to the Latin; the Latin letters are derived from the Greek; and the Greek are in substance identical with the Phenician; while the Phenician alphabet is the oldest, or one of the oldest, in the world.

In the pronunciation, too, you may in the main follow the best English usage. Every modern nation pronounces the Latin as it pronounces its own tongue. Thus there are divers methods of pronunciation. This diversity would be inconvenient, if the Latin were, like the French, a general medium of verbal intercourse. At one time it was so. And then there prevailed one recognised manner of pronunciation. Now, however, for the most part, Latin is read, not spoken. Consequently the pronunciation is not a matter of consequence. Even in our own country there are diversities. but such diversities are secondary matters. To one or two remarks, however, you should carefully attend. In Latin the vowels are what is called long or short. In other words, on some the accent or stress of the voice is thrown, on others it is not thrown. The vowel *a* for instance is mostly long, the vowel *i* is mostly short. A long vowel is said to be equal to two short vowels. We English people, however, have no other way of marking a long vowel, except by throwing on it, the accent or stress of the voice. It is also a fact, that the same vowel is sometimes short and sometimes long; in other words, the same vowel sometimes has, and sometimes has not the accent on it; thus the *i* in dominus, *a lord*, is without the accent, while the *i* in doctrina, *learning*, has the accent; the former, therefore is pronounced thus, dóminus, the latter thus, doctrína. Now observe that these words are trisyllables, as dom, i, nus. Of these three syllables the last, namely us, is called the ultimate; the second, i, is called the penult; the third, or dom, is called the antepenult. And the general rule for pronouncing Latin words is, that the accent is thrown on the penult, or if not on the penult, then on the antepenult. In doctrína the accent is on the penult, or last syllable but one. In dóminus, the accent is on the antepenult, or last syllable but two. In order that you may know where to lay the stress of your voice, I shall mark, as in dóminus and doctrína, on which syllable the accent lies. You will then understand that when I put a mark thus ´ over a vowel, I mean thereby that you should let your voice rest, as it were on that vowel. For example, in the word incur, the accent you know is on the last syllable, for you throw the stress of the voice on the syllable cur. This is indicated thus, incúr. So in the Latin amícus, *a friend*, the accent is on the *i*, and the word is to be pronounced thus amícus, the accent being on the penult. There is another way of marking the same fact; it is by the use of a short strait line, as ¯, and a curve, as ˘. The former denotes a long or accented syllable, for instance doctrīna; the latter denotes a short or unaccented syllable, for instance, domĭnus. You thus see that doctrina and doctrína, dóminus and domĭnus point out the same thing, namely, that in pronouncing doctrina you must lay the stress of the voice on the *i*, and in pronouncing dóminus you must lay it on the *o*.

I must point out to you another practice. In Latin, as you will presently learn, the endings of words have a good deal to do with their meanings. It is, on that account, usual to pronounce them at least very distinctly. Indeed, I might say, that on every terminating syllable a sort of secondary accent is laid. Thus, dominus is pronounced dómĭnús. So in other forms of the word, thus, dómĭní, dómĭnó, dómĭnúm. The object is to mark the distinction between, say, dominus and dominis, a distinction of great consequence. Another form of this word is dominos. For the same reason a stress is laid on the termination os, which accordingly is pronounced as if it were oase. Words, too, which end in *es* have a secondary accent on the *e*; as Vulpes, *a fox*, pronounced vulpes. In a few cases the vowel is what we call doubtful, that is, it is sometimes short and sometimes long. This peculiarity is marked thus, ⌣ as in tenĕbrae, *darkness*, when the accent may be on the penult, as tenĕbrae, or on the antepenult, as tenébrae. Observe, also, that a vowel at the end of a word is always pronounced in Latin. Take, as an example, docére, *to teach*, which is pronounced as it is marked, that is, with an accent on the last syllable no less than on the last syllable but one. The Latin language has no silent e, as we have: for instance, in wife. Practise yourself, according to these rules, in pronouncing thus the opening lines of that fine poem, Virgil's Aeneid. As I am anxious that you should not pass anything without knowing its meaning, I subjoin the translation made by the English poet Dryden.

"Arma virúmque cáno, Trójaé quí prímus ab óris
Italíam, fáto prófugús, Lavínia vénit
Líttora; múltum flé ét térris jáctatús et álto,
Vi supérum, saévaé memórem Júnónis ob íram;
Múlta quóque ét béllo pássus dúm cónderét úrbem,
Inférrétque Déós Látio; genus únde Látínum,
Albáníque patrés, átque áltaé moénia Rómae."

"Arms and the man I sing, who forc'd by fate,
And haughty Juno's unrelenting hate,
Expell'd and exil'd, left the Trojan shore,
Long labours, both by sea and land, he bore,
And in the doubtful war, before he won
The Latin realm, and built the destined town—
His banish'd gods restor'd to rites divine,
And settled sure succession in his line,
From whence the race of Alban fathers come,
And the long glories of majestic Rome."

LESSONS IN GEOMETRY.

In pronouncing the third line, you must cut off the um before the vowel *i*; and the *e* in ille before the *e* in et. Also in the fifth line drop the *e* in quoque before the *e* in el. In the last line, too, the *e* in atque is dropped or elided before the vowel *a* in altae; pronounced as if written qualtae. Accuracy of pronunciation, however, is not easily acquired from any written or printed directions. The living tongue is the only adequate teacher. And it will be well if you can get some grammar school-boy to read to you and hear you read the passage I have given above from Virgil, and the exercises, or some of them, which ensue. Although the pronunciation of Latin is of secondary importance, yet you must try to be as correct as you can, if only from the consideration that what is worth doing at all, is worth doing well. But should you, as you justifiably may, hope by these lessons to prepare yourself for becoming even a teacher of Latin—say in a school—you would in that capacity find the pronunciation considered as a matter of consequence; indeed a disproportionate value is, especially in the old grammar schools, attached to the established methods of pronunciation. After all, we cannot pronounce the Latin as it was pronounced by the Latins themselves, nor can the best trained lips pronounce their poetry so as to reproduce its music.

In regard to the exercises which I am about to give, you should first learn the vocabulary by heart. If yours is a mechanical trade, you may repeat the words over again and again while engaged in labour. Or you may make the words your own while walking to and from your employment. Among my personal friends, is a gentleman who acquired the greater part of the words of the French language, while rising and dressing in the morning. Thousands of words have I myself learnt while walking for recreation.

Having thoroughly mastered the vocabulary, take a slate and write down the Latin into English; then write the English into Latin. Look over what you have done carefully. Correct every mistake and error. If you look into the exercises you will find that the English will assist you in writing the Latin, and the Latin will assist you in writing the English. When you have got both the Latin and the English into as correct a state as you can, copy them neatly into a note-book. Having done so, read them carefully over, and compare each instance with the rule or the direction, and also the example. Leave nothing until you understand the reason. All the examples or illustrations that I give, as well as the chief rules, should be committed to memory. Before you proceed to a second lesson, ascertain that you are master of the first. It would be useful to write out the rules in one consecutive view, in order that, having them all at once under your eye, you may study them in their connexion and as a whole, so as to see their bearing one upon another, and the general results to which they lead. Such a practice would have a very beneficial effect on your mind, by habituating it to arrangement and order, and might be expected to afford you valuable aid, both in other studies and in your business pursuits. Carefully avoid haste and slovenliness. Do your best in all that you undertake. "Well" not "much" should be your watchword. Repeated reviews of the ground passed over are very desirable. Every Saturday you should go carefully over what you have done during the week. At the end of every month the work of the month should be reviewed. On arriving at a natural division of our subject, as for instance, when we have treated of the nouns, you should go over, and put together in your mind the substance of what has been said thereon. "Be not weary in well doing, for in due season you will reap, if you faint not. (Gal. vi. 9).

VOCABULARY.

Curro, *I run*. The chief parts are curro, *I run*; currere, *to run*; cucurri, *I have run*; cursus, *run*. The English representative, or the element in English derived from the parts, is curr; also curs or cours. Con, from cum, means *with*; dis signifies *in different directions*; ex signifies *out of*.

EXERCISE—LATIN-ENGLISH.

Curro and its parts give rise to several English words, as *current*, ("the current coin of the realm;") *currency* ("the circulating medium.") Another example is found in the phrase "account current."

EXERCISE—ENGLISH-LATIN.

Find English words derived from some part of curro; find English words derived from curro, with in prefixed; also with con prefixed; also with dis prefixed; also with ex prefixed.

REMARK.—In order to make my meaning quite clear, I will myself do this exercise in part. From cursus comes the English word *course*; from in and curs comes *incursion*; from ex and curs comes *excursion*. If the reader is acquainted with, or is learning French, he will do well as he passes on, to find out French words corresponding to, and derived from, Latin words; as in courir, French *to run*; cours, a course. By comparison he may occasionally find that the same sound or word has a different meaning in French from what it has in Latin or in English. Thus, concursus in Latin means a coming together, as to a meeting, a *concours* of people; but the corresponding French, concours, signifies *co-operation*. So concurrence in English is *agreement*, but in French *competition*. By practising comparisons such as this, you will not only meet with many curious facts, but be assisted to understand the nature of language itself, as well as receive good mental discipline. If it seems strange to you that the same letters curr or curs should bear dissimilar meanings, a little reflection will take away your surprise. Go to the primary meaning of curr. Its primary meaning is *to run*. Now, men may run into, or run out of, or run together, or run about, for different purposes. For instance, they may run together in harmony, and then they concur; or they may run together in rivalry, and then they are in what the French call concurrence, that is, competition.

I have thus, my fellow student, opened out before you an immense field. It is only a hint or two that I can give; but if you follow these intimations, you will in time become not only a Latin scholar, but a good linguist.

LESSONS IN GEOMETRY.—No. I.

THE term *Geometry*, which comes from the Greek word *Geometria*, literally signifies *land-measuring*, and was originally applied to the practical purpose which its name signifies, in the land of Egypt, the cradle of the arts and sciences. Herodotus, the oldest historian, with the exception of Moses, whose works have reached us, gives the following account of its origin: "I was informed by the priests at Thebes, that king Sesostris made a distribution of the territory of Egypt among all his subjects, assigning to each an equal portion of land, in the form of a quadrangle, and that from these allotments he used to derive his revenue, by exacting every year a certain tax. In cases, however, where a part of the land was washed away by the annual inundations of the Nile, the proprietor was permitted to present himself before the king, and signify what had happened. The king then used to send proper officers to examine and ascertain, by admeasurement, how much of the land had been washed away, in order that the amount of the tax to be paid for the future might be proportional to the land which remained. From this circumstance, I am of opinion, that geometry derived its origin; and from hence it was transmitted into Greece." The existence of the pyramids, the ruins of the temples, and the other architectural remains of ancient Egypt, supply evidence that they possessed some knowledge of geometry, even in the higher sense in which we now use the term; although it is possible that the geometrical properties of figures, necessary for the construction of such works, might have been known only in the form of *practical rules*, without any scientific arrangement of geometrical truths, such as are presented to us in the Elements of Euclid.

The word geometry, used in its highest and most extensive meaning, signifies the *science of space*; or that science which investigates and treats of the properties of, and relations existing among, definite portions of space, under the abstract division of lines, angles, surfaces, and volumes, without any regard to the physical properties of the bodies to which they belong. In this sense, it appears to be very doubtful whether the Egyptians or Chaldeans knew anything of the science. It is to the Greeks, therefore, that we must look for the real origin of geometry, as an abstract science. Thales, the Greek philosopher, born 640 B.C., is reported, by ancient historians to have astonished even the Egyptians by his knowledge of this science. The founder of scientific geometry in Greece, however, appears to have been Pythagoras, who was born about 568 B.C. He discovered the celebrated 47th proposition of the first book of Euclid's Elements, and various other important theorems. He was great also in valuable astronomy, having anticipated the Copernican system of the world. Of Plato, another great geometrician, and founder of the academy at Athens, we have already spoken in our first number. He was the first who made some advances into what is called the higher geometry. The next name, super-eminent in the science of geometry, is that of Euclid, whose Elements have been the *principal text-book* for learners, during a period of more than 2000 years. He flourished at Alexandria, in Egypt, about B.C. 300, during the reign of Ptolemy Lagus, who was one of his pupils, and to whom he made the celebrated reply, when asked if there was a shorter way to geometry than by studying his Elements:—"No, sire, there is no *royal road* to geometry."

The prince of ancient mathematicians, however, was the celebrated Archimedes, born at Syracuse, B.C. 287, about the period of the death of Euclid. His discoveries in geometry, mechanics and hydrostatics, form a remarkable era in the history of the mathematical sciences; and even the remains of his works which are still extant, constitute the most valuable part of the ancient Greek geometry. He was the first who attempted to solve the celebrated problem of the *rectification of the circle*; that is, finding a *straight line exactly equal* to the circumference. He found out the beautiful ratios of the cylinder to its inscribed sphere and cone, and the quadrature of one of the conic sections. We have, in our second lesson on arithmetic, alluded to his discoveries in that science. His discoveries in physics or natural philosophy are simple, true, and beautiful. The story of the determination of the specific gravity of the golden crown of his cousin, Hiero king of Syracuse, is well known; and the very natural shout of "*Heureka, heureka!*"—*I have found it, I have found it!* on coming out of the bath, has become a "household word." Scarcely less celebrated was the famous Apollonius of Perga, in Pamphylia, who flourished at Alexandria in the reign of Ptolemy Euergetes, (from B.C. 247 to 222) another king of the same Ptolomean dynasty, and who was called by his cotemporaries the "Great Geometer." He wrote several books, full of discoveries, on the higher geometry, and greatly extended the domains of the plane geometry. Other geometricians of eminence arose in the school of Alexandria, and bequeathed the precious remains of their genius to happier times. Claudius Ptolemæus, the author of the great work on astronomy called *Megalē Syntaxis*, the *Great Construction*, or Almagest; Pappus, the author of the *Mathematical Collections*; and others, including Theon and his daughter Hypatia, bring us down to the period when the Alexandrian library was burnt by command of the Mohammedan barbarian Caliph Omar, and the labour and learning of ages were irrevocably destroyed. The dark ages supervened, and little was done in the advancement of science until the glorious invention of printing, and the general revival of literature about the middle of the fifteenth century.

The ancient Greek geometry was speedily made known to the moderns through the medium of translations of, and commentaries upon, the writings of the great masters. The Elements of Euclid, indeed, were reckoned so perfect, that no attempt was made to supersede them; and the only object of writers on geometry in general was to explain his works, and to make what additions they could to the science, in the same masterly style of composition. A host of names of eminent authors might be mentioned, who succeeded in establishing the *Greek geometry*, and in extending its domains. The principal of these, however, was Dr. Robert Simson, professor of mathematics in the University of Glasgow, who flourished in the middle of the last century. His grand endeavour was to present to modern Europe the Elements of Euclid, as they originally appeared in ancient Greece. In this he succeeded to admiration, and his edition of this great work maintains its reputation to the present moment. He was also an original writer of great eminence; and but for the eclat of the *new geometry*, invented by Leibnitz and Newton, he would have shone as a star of the first magnitude. On this interesting subject, and others connected with it, we cannot now enter; but we trust to be able, in future numbers of this work, to bring before our readers both its history and its application, as one of the greatest of our modern engines in the discovery of scientific truth, and in the development of the philosophy of nature.

In giving our first lessons on geometry, we think it advisable to follow what seems to have been the natural course of events in the history of this science. The present advanced state of our geometrical knowledge was preceded in early times by a species of practical geometry gathered from experience, and suited to the wants of those who required its application, before any attempt was made to enter very deeply into the study of the theory. The latter was left to the schools of the philosophers and the academy of Plato. Accordingly, we shall precede our disquisitions on the Elements of Euclid and other geometers, both ancient and modern, by a short system of practical rules and easy explanations in this important science; and we shall endeavour to make the subject both simple and clear by plain definitions, suitable diagrams, and palpable demonstrations, after the manner of the French writers on this subject, who have even in their more elaborate treatises to a great extent abandoned the system of Euclid.

DEFINITIONS.

Extension, or the space which anybody in nature occupies, has three dimensions, viz., length, breadth, and thickness. This is Euclid's definition of a *geometrical solid*.

A *point* is the beginning of extension, but no part of it; hence it is said to have position in space, but no magnitude.

A *line* is extension in one direction only; hence, it is said to have length without breadth. Hence, also, the extremities of a line are points; and lines intersect or cross each other only in points.

A *straight line* is said, by Euclid, to be that which lies *evenly* between its extreme points; and, by Archimedes, to be the *shortest distance* between any two points. Both of these definitions are defective; the defect is supplied thus: A straight line is such, that if any two points be taken in it, the part which they intercept (or which lies between them), is the shortest line that can be drawn between those points.

A *crooked line* is one composed of straight lines joined at their extremities in any manner whatever, except that of uniform direction. A *curved line*, or curve, is a line whose direction varies at every point.

Straight lines, or curve lines, are generally denoted, in speaking and writing, by two letters placed commonly at their extremities; but, they may be placed anywhere on the lines at a distance from each other. Thus, in fig. 1, the letters A, B, denote one straight line; the letters C, D, another; and the letters E, F, a third; and these straight lines are respectively called the straight lines A B, C D, and E F. A straight line, as A B, may be divided into any number of equal parts, to serve as a standard for measuring other straight lines.

A combination of straight, crooked, and curved lines is represented in fig. 2; A B, B C, C D, and D A, are each straight lines; the combination A D C B, beginning at A, and terminating at B, is a crooked line; and the line A M B, beginning at A, and ending at B, is a curved line.

A *surface*, or, as it is sometimes called, a *superficies*, is extension in two directions; hence, it is said to have only length and breadth. Hence, also, the extremities or boundaries of a surface are lines; and surfaces intersect or cross each other in lines.

A *plane surface*, or *plane*, is a surface in which any two points being taken, the *straight line* between them lies wholly in that surface; or, it is that surface with which a *straight line* wholly coincides, when applied to it in every direction. Any other surface, not composed of plane surfaces, is called a *curved surface*.

LESSONS IN GEOMETRY.

Parallel straight lines are such as lie in the same plane, and which though produced ever so far both ways, do not meet (fig. 3).

An *angle* is the inclination of two straight lines to each other, which meet in a point, and are not in the same direction. The point in which they meet is called their *vertex*, and each of them a *side* or *leg* of the angle. The angle itself is generally called a *plane rectilineal angle*, because it necessarily lies in a plane, and is formed of *straight lines*. *Curvilineal angles* are such as are formed on the surface of a sphere or globe; but the consideration of such angles belongs to the higher geometry. The magnitudes of angles do not depend on the lengths of their legs or sides, but on the degree or amount of aperture between them, taken at the same distance from the vertex.

An angle is generally represented by three letters, one of which is *always placed* at the *vertex*, to distinguish it particularly from every other angle in a given figure, and the other two are placed somewhere on the legs of the angle, but generally at their extremities; and in reading or in speaking of the angle, the letter at the vertex is always placed between the other two, and uttered or written accordingly. Thus, in fig. 4, which represents an angle, the name of the angle is either B A C or C A B: the point A is called its vertex; and the straight lines B A, C A, its sides or legs.

Angles are divided into two kinds, *right* and *oblique*, and oblique angles are divided into two species, *acute* and *obtuse*.

When one straight line meets another, at any point between its extremities, and makes the adjacent or contiguous angles equal to each other, each of them is called a *right angle*, and the legs of each of these angles are said to be *perpendicular* to one another. Thus, in fig. 5, the straight line A B meets the straight line C D in the point A, and makes the adjacent angles C A B, D A B, equal to each other; each of these angles is therefore called a *right angle*; and the straight line A B is said to be *perpendicular* to the straight line A C, or D A, and consequently A C or A D is perpendicular to A B.

When one straight line meets another, at any point between its extremities, and makes the adjacent angles unequal to each other, each of them is called an *oblique* angle; that which is greater than a right angle is called an *obtuse angle*; and that which is less than a right angle is called an *acute* angle. Thus, in fig. 6, the straight line A B meets the straight line C D, in the point A, and makes the adjacent angles unequal to each other; each of these angles is therefore called an *obtuse angle*; the angle C A B, which is greater than a right angle, is called *obtuse*; and the angle D A B, which is less than a right angle, is called *acute*.

A *plane figure* in geometry, is a portion of a plane surface, inclosed by one or more lines, or boundaries. The sum of all the boundaries is called the *perimeter* of the figure, and the portion of surface contained within, is called its *area*.

A *circle* is a plane figure contained or bounded by a *curve* line, called the *circumference* or *periphery*, which is such that all straight lines drawn from a *certain point* within the figure to the circumference are equal to each other. This point is called the *centre of the circle*, and each of the straight lines is called the *radius*. The straight line drawn through the centre and terminated at both ends in the circumference, is called the *diameter of the circle*. It is plain, from the definition that all the radii must be equal to each other; that all the diameters must be equal to each other, and that the diameter is always double the radius. In speaking or writing, the circle is usually denoted by three letters placed, at any distance from each other, around the circumference; thus, in fig. 7, the circle is denoted by the letters A C B, or A E B; or, by any three of the other letters on the circumference. The point o is the centre, either of the straight lines O A, O B, O C, O E, is a radius, and the straight line A B is a diameter.

An *arc* of a circle is any part of its circumference; the *chord of an arc* is the straight line which joins its extremities. A *segment* of a circle is the surface inclosed by an arc and its chord. A *sector* of a circle is the surface inclosed by an arc, and the two radii drawn from its extremities. Thus, in fig. 7 the portion of the circumference A M C, whose extremities are A and C, is an arc; and the remaining portion A B C, having the same extremities is also an arc; the straight line A C is th. chord of either of these arcs. The surface included between the arc A M C and its chord A C, is the segment A M C; there is also the segment A B C. The surface included between the radii O C, O B, and the arc C B, is called the sector C O B; the remaining portion of the circle is also a sector.

A *semicircle* is the segment whose chord is a diameter. Thus in fig. 7. A C B, or A E B is a semicircle. The term semicircle, which literally means half-a-circle, is restricted in geometry to the segment thus described; but there are many other ways of obtaining half a circle.

Plane *rectilineal* figures are described under various heads; as trilateral or triangular; quadrilateral or quadrangular; and multilateral or polygonal.

A triangle (fig. 8) is a plane rectilineal figure contained by three straight lines, which are called its sides. No figure can be formed of two straight lines; hence, an angle is not a figure, its legs being unlimited as to length. Triangles are divided into various kinds, according to the relation of their sides or of their angles; as equilateral, isosceles, and scalene; right-angled, obtuse-angled, and acute-angled.

An *equilateral* (equal sided) triangle, is that which has *three* equal straight lines or sides (fig. 9).

An *isosceles* (equal-legged) triangle, is that which has only *two* equal sides (fig. 10).

A *scalene* (unequal) triangle, is that which has all its sides unequal (fig. 11).

A *right-angled* triangle is that which has one of its angles a right angle (fig. 11), in which the angle at A is the right angle. The side opposite to the right angle is called the *hypotenuse* (the subtense, or line stretched under the right angle) and the other two sides are called the *base* and the *perpendicular*; the two latter being interchangeable according to the position of the triangle.

An *obtuse-angled* triangle is that which has one of its angles an obtuse angle (fig. 8).

An *acute-angled* triangle is that which has all its angles acute; figs. 9 and 10 are examples as to the angles, but there is no restriction as to the sides.

In any triangle, a straight line drawn from the vertex of one of its angles perpendicular to the opposite side, or to that side produced (that is extended beyond either of its extremities in a continued straight line), is called the perpendicular of the triangle; as in fig. 12, where the dotted line is the perpendicular of the triangle; and in fig. 13, where the dotted line drawn from the point O to the dotted part of the base produced is the perpendicular of the triangle.

A *quadrilateral figure*, or quadrangle, is a plane rectilineal figure contained by four straight lines, called its sides. The straight line which joins the vertices of any two of its opposite angles, is called its *diagonal*. Quadrangles are divided into various kinds, according to the relation of their sides and angles; as parallelograms, including the rectangle, the square, the rhombus, and the rhomboid; and trapeziums, including the trapezoid.

A *parallelogram* is a plane quadrilateral figure, whose opposite sides are parallel; thus, fig. 14, A C B D, is a parallelogram, and A B, C D, are its diagonals.

Fig. 15. A *rectangle* is a parallelogram, whose angles are right angles (fig. 15).

A *square* is a rectangle, whose sides are all equal (fig. 16).

A *rhomboid* is a parallelogram, whose angles are oblique (fig. 14).

A *rhombus*, or lozenge, is a rhomboid, whose sides are all equal (fig. 17).

A *trapezium* is a plane quadrilateral figure, whose opposite sides are not parallel (fig. 18).

A *trapezoid* is a plane quadrilateral figure, which has two of its sides parallel (fig. 19).

A *multilateral* figure or *polygon*, is a plane rectilineal figure, of any number of sides. The term is generally applied to any figure whose sides exceed *four* in number. Polygons are divided into *regular* and *irregular*; the former having all their sides and angles equal to each other; and the latter having any variation whatever in these respects. The sum of all the sides of a polygon is called its *perimeter*, and when viewed in position its *contour*. Irregular polygons are also divided into *convex* and *non-convex*; or, those whose angles are all *salient*, and those of which one or more are *re-entrant*. The irregular polygon (fig. 20), has its angles at B, C, and D, salient; and its angles at A and E, re-entrant.

Polygons are also divided into classes, according to the number of their sides; as, the *pentagon* (fig. 21), having five sides; the *hexagon* (fig. 22), having six sides; the *heptagon* having seven sides; the *octagon* having eight sides; and so on. According to this nomenclature, the triangle is called a *trigon*, and the quadrangle a *tetragon*.

QUESTIONS ON THE PRECEDING LESSON.

What is a geometrical solid? what is a point? a line? a straight line? a crooked line? a curve?

How are lines denoted? what is a surface? a plane? an angle? What are parallel straight lines? how are angles denoted? how are they divided? what is a right angle? an oblique angle? an acute angle? an obtuse angle?

What is a plane figure? its perimeter? its area? a circle? its circumference? its centre? its radius? its diameter?

How is a circle denoted? what is an arc? a chord? a segment? a sector? a semicircle?

How are plane rectilineal figures divided? what is a triangle? an equilateral triangle? an isosceles? a scalene? a right-angled triangle? an obtuse-angled? an acute-angled? the perpendicular of a triangle?

In a right-angled triangle, what are the hypotenuse, the base, and the perpendicular?

What is a quadrilateral figure? how are quadrangles divided? what is a diagonal? a parallelogram? a rectangle? a square? a rhombus? a rhomboid? a trapezium? a trapezoid? a polygon?

How are polygons divided? what is the difference between regular and irregular polygons? what is perimeter? contour? salient? re-entrant? pentagon? hexagon? heptagon? trigon? tetragon?

LESSONS IN ENGLISH GRAMMAR.—No. II.

ETYMOLOGY.

SUPPOSING that you have acquired a pretty good knowledge of the *sounds* of the different letters in the alphabet, you should next apply yourself to the study of the most correct way of putting them together, so as to form words rightly spelled, and sentences properly constructed. To do this you must find out how words have been formed—how many different sorts of words there are—what is their exact meaning—and the way in which they may be changed or altered, according to the ideas which the writer or speaker may wish to express. This is the *second* part of English Grammar, and it is called ETYMOLOGY.

Words may be divided into two classes; first, those which are *primitive*; secondly, those which are *derived*.

Primitives, or original words, are words which have been purposely formed to express one idea; they are words which have not been taken from any other word, and which cannot be reduced so as to be more simple. Thus, the words *man*, *book*, *child*, *house*, &c., express a complete sense, and nothing can be taken from them.

Derivatives are words which are drawn out of others, or which take part or parts of others, or which are formed by joining two words together, so as to make a new word meaning something different from the others; as *mankind*, *bookbinder*, *childlike*, *housekeeper*, &c. All these words you will see may be reduced; *mankind* may be reduced to *man*, and still express a complete sense; and so may the other words.

There are *ten* sorts of words in the English language: these are commonly called PARTS OF SPEECH, and the names given to them are as follow:—Article, Noun, Pronoun, Adjective, Verb, Participle, Adverb, Conjunction, Preposition, Interjection. Each of these must be studied separately. That you may have a general view of the whole subject, a brief mention of them will be made here, though each will afterwards be explained more fully. It is supposed that in the English language there are about *sixty thousand* words; of course, each of these words belongs to one or other of the following ten *parts of speech*.

1. The ARTICLE is placed before a noun, to point it out, and to fix its exact meaning.

2. The NOUN is the name of anything.

3. The PRONOUN is used for, or instead of a noun, to prevent its being repeated too often.

4. The ADJECTIVE expresses the particular quality or property of the noun.

5. The VERB expresses action, being, or suffering.

6. The PARTICIPLE is a word derived from a verb, and partakes of the nature both of a verb and an adjective.

7. The ADVERB describes the quality, or circumstance, or peculiar meaning of other words, and is joined either to a verb, an adjective, a participle, or another adverb.

8. The CONJUNCTION joins the several words or parts of sentences together.

9. The PREPOSITION is commonly set before words to connect them, or to show their relation.

The INTERJECTION expresses some sudden emotion of mind.

I. THE ARTICLE.

THE ARTICLE is a part of speech set before nouns, to point them out, and to fix their exact meaning. There are in the English language two articles, *a* or *an*, and *the*. The *a* and *an* are reckoned but as one, because *a* becomes *an* when it is placed before a vowel; that is, before *a*, *e*, *i*, *o*, and *u* short, as *an* urn; also before a mute, or an *h* that is not sounded, as *an* hour; if the *h* be sounded, the article *a* only is used, as, *a* haven. The article *a* is used before all words beginning with a consonant, as, *a* shoe, *a* boot; also before *u* long, that is, when it has the sound of *you*, as in, *a* useful book, not *an* useful book, or, *a* union, not *an* union.

Articles are divided into two classes, definite and indefinite. An *indefinite* article is one which does not define the particular meaning or application of the word before which it is placed; or which speaks of things in general, things which are common, or of which there are many of the same sort. *A* and *an* are indefinite for this reason; as if you were to say, *a* book, *a* man, *an* apple, you would not be understood as meaning any particular book, or man, or apple.

The is called the *definite* article, because it defines your meaning, and fixes it to one particular thing; as, *the* book, *the* man, *the* apple; that is, some particular book, or man, or apple. If you were to enter a coffee-room, and say to the waiter, "Lend me *a* paper," he would bring you the first that came to hand; but if you saw the *Times* in his hand, and said, lend me *the* paper," he would understand you as asking for that particular paper. For this reason the definite article is sometimes called the *demonstrative* article, as, when pointing to an individual, we say, "That is *the* man I wish to employ;" or "This is *the* book I want you to lend me."

The article *the* may be set before nouns both of the singular and plural number, because we can speak definitely of many as well as of one; as, *the* men, *the* books, *the* apples.

LESSONS IN ARITHMETIC.

The articles are sometimes placed before an adjective, when it precedes a noun, as, *an* admirable painting, or, *The* better day *the* better deed.

The definite article *the* is sometimes set before adverbs in the comparative and superlative degrees, as, *The* more *the* merrier; or, *The* oftener I look at Raffaelle's paintings, *the* more I admire them.

Articles are sometimes found joined to proper names, for the purpose of giving them distinction or eminence; thus we say of some large town, it is quite *a* London, that is, a place as busy or as bustling as London; or, *the* Howards, that is, the family of the Howards; or, he is *a* Wellington, that is, a man as distinguished for skill and bravery as the Duke of Wellington; or, *the* Cæsars, that is, the Roman emperors of the name of Cæsar.

Some nouns are used without articles; such as proper names, *Andrew, London, Paris*; or names of attributed or mental qualities, as, *beauty, goodnature, virtue, charity*, &c.; or words in which nothing is implied but the mere existence of the thing, as, This is not silk, but cotton; or, This is not gold, but silver gilt. There are also nouns which will not admit the use of the article, as when words are to be taken in their largest and most general sense; thus we say, *Man* is a rational, an accountable creature; that is, *all men*, without exception, are rational and accountable.

(*Questions on the foregoing Lesson will be given in our next.*)

LESSONS IN ARITHMETIC.—No. II.

The difficulty of inventing names for all numbers even to a limited extent, and of remembering them after they were invented, evidently led to the classification and arrangement exhibited in our system of numeration, which was explained in the first lesson. The next difficulty would be that of performing calculations by the help of the mere names—a process which, in such a case, must either be done mentally, or with the assistance of the ten fingers. The use of small stones or pebbles (in Latin, *calculi*), for the purpose of making *calculations*, is indicated by the origin of the word itself. The necessity of inventing signs or characters to represent numbers, and to facilitate the process of computation, would become more and more obvious as society advanced in civilisation. At first, men would most naturally employ the letters of the alphabet, in every language, as the readiest marks for numbers. Hence, we find that this practice was adopted by the Hebrews, the Greeks, the Romans, and various other nations of antiquity. In the two oldest collections of writings in the world, the *Bible*, and the works of *Homer*—the one written in Hebrew and the other in Greek—the letters of the alphabets of these two languages are respectively used to denote the whole or parts of these books, in their proper numerical order. The letters of the alphabet in any language, however, would go but a little way in expressing numbers by signs, unless some system of classification and arrangement were adopted, or some method of increasing their value, according to a fixed scale, introduced.

For the purpose of expressing large numbers by signs, the Hebrews divided the letters of their alphabet into three classes of nine characters each, to denote *units, tens,* and *hundreds*, respectively; and as this alphabet contained only 22 letters, they adopted *five* of its letters, which had a *final form* (that is, a peculiar form when they terminated a word), to complete the class of hundreds. The whole collection of signs was then arranged, as in the following table:—

HEBREW SYSTEM OF NOTATION.

Signs.	Names.	Values.	Signs.	Names.	Values.	Signs.	Names.	Values.
א	Aleph	1	י	Yodh	10	ק	Qoph	100
ב	Beth	2	כ	Kaph	20	ר	Resh	200
ג	Gimel	3	ל	Lamedh	30	ש	Shin	300
ד	Daleth	4	מ	Mem	40	ת	Tav	400
ה	He	5	נ	Nun	50	ך	Kaph	500
ו	Vav	6	ס	Samekh	60	ם	Mem	600
ז	Zayin	7	ע	Ayin	70	ן	Nun	700
ח	Cheth	8	פ	Pe	80	ף	Pe	800
ט	Teth	9	צ	Tsadhe	90	ץ	Tsadhe	900

In combining different numbers, the greater is put first, according to the Hebrew mode of writing; thus, יא, 11; and קכא, 121. The number 15 is marked by the letters טו, instead of the letters יה, because the latter commence the name of God in Hebrew. The *thousands* are denoted by the *units with two dots* above—thus, א̈, 1,000. *Gesenius*, in his grammar, says that this numeral use of the letters did not occur in the text of the Old Testament, but was first found on the coins of the Maccabees in the middle of the second century before the Christian era.

The Greeks, in the same manner as the Hebrews, divided the letters of their alphabet into three classes of nine characters each, to denote *units, tens,* and *hundreds,* respectively; and as this alphabet contained only 24 letters, they adopted three marks which were formerly used as letters in the more ancient Greek alphabet, introducing one into the class of *units,* one into that of *tens,* and one into that of *hundreds.* The whole of the characters thus arranged are shown in the following table:—

GREEK SYSTEM OF NOTATION.

Signs.	Names.	Values.	Signs.	Names.	Values.	Signs.	Names.	Values.
α	Alpha	1	ι	Iota	10	ρ	Rho	100
β	Beta	2	κ	Kappa	20	σ	Sigma	200
γ	Gamma	3	λ	Lambda	30	τ	Tau	300
δ	Delta	4	μ	Mu	40	υ	Upsilon	400
ε	Epsilon	5	ν	Nu	50	φ	Phi	500
ς	Bau	6	ξ	Xi	60	χ	Chi	600
ζ	Zeta	7	ο	Omicron	70	ψ	Psi	700
η	Eta	8	π	Pi	80	ω	Omega	800
θ	Theta	9	ϟ	Koppa	90	ϡ	Sampi	900

The *thousands* in the Greek system of notation were denoted by the same letters as the *units, with a dash,* or accentual mark under; thus, ͵α, 1,000. *Myriads*, or *tens of thousands*, were denoted by the same letters with the letter M under—as $\frac{α}{M}$ 10,000. Instead of placing the letter M under, sometimes the letters M^υ were placed to the right of the number of myriads, and sometimes only a point, instead of either, was placed in the same position, to indicate the same thing. Archimedes extended this notation, by taking the square of the myriad as a new unit or period, and forming a series of periods containing eight figures in each; so that he was enabled to express a number sufficient to denote all the sands of the sea. This system of notation, in some respects, anticipated the modern systems; and in others, surpassed them; but, unfortunately, it was confined to the knowledge of the learned. The same mathematician, one of the mightiest geniuses of antiquity, anticipated the discovery of logarithms, by a few happy thoughts, which were allowed to lie dormant for 2,000 years, until Napier *promulgated* his immortal invention, in 1614, and in his turn forestalled the discoveries of later times.

The origin of the notable improvement in notation, by which the *nine* characters for *units* only were employed, and the *eighteen* for *tens* and *hundreds*, thrown aside, is still a doubtful question, although it has generally been attributed to the Arabs or Moors of Spain, and examples of a similar notation are to be found in India. This improvement consists in giving to these nine characters a *relative value*—that is, a value depending on their positions, as well as an *absolute value* depending on their names. Thus denoting the place of *units* by a certain fixed mark or character, and placing each of the nine primary characters to the left of it, their values are increased tenfold, so that no new characters are necessary to denote the *tens*; again, denoting the place of *tens* and *units* by two of the same fixed marks or characters, and placing each of the nine primary characters to the left of these, their values are increased a hundred-fold, so that no new characters are necessary to denote the *hundreds*. It is evident that this process may be extended indefinitely, and applied so as to denote not only all the numbers whose names are expressed or indicated in our system of numeration, but all numbers whatsoever, although far beyond the reach of our numerical nomenclature. The first nine letters of any alphabet would, of course, answer the purpose of denoting the *units,* and a dot or any new letter might be employed to denote the vacant places of units, tens, &c., as they occur. The nine characters, and the cipher (which stands for nothing by itself, and is only employed to increase the value of other numbers), now usually adopted in all civilised countries, are the following—viz.,

0 1 2 3 4 5 6 7 8 9

cipher, one, two, three, four, five, six, seven, eight, nine.

M. Chasles, a French writer who has recently made some curious researches in the history of the mathematics, maintains that these characters have descended to us from the Greeks and the Romans, with the whole system of decimal notation. He asserts that a very obscure passage in the writings of Boethius, a Roman philosopher and senator, who flourished at the end of the fifth century, has a direct reference to our decimal system of notation; that various manuscript treatises written between the tenth and twelfth centuries relate to the same subject; that the celebrated Gerbert (afterwards Pope Sylvester II.) had greatly contributed to introduce and extend the knowledge of the decimal system, in the east, towards the end of the tenth century; and that the apparatus employed to facilitate operations in this system, which was unquestionably constructed on the decimal scale, was universally denominated the *abacus Pythagoricus*, or *Pythagoras's board*, until the beginning of the twelfth century. In the early part of this century, the *cipher*, which had been preceded in the Greek notation by a *dot* or *period*, was known at first by the names of *rota*, *rotula*, *sipos*, and afterwards by those of *circulus* and *cifra*, or *ciphra*. The term *cipher*, however, is applicable to all the characters used in our system of notation; and the art of arithmetic itself is hence called *ciphering*. This word is evidently derived from the Hebrew verb *saphar*, *to number*; and it is not improbable that even the art of numbering itself, as well as the symbols employed in it, may have spread over the east from the people who originally spake this language.

At the revival of literature, the invention of the arithmetical characters was ascribed to the Indians, from whom it was pretended they came to us, through the Arabians; and the characters themselves were denominated *figuræ Indorum*. In this way all trace of the ancient system of notation, preserved in the *abacus Pythagoricus*, was insensibly lost in the writings of the moderns, while some ideas, no doubt taken from the Arabic literature, were introduced. Hence, at the present time, all remembrance of the abacus, and of the real origin of our system of notation, has disappeared, and their origin is referred to the Arabians and the Hindoos. Many passages, however, in the works of writers on the subject, even so late as the sixteenth century, show that the Greek and Latin origin of our decimal system was not then completely forgotten. It is also important to observe, that those who ascribe its origin to the Arabians, or the Asiatics, do not assert that we have preserved the characters employed by the inventors; and it may, indeed, be shown that the characters we now use are extremely analogous to those of Boethius, as well as to those which were employed in the treatises on the *abacus* written during the middle ages. The following are the characters which M. Chasles has discovered in a manuscript of the twelfth century, which treats of the *abacus Pythagoricus*, viz.:—

1 2 3 4 5 6 7 8 9

From the preceding observations, it is evident that the Romans, especially those who were initiated into the doctrines of Pythagoras, employed in their mathematical calculations a system of notation and a set of characters very similar to our own, and very different from those which they used in their ordinary writings, and which are denominated *Roman figures*. As these are, to this day, very often used for various common purposes among ourselves, such as paging certain portions of a book, marking dates, numbering chapters, &c., it will be useful to give the following table of their values:—

VULGAR SYSTEM OF ROMAN NOTATION.

Signs.	Values.	Signs.	Values.	Signs.	Values.
I	1	X	10	C	100
II	2	XX	20	CC	200
III	3	XXX	30	CCC	300
IV or IIII	4	XL	40	CCCC or CD	400
V	5	L	50	D or IƆ	500
VI	6	LX	60	DC	600
VII	7	LXX	70	DCC	700
VIII	8	LXXX	80	DCCC	800
IX	9	XC	90	DCCCC	900

Combinations of these numbers are formed by placing those of highest value first in order; thus XI, 11; XII, 12; CXXI, 121, &c. The *thousands* are denoted by the letter M or the combination CIƆ; the *tens of thousands* by CCIƆƆ; and so on. In this system, there is very considerable regularity and ingenuity, although it is not adapted for the purposes of calculation. The letter I, repeated any number of times denotes so many *units*; when placed to the right of another character, it adds a *unit* to the number represented by that character; when placed to the left, it takes away a *unit*. The letter X repeated any number of times, denotes so many *tens*; when placed to the right of a character of greater value, it adds *ten* to the number represented by that character; when placed to the left, it takes away *ten*. The letter C repeated any number of times, denotes so many *hundreds*; when placed to the right of a character of greater value, it adds a *hundred*; and when placed to the left, it takes away a *hundred*; and so on, with M &c. The letter Ɔ placed right and left, in the former case inverted, increases the value of CIƆ *tenfold*. A bar placed over any character or number increases its value a *thousand fold*. In some few cases, it has been ascertained that the Romans employed these literal characters even with values depending on their position; thus, in Pliny, we find XVI.XX.DCCC.XXIX used for the number 1,620,829.

The following tables, especially the first, which combines the system of numeration with that of notation, will be found of the greatest utility.

TABLE I.—ENGLISH SYSTEM OF NUMERATION AND NOTATION.

SEXTILLIONS. / QUINTILLIONS. / QUADRILLIONS. / TRILLIONS. / BILLIONS. / MILLIONS. / UNITS.

Septillions. Hundreds of thousands of... Tens of thousands of... Thousands of... Hundreds of... Tens of... Sextillions. Hundreds of thousands of... Tens of thousands of... Thousands of... Hundreds of... Tens of... Quintillions. Hundreds of thousands of... Tens of thousands of... Thousands of... Hundreds of... Tens of... Quadrillions. Hundreds of thousands of... Tens of thousands of... Thousands of... Hundreds of... Tens of... Trillions. Hundreds of thousands of... Tens of thousands of... Thousands of... Hundreds of... Tens of... Billions. Hundreds of thousands of... Tens of thousands of... Thousands of... Hundreds of... Tens of... Millions. Hundreds of thousands of... Tens of thousands of... Thousands of... Hundreds of... Tens of... Units.

1; 0 0 0, 0 0 0; 0 0 0, 0 0 0; 0 0 0, 0 0 0; 0 0 0, 0 0 0; 0 0 0, 0 0 0; 0 0 0, 0 0 0; 0 0 0, 0 0 0.

LESSONS IN FRENCH.

TABLE II.—FRENCH SYSTEM OF NUMERATION AND NOTATION.

	SEXTILLIONS.	QUINTILLIONS.	QUADRILLIONS.	TRILLIONS.	BILLIONS.	MILLIONS.	THOUSANDS.	UNITS.
Hundreds of... Tens of...	Sextillions.	Quintillions.	Quadrillions.	Trillions.	Billions.	Millions.	Thousands.	Units.

1,0 0 0, 0 0 0, 0 0 0, 0 0 0, 0 0 0, 0 0 0, 0 0 0, 0 0 0.

The use of these tables is to enable the learner to read any number that may be placed before him, or that may occur in calculation, or to write any number that may be proposed in words, with ease and certainty, according to the particular system he chooses to adopt, or that may be recommended to him. As we are partial to the English system, on account of its greater ability to grasp large numbers, we add the following rules, which have special reference to Table I., and which must be committed to memory:—

PROBLEM 1.—*To read or express in words any proposed number expressed in figures.*—Rule: Point the proposed number off by commas into periods of six figures each, from right to left, and then into half periods of three figures each. Apply to the number thus divided the names which belong to the respective figures and places of figures in each period, reading them from left to right—that is, from the highest name to the lowest—taking care to avoid repetitions of the same word, and observing that wherever a cipher occurs, the name which belongs to that place must be omitted.

It will be of importance to remember, that in the application of this table, the name *hundred* is applied to that of every *third* figure, and the *additional* name *thousand* to that of every *sixth* figure, reckoned from right to left. After the name *hundred*, in reading from left to right, the name *ten* immediately follows; and after the name *hundred thousand*, that of *ten thousand*, in the same order. After the name *ten*, in reading from left to right, the name of the period in which it occurs is applied; and after the name *ten thousand*, that of *thousand* is applied.

The following examples will show the application of this rule.

EXAMPLE 1.—Read, or express in words, the number
146385297831276543

Here, the number pointed according to the rule will stand thus: 146,385;297,831;276,543.

In this number there are three complete periods, and six half periods. By referring to the table, we see that the name of the first period, reckoning from left to right, is *billions*, the next *millions*, and the next *units*. Hence, remembering the above rule, it is read or expressed in words, thus:

One hundred and forty-six thousand three hundred and eighty-five billions, two hundred and ninety-seven thousand eight hundred and thirty-one millions, two hundred and seventy-six thousand five hundred and forty-three.

The name *units* is generally omitted at the end of a number when read in the preceding manner. The number in the table itself is read thus: *one septillion.*

EXAMPLE 2.—Read or express in words the number
101000230200001.

This number, pointed according to the rule, will stand thus: 101;000,230;200,001.

In this number there are two periods and a half; hence, it is read or expressed in words as follows:

One hundred and one billions, two hundred and thirty millions, two hundred thousand and one.

PROBLEM 2.—*To write or express in figures any proposed number expressed in words.*—Rule: Write in one line as many ciphers, from right to left, as will reach from units to the highest name in the proposed number, and point them off according to the table, as before. Write below these ciphers the figures which express the names that are applied to each place in the given number, according as they stand in the table, and fill up the blank places in this line of figures with ciphers; then the proposed number will be properly expressed in figures.

EXAMPLE 1.—Write or express in figures the number; *Three hundred and forty-five thousand six hundred and seventy-two billions, one hundred and thirty-eight thousand seven hundred and ninety-two millions, five hundred and eighty-three thousand six hundred and forty-one.*

Here, the highest name in the proposed number being *hundreds of thousands of billions*, we write eighteen ciphers, as follows; and then write below them the figures which express the names belonging to each place, according to rule; thus:
000,000;000,000;000,000.
345,672;138,792;583,641.

EXAMPLE 2.—Write or express in figures, the number; *One hundred billions, two thousand and thirty-two millions, one hundred and one.*

Here, as before, the highest name being *hundreds of billions*, we write fifteen ciphers as follows; and then write below them the figures which express the names belonging to each place, according to rule, filling up the blank places with ciphers; thus:—
000;000,000;000,000.
100;002,032;000,101.

QUESTIONS ON THE PRECEDING LESSON.

1. Write out the names of all the numbers from one to a hundred, and express them in figures.
2. Write out the names of the numbers which immediately follow one hundred; one hundred and ninety-nine; four hundred and ninety-nine; nine thousand nine hundred and ninety-nine; and a million.
3. Express, in figures, the numbers named in the preceding example, and those which immediately follow them.
4. Write the names of the numbers which are next to the following numbers, and express both sets in figures: one million and ninety-nine; one million five thousand nine hundred and ninety-nine; and nine millions nine hundred and ninety-nine thousand nine hundred and ninety-nine.
5. Read or express the following numbers in words:—

202	20030208	100010001000
1001	1010101	3000000000000
15608	9999999	777666555444
306042	347125783	123456789123
5678914	202021010	48484848484848
25312478	9090909090	10210230430400

6. Write or express the following numbers in figures:—
Four hundred and four.
Three thousand and thirty-two.
Twenty-four thousand and eighty-six.
Six hundred and five thousand, and nineteen.
Eleven thousand, eleven hundred and eleven.
Three hundred and forty-one thousand, seven hundred and eighty-two.
Eighty millions, two hundred and three thousand and two.
Two hundred and two millions, twenty thousand two hundred and two.
Nine thousand nine hundred and ninety-nine millions, nine hundred and ninety-nine thousand, nine hundred and ninety-nine.
Write also the number which follows this last one in order
Twenty thousand millions.
Two hundred thousand and twenty millions, two thousand.
One trillion.
The next number to thirty thousand billions, nine hundred and ninety-nine thousand.

LESSONS IN FRENCH.—No. II.

By Professor LOUIS FASQUELLE, LL.D.

THE following reading and pronouncing exercises belong to Lesson I., given in our last number, and must be carefully performed in connexion with that lesson, which should have been headed SECTION I. for the sake of reference.

EXERCISE 1.—THE VOWELS.

(a) Table, *table*; fable, *fable*; chat, *cat*; éclat, *splendour*; arbre, *tree*; tard, *late*; balle, *ball*.
(â) âme, *soul*; blâme, *blame*; bâtir, *to build*; pâte, *paste*; âge, *age*; mât, *mast*.
(e) me, *me*; de, *of*; que, *that*; elle, *she*; malle, *mail*; parle, *speak*; fourchette, *fork*; salle, *hall*.

Appendix 3
National Home Reading Union program (1890)

Source: The Bodleian Libraries, The University of Oxford, 26271 e.3.

NATIONAL Home Reading Union.

Vice-Presidents:

The Archbishop of Canterbury.
The Duke of Argyle.
The Marquis of Ripon.
The Earl and Countess of Aberdeen.
The Earl of Meath.
The Earl and Countess of Roseberry.

The Bishops of Durham, London, Carlisle, Manchester, Newcastle, Ripon, and Rochester.
Professor Bryce, M.P.
T. Burt, Esq., M.P.
Sir Matthew White-Ridley, M.P.
Sir Henry Roscoe, M.P.
R. Yerburgh, Esq., M.P.

Sir John Lubbock, M.P.

AND MANY OTHERS.

Chairman of the Council:
The Rev. Dr. Percival,
Head Master of Rugby.

Chairman of the Executive Committee:
Dr. A. Hill,
Master of Downing College, Cambridge.

Hon. Secretary:
The Rev. Dr. Paton
(Nottingham).

General Treasurer:
Sir O. Roberts.
(London).

General Secretary:
T. F. Hobson, Esq., M.A.
(Oxford).

Blackpool Committee:
Rev. J. Wayman *(Secretary).*
R. Handley, Esq. *(Treasurer).*

THE SECOND

SUMMER ASSEMBLY

WILL BE HELD AT

BLACKPOOL, Lancashire,

From July 15th, to July 25th, 1890.

PRINTED AT THE "TIMES" OFFICE, CHURCH STREET, BLACKPOOL.

138 *Appendix 3*

❖ PROGRAMME. ❖

THE Second Blackpool Summer Assembly of the National Home Reading Union will commence on TUESDAY, July 15th, 1890, with an INAUGURAL MEETING in the OPERA HOUSE. Among those who are expected to be present and address the Meeting are Sir HENRY ROSCOE, M.P., R. YERBURGH, Esq., M.P., the MASTER OF DOWNING COLLEGE, Cambridge, Professor G. CAREY FOSTER, F.R.S., the Rev. Dr. PATON, and the Rev. J. GUINNESS ROGERS. The Chair will be taken at 3 p.m. by Sir MATTHEW WHITE-RIDLEY, M.P. The INAUGURAL ADDRESS will be delivered by   , and the Certificates won by Members of the Union during the Reading Season just concluded will be presented by

At 7-30 p.m. on TUESDAY, July 15th, there will be a RECEPTION by the MAYOR OF BLACKPOOL (J. Bickerstaffe, Esq.), in the INDIAN PAVILION, NORTH PIER. Selections of Vocal and Instrumental Music will be given, and a few speeches of welcome will be made.

On WEDNESDAY, July 16th, THURSDAY, July 17th, FRIDAY, July 18th, and SATURDAY, July 19th, the following COURSES OF LECTURES will be delivered :—

Morning, 10—11.	**Four English Statesmen of Early Times** (Alfred the Great, William the Conqueror, Henry II, and Stephen Langton), by the Rev. T. J. LAWRENCE, M.A., L.L.M., late Deputy Professor of International Law, Cambridge, and Cambridge University Extension Lecturer in History.
11-30—12-30.	**Some Problems of Plant Life**, by E. A. PARKYN, Esq., M.A., Cambridge University Extension Lecturer in Physiology and Botany.
Afternoon, 4—5.	**Vocal Music for Children**, by FRANK SHARP, Esq., Instructor in Singing to the Dundee School Board.
Evening, 7—8.	**Vocal Music for Adults**, by FRANK SHARP, Esq.
8—9.	**Choir Practice**, by FRANK SHARP, Esq.
8—9.	**Hindu Mythology**, by the REV. W. J. WILKINS, B.A., Author of "Hindu Mythology" and "Modern Hinduism."

In addition to the COURSES there will be SINGLE LECTURES in the Opera House at 2-30 p.m., the Subjects and Lectures being as follows :—

On WEDNESDAY, July 16, **Life's Lowest Forms**, by SIR HENRY ROSCOE, M.P.

On THURSDAY, July 17, **The Great Cathedrals and their Builders**, by Professor BALDWIN BROWN.

On FRIDAY, July 18th, **Missing Links**, by Professor MILNES MARSHALL.

On SATURDAY, July 19th, **Musical Critics**, by W. H. JUDE, Esq., Principal of the Liverpool Organ College.

N.B.—This last Lecture will be delivered in the Indian Pavilion, North Pier.

On SUNDAY, July 20th, SERMONS will be preached on behalf of the Union, in the Principal Places of Worship in Blackpool. Among the Preachers will be the Rev. Canon BARKER, the Rev. J. GUINNESS ROGERS, and the Rev. J. SCOTT LIDGETT. At 2-45 p.m., JAMES HATCH, Esq., M.T.C., will conduct a CHILDRENS SERVICE OF SACRED SONG in the Victoria Street Congregational Church.

MONDAY, July 21st., will be devoted to EXCURSIONS. The Summer Assembly Committee are endeavouring to arrange for at least three—one by water to Barrow for Furness Abbey, Walney Island, and other places of interest; one by road to Grisedale, where the pipe track from Thirlmere to Manchester can be seen; and one by rail to Manchester for the Ship Canal, the Town Hall, the Owens College, &c. The Committee will be grateful if those who apply for Tickets for the Summer Assembly will say at the same time whether they wish to join any of these Excursions. The cost of conveyance will probably be from 2s. to 5s., according to the Excursion chosen. Full particulars will be given in the Official Programme.

On TUESDAY, July 22nd, WEDNESDAY, July 23rd, THURSDAY, July 24th, and FRIDAY, July 25th, the following COURSES OF LECTURES will be delivered:—

Morning, 10—11. The Puritan Literature of the Seventeenth Century, by J. CHURTON COLLINS, Esq., M.A., Oxford University Extension Lecturer in English History.

11-30—12-30. The Chemistry of Food, by C. W. KIMMINS, Esq., M.A. (Cambridge), D.Sc. (London), Cambridge University Extension Lecturer in Chemistry and Botany.

Afternoon, 4—5. Vocal Music for Children, by FRANK SHARP, Esq., Instructor in Singing to the Dundee School Board.

Evening, 7—8. Vocal Music for Adults, by FRANK SHARP, Esq.

8—9. Choir Practice, by FRANK SHARP, Esq.

8—9. The Makers of Modern Italy (Mazzini, Cavour, Garibaldi), by J. A. R. MARRIOTT, Esq., M.A., Oxford University Extension Staff-Lecturer in History, Economics and Literature.

N.B.—The Course on the "Makers of Modern Italy" and Mr. SHARP'S "Vocal Music" Courses will terminate on Thursday July 24th.

In addition to the COURSES there will be SINGLE LECTURES in the Opera House, at 2-30 p.m., the Subjects and Lecturers being as follows:—

On TUESDAY, July 22nd, The Parthenon Marbles, by Miss JANE E. HARRISON, Newnham College, Cambridge,

On WEDNESDAY, July 23rd, The True Use of Poetry, by J. CHURTON COLLINS, Esq., M.A., Balliol College, Oxford.

On THURSDAY, July 24th, Tennyson, the Poet of the Age, by the Rev. H. R. HAWEIS, M.A.

On FRIDAY, July 25th, An Evening with the Telescope, by Sir ROBERT S. BALL, Astronomer Royal of Ireland.

N.B.—This last Lecture will be delivered at   p.m.

On FRIDAY, July 25th, a FAREWELL CONVERSAZIONE will be given in the PALACE GARDENS, from 7 to 10-30 in the evening. Edison's latest Phonograph will be exhibited. H. N. LAWRENCE, Esq., M.I.E.E., will give a Demonstration with experiments on The Human Body as an Electric Generator. All the attractions of the Palace Gardens, including a grand display of fireworks, will be at the disposal of Assembly Ticket Holders.

Throughout the gathering the Science Lectures will be illustrated by specimens, diagrams, and experiments. In some of them the oxy-hydrogen lantern will be used. Most of the afternoon lectures will be illustrated in a similar way. Full particulars will be found in the detailed Official Programme.

PRICES OF TICKETS.

	s.	d.
For the whole Assembly, including all Lectures, Entertainments, and Meetings	10	0
For the Five Days, from Tuesday, July 15th, to Saturday, July 19th (both inclusive); or for the Five Days from Monday, July 21st, to Friday, July 25th (both inclusive)	5	0
For any Course of Lectures on any Single Subject	2	0
For any Single Day (no Day Tickets will be issued for Sunday, July 20th, or Monday, July 21st)	2	0
For any Single Lecture, Entertainment, or Meeting (Stalls at the Opera House, 6d. extra.)	1	0
Second Seats for Afternoon Lectures and Lectures delivered in the Indian Pavilion	0	6

N.B.—Members of the National Home Reading Union may obtain Tickets for themselves alone at the following Reduced Rates:—

	s.	d.
For the Whole Assembly	9	0
For the First Five Days, or for the Second Five Days	4	6

No other reduction will be made. Members Tickets must not be transferred to Non-Members. The Committee reserve to themselves the right to exclude any Non-Member attempting to use a Member's Ticket.

All applications for Tickets should be made to the Rev. J. WAYMAN, The Manse, Blackpool.

A detailed Official Programme will be issued in a pamphlet form on July 3rd. It will contain a Time Table of Lectures, Meetings, Excursions and Entertainments, full information on all subjects connected with the Summer Assembly, a short guide to Blackpool, a Railway Time Table, a Postal Guide, and a few hints as to prices and accommodation. The price will be 2d., by post 2½d. All who intend to come to the gathering should send 2½d., in stamps, for this Official Programme to the Rev. J. WAYMAN, The Manse, Blackpool, on or after July 3rd. At the same time an interleaved Pamphlet containing a short syllabus or outline of the Lectures to be delivered during the Assembly will be ready. The price will be 6d., by post 7d.

Appendix 4
Excerpt from George Gissing's *Thyrza* (1887)

Gissing, George. *Thyrza*. Ed. Pierre Coustillas. Brighton: Victorian Secrets, 2013. Print. Chapter 37: 464–70. Reprinted Courtesy of Victorian Secrets.

Walter Egremont to Mrs. Ormonde

'Were I to spend the rest of my natural life in this country—which assuredly I have no intention of doing—I think I should never settle down to an hour's indulgence of those tastes which were born in me, and which, in spite of all neglect, are in fact as strong as ever. I cannot read the books I wish to read; I cannot even think the thoughts I wish to think. As I have told you, the volumes I brought out with me lay in their packing-cases for more than six months after my arrival, and for all the use I have made of them in this second six months they might be still there. The shelves in the room which I call my library are furnished, but I dare not look how much dust they have accumulated.

'I read scarcely anything but newspapers—ye gods! it is I who write the words! Newspapers at morning, newspapers at night. Yes, one exception; I have spent a good deal of time of late over Walt Whitman (you know him, of course, by name, though I dare say you have never looked into his works), and I expect that I shall spend a good deal more; I suspect, indeed, that he will in the end come to mean much to me. But I cannot write of him yet; I am struggling with him, struggling with myself as regards him; in a month or so I shall have more to say. It is perfectly true, then, that till quite recently I have read but newspapers. The people about me scarcely by any chance read anything else, and the influence of surroundings has from the first been very strong upon me. You have complained frequently that I say nothing to you about my *self*; it is one of the signs of my condition that with difficulty I think of that self, and to pen words about it has been quite impossible. I long constantly for the old world and the old moods, but I cannot imagine myself back into them. I would give anything to lock my door at night, and take down my Euripides; if I get as far as the shelf, my hand drops.

'I begin to see a meaning in this phase of my life. I have been learning something about the latter end of the nineteenth century, its civilisation, its possibilities, and the subject has a keen interest for me. Is it new, then? you will ask. To tell you the truth, I knew nothing whatever about it until I came and began to work in America.

I am in the mood for frankness, and I won't spare myself. All my so-called study of modern life in former days was the merest dilettantism, mere conceit and boyish pedantry. I travelled, and the fact that wherever I went I took a small classical library with me was symbolical of my state of mind. I saw everything through old-world spectacles. Even in America I could not get rid of my pedantry, as you will recognise clearly enough if you look back to the letters I wrote you at that time. I came then with theories in my head of what American civilisation must be, and everything that I saw I made fit in with my preconceptions. This time I came with my mind a blank. I was ill, and had not a theory left in me on any subject in the universe. For the first time in my life I was suffering all that a man can suffer; when the Atlantic roared about me, I scarcely cared whether it engulfed me or not. Getting back my health, I began to see with new eyes, and have since been looking my hardest. And I have still not a theory on any subject in the universe.

'In fact, I believe that for me the day of theories has gone by. I note phenomena, and muse about them, and not a few interest me extremely. The interest is enough. I am not a practical man; I am not a philosopher. I may, indeed, have a good deal of the poet's mind, but the poet's faculty is denied to me. It only remains to me to study the word in its relations to my personality, that I may henceforth avoid the absurdities to which I have such a deplorable learning.

'Do you know what I ought to have been?—A schoolmaster. That is to say, if I wished to do any work of direct good to my fellows in the world. I could have taught boys well, better than I shall ever do anything else. I could not only have taught them—the "gerund-grinding" of Thomas Carlyle—but could have inspired them with love of learning, at all events such as were capable of being so inspired. My class of working men in Lambeth exercised this faculty to some extent. When I was teaching them English Literature, I was doing, as far as it went, good and sound work. When I drifted into "Thoughts for the Present"—Heaven forgive me!—I made an ass of myself, that's the long and short of it. My ears tingle as I remember those evenings.

'I am infinitely more human than I was; I can even laugh heartily at American humour, and that I take to be a sign of health. Health is what I have gained. The devotion of eight or ten hours a day to the work of the factory has been the best medicine anyone could have prescribed to me. It was you who prescribed it, and it was your crowning act of kindness to me, dear Mrs. Ormonde. It is possible that I have grown coarser; indeed, I know that I associate on terms of equality and friendliness with men from whom I should formerly have shrunk. I can get angry, and stand on my rights, and bluster if need be, and on the whole I think I am no worse for that. My ear is not offended if I hear myself called "boss"; why should it be? it is a word as well as another. Nay, I have even felt something like excitement when listening to political speeches, in which frequent mention was made of "the great State of Pennsylvania." Well, it *is* a great State, or the phrase has no meaning in any application. Will not this early life of the New World some day be studied with reverence and enthusiasm? I try to see things as they are.

'Social problems are here in plenty. Indeed, it looks very much as if America would sooner have reached an acute stage of social conflict than the old countries;

naturally, as it is the refuge of those who abandon the old world in disgust. American equality is a mere phrase; there is as much brutal injustice here as elsewhere. But I can no longer rave on the subject; the injustice is a *fact*, and only other facts will replace it; I concern myself only with facts. And the great fact of all is the contemptibleness of average humanity. I will submit for your reverent consideration the name of a great American philanthropist—Cornelius Vanderbilt. Personally he was a disgusting brute; ignorant, base, a boor in his manners, a blackguard in his language; he had little if any natural affection, and to those who offended him he was a relentless barbarian. Yet the man was a great philanthropist, and became so by the piling up of millions of dollars. Of course he did that for his own vulgar satisfaction, though personally he could not use the money when he had it; no matter, he has aided civilisation enormously. He as good as created the steamship industry in America; he reorganised the railway system with admirable results; by adding so much to the circulating capital of the country, he provided well-paid employment for unnumbered men. Thousands of homes should bless the name of Vanderbilt—and what is the state of a world in which such a man can do such good by such means? Well, I have nothing to say to it. It is merely part of the tremendous present, which interests me.

'And I once stood up in my pulpit, and with mild assurance addressed myself to the task of improving the world! Do not make fun of me when we meet again, dear friend; I am too bitterly ashamed of myself.

'It seems a long time since you told me anything of Thyrza. I do not like to receive a letter from you in which there is no mention of her name. Does she still find a resource in her music? Are you still kind to her? Yes, kind I know you are, but are you gentle and affectionate, doing your utmost to make her forget that she is alone? You do not see her very frequently, I fear. I beg you to write to her often, the helpful letters you can write to those whom you love. She can repay you for all trouble with one look of gratitude.'

(Three months later.)

'I am sending you Whitman's "Leaves of Grass." I see from your last letter that you have not yet got the book, and have it you must. It is idle to say that you cannot take up new things, that you doubt whether he has any significance for *you*, and so on. You have heart and brain, therefore his significance for you will be profound.

'I would not write much about him hitherto; for I dreaded the smile on your face at a new enthusiasm. I wished, too, to test this influence upon myself thoroughly; I assure you that it is easier for me now to be skeptical than to open my heart generously to any one who in our day declares himself a message-bringer to mankind. You know how cautiously I have proceeded with this American *vates*. At first I found so much to repel me, yet from the first also I was conscious of a new music, and then the clamour of the vulgar against the man was quite enough to oblige me to give him careful attention. If one goes on the assumption that the ill word of the mob is equivalent to high praise, one will not, as a rule, be far wrong, in matters of literature. I have studied Whitman, enjoyed him, felt his force and his value. And, speaking with all seriousness, I believe that he has helped me, and will help me, inestimably, in my endeavour to become a sound and mature man.

'For in him I have met with one who is, first and foremost, a man, a large, healthy, simple, powerful, full-developed man. Read his poem called "A Song of Joys"—what glorious energy of delight, what boundless sympathy, what *sense*, what *spirit*! He knows the truth of the life that is in all things. From joy in a railway train—"the laughing locomotive! To push with resistless way and speed off in the distance"—to joy in fields and hillsides, joy in "the dropping of raindrops in a song," joy in the fighter's strength, joy in the life of the fisherman, in every form of active being—aye, and

> Joys of the free and lonesome heart, the tender, gloomy heart,
> Joys of the solitary walk, the spirit bow'd yet proud, the suffering and the struggle;
> The agonistic throes, the ecstasies, joys of the solemn musings day or night;
> Joys of the thought of Death, the great spheres Time and Space!

What would not I give to know the completeness of manhood implied in all that? Such an ideal of course is not a new-created thing for me, but I never *felt* it as in Whitman's work. It is so foreign to my own habits of thought. I have always been so narrow, in a sense so provincial. And indeed I doubt whether Whitman would have appealed to me as he now does had I read him for the first time in England and under the old conditions. These fifteen months of practical business life in America have swept my brain of much that was mere prejudice, even when I thought it worship. I was a pedantic starveling; now, at all events, I *see* the world about me, and all the goodliness of it. Then I am far healthier in body than I was, which goes for much. It would be no hardship to me to take an axe and go off to labour on the Pacific coast; nay, a year so spent would do me a vast amount of good.

'I wonder whether you have read any of the twaddle that is written about Whitman's grossness, his materialism, and so forth? If so, read his poems now, and tell me how they impress you. Is he not *all* spirit, rightly understood? For to him the body with its energies is but manifestation of that something invisible which we call human soul. And so pure is the soul in him, so mighty, so tender, so infinitely sympathetic, that it may stand for Humanity itself. I am often moved profoundly by his words. He makes me feel that I am a very part of the universe, and that in health I can deny kinship with nothing that exists. I believe that he for the first time has spoken with the very voice of Nature; forests and seas sing to us through him, and through him the healthy, unconscious man, "the average man," utters what before he had not voice to tell of, his secret aspirations, his mute love and praise.

'Look you! I write a sort of essay, and in doing so prove that I am myself still. Were it not that I have mercy on you, I could preach on even as I used to do to my class in Lambeth. Ha, if I had known Whitman then! I believe that by persuading those men to read him, and helping them to understand him, I should really have done an honest day's work. There were some who could have relished his meaning, and whose lives he would have helped. For there it is; Whitman helps one; he is a tonic beyond all to be found in the druggist's shop. I imagine that to live with the man himself for a few days would be the best thing that could befall an invalid; surely vital force would come out of him.

'He makes one ashamed to groan at anything. Whatever comes to us is in the order of things, and the sound man accepts it as his lot. Yes, even Death—of which he says noble things. The old melodious weeping of the poets—Moschus over his mallows, and Catullus with his "*Soles occidere et redire possunt*"—Whitman has no touch of that. Noble grief there is in him, and noble melancholy can come upon him, but acquiescence is his last word. He holds that all is good, because it exists, for everything plays its part in the scheme of nature. When his day comes, he will die, as the greatest have done before him, and there will be no puny repining at the order of things.

'Has he then made me a thorough-going optimist? Scarcely, for the willow cannot become the oak. Your old name for me was "The Idealist," and I suppose in a measure I deserved it; I know I did in the most foolish sense of the word. And in my idealism was of course implied a good deal of optimism. But shall I tell you what was there in a yet larger measure? That which is termed self-conceit. An enemy speaking of me now—Dalmaine for example, if he chose to tell the truth—would say that a business-life in America has taken a great deal of the humbug out of me. I shall always be rather a weak mortal, shall always be marked by that blend of pessimism and optimism which necessarily marks the man to whom, in his heart, the beautiful is of supreme import, shall always be prone to accesses of morbid feeling, and in them, I dare say, find after all my highest pleasure. Nay, it is certain that Moschus and Catullus will always be more loved by me than Whitman. For all this, I am not what I was, and I am a completer man than I was. I shall remain here yet nine months, and who can say what further change may go on in me?

'Now to another subject. It gladdens me to hear what you say of Thyrza, that she seems both well and happy. I envy you the delight of hearing her sing. It is a beautiful thing that in this way she has found expression for that poetry which I always read in her face. By-the-by, does she still meet her sister away from the place where she lives? Is that still necessary? However, all these details are in your judgment. The great thing is that she is happy in her life, that she has found a great interest.

'I wish to know—I beg you to answer me—whether she has ever spoken of me. When I used to press you to speak on this subject, you always ignored that part of my letter. Need you still do so? Will you not tell me whether she has asked about me, has spoken in any way of me? To be sure, you must betray no confidences; yet perhaps it will not be doing so.

'Read Whitman; try to sympathise with me as I now am. You know that I am anything but low-spirited, yet in very truth I have no single companion here to whom I can speak of intimate things, and, except on business, I write absolutely to no one in England save to you. And intellectual sympathy I do need; I scarcely think I could live on through my life without it.

'Another thing, and the last. You have never once spoken of Miss Newthorpe, nor have I, in all this long time. I pray you tell me something of her. It is very likely that she's married—to whom, now? Her husband should be an interesting man, one I should like some day to know. Or is she another example of the unaccountable things women will do in marriage. Pray Heaven not!'

Works Cited

Ablow, Rachel. "Introduction." *The Feeling of Reading: Affective Experience and Victorian Literature*. Ed. Rachel Ablow. Ann Arbor: U of Michigan P, 2010. 1–10. Print.

ABRACADABRA: A Fragment of University History. Oxford: George Shrimpton, 1877. Print.

Adams, Pauline. *Somerville for Women: An Oxford College 1879–1993*. New York: Oxford UP, 1996. Print.

Altick, Richard D. *The English Common Reader: A Social History of the Mass Reading Public, 1800–1900*. 2nd ed. Columbus: Ohio State UP, 1998. Print.

Armstrong, Isobel. *Victorian Poetry: Poetry, Poetics and Politics*. New York: Routledge, 1993. Print.

Arnold, Matthew. "The Buried Life." *Victorian Literature 1830–1900*. Ed. Dorothy Mermin and Herbert Tucker. Fort Worth: Harcourt, 2002. 710–11. Print.

———. *Culture and Anarchy*. New Haven: Yale UP, 1994. Print.

———. *The Letters of Matthew Arnold, Vol. 3: 1866–1870*. Ed. Cecil Y. Lang. Charlottesville: UP of Virginia, 1998. Print.

———. *Literature and Science*. Ed. William Savage Johnson. Boston: Houghton Mifflin, 1913. Print.

———. "The Scholar-Gipsy." *Victorian Literature 1830–1900*. Ed. Dorothy Mermin and Herbert Tucker. Fort Worth: Harcourt, 2002. 711–14. Print.

———. "Stanzas from the Grande Chartreuse." *Victorian Literature 1830–1900*. Ed. Dorothy Mermin and Herbert Tucker. Fort Worth: Harcourt, 2002. 714–16. Print.

Association for Experiential Education. "What Is Experiential Education?" *Association for Experiential Education*, n.d. Web. 24 June 2015. <http://www.aee.org/what-is-ee>.

Association of American Colleges and Universities. *High-Impact Educational Practices*. Washington, D.C.: Association of American Colleges and Universities, 2008. Print.

Atwood, Sara. *Ruskin's Educational Ideals*. Burlington: Ashgate, 2011. Print.

Austen, Jane. *Emma*. New York: Oxford UP, 2003. Print.

———. "History of England." *Juvenilia*. Ed. Peter Sabor. New York: Cambridge UP, 2006. 176–89. Print.

———. *Jane Austen's Letters*. Ed. Deirdre Le Faye. New York: Oxford UP, 2011. Print.

———. "Love & Freindship." *Juvenilia*. Ed. Peter Sabor. New York: Cambridge UP, 2006. 101–41. Print.

———. *Mansfield Park*. New York: Oxford UP, 2003. Print.

———. *"My Dear Cassandra": The Letters of Jane Austen*. Ed. Penelope Hughes-Hallett. London: Collins & Brown, 1990. Print.

———. *Northanger Abbey*. New York: Bantam, 1985. Print.

———. *Persuasion*. Ed. Patricia Meyer Spacks. New York: Norton, 1995. Print.

———. "Plan of a Novel, According to Hints from Various Quarters." *Jane Austen: Later Manuscripts*. Ed. Janet Todd and Linda Bree. New York: Cambridge UP, 2008. 226–9. Print.

———. *Sense and Sensibility*. New York: Penguin, 2003. Print.

Austen-Leigh, William. *Jane Austen, A Family Record*. Ed. Deirdre Le Faye. New York: Cambridge UP, 2004. Print.

Best, Stephen and Sharon Marcus. "Surface Reading: An Introduction." *Representations* 108.1 (2009): 1–21. Web. 3 June 2015.

"Biography—no. 2: George Stephenson." *The Popular Educator* 1 (1852): 75–6. Print.

"Biography—no. 7: John Harrison, the First Chronometer Maker." *The Popular Educator* 1 (1852): 373–5. Print.

Birch, Dinah. *Our Victorian Education*. Malden: Blackwell, 2008. Print.

Blake, Kathleen. "Elizabeth Barrett Browning and Wordsworth: The Romantic Poet as a Woman." *Victorian Poetry* 24.4 (1986): 387–98. Print.

Boardman, Elizabeth. *RE: C19 Curriculum*. Message to the author. 22 Aug. 2012. E-mail.

Bok, Derek. "The Future of Harvard: Harvard Can Provide Educational Leadership." *Boston Globe*, 15 Oct. 2011: K11. Web. 22 May 2015.

Bourdieu, Pierre. *The State Nobility: Elite Schools in the Field of Power*. Stanford: Stanford UP, 1996. Print.

Brantlinger, Patrick. *The Reading Lesson: The Threat of Mass Literacy in Nineteenth-Century British Fiction*. Bloomington: Indiana UP, 1998. Print.

Brock, M.G. and M.C. Curthoys, eds. *The History of the University of Oxford: Nineteenth-Century Oxford, Part 1*. 6 vols. Oxford: Clarendon, 1997. Print.

———. *The History of the University of Oxford: Nineteenth-Century Oxford, Part 2*. Oxford: Clarendon, 2000. Print.

Brown, Julia Prewitt. *The Bourgeois Interior: How the Middle Class Imagines Itself in Literature and Film*. Charlottesville: U of Virginia P, 2008. Print.

———. *Jane Austen's Novels: Social Change and Literary Form*. Cambridge: Harvard UP, 1979. Print.

Browning, Elizabeth Barrett. *Aurora Leigh*. Ed. Margaret Reynolds. New York: Norton, 1996. Print.

———. "The Cry of the Children." *The Norton Anthology of English Literature*. Ed. Carol Christ and Catherine Robson. 8th ed. Vol. E. New York: Norton, 2006. 1079–82. Print.

———. *The Letters of Elizabeth Barrett Browning to Mary Russell Mitford, 1836–1854*. Ed. Meredith B. Raymond and Mary Rose Sullivan. Winfield: Wedgestone, 1983. Print.

Burrows, Montagu. *Pass and Class: An Oxford Guide-Book through the Courses of Literae Humaniores, Mathematics, Natural Science, and Law and Modern History*. Oxford: J.H. & J. Parker, 1861. Print.

Butler, Ruth F. *A History of Saint Anne's Society, Formerly the Society of Oxford Home-Students, Vol. 2: 1921–1946*. Oxford: Oxford UP, 1949. Print.

Carlyle, Thomas. "Signs of the Times." *The Spirit of the Age: Victorian Essays*. Ed. Gertrude Himmelfarb. New Haven: Yale UP, 2007. 31–49. Print.

Caswall, Edward. *A New Art Teaching How to Be Plucked, Being A Treatise after The Fashion of Aristotle; Writ for The Use of Students in The Universities*. 3rd ed. Oxford: J. Vincent, 1835. Print.

Christ Church College. *Examination Papers, Christ Church*. Oxford University, 1859–1874. Print.

Collins, Philip. "Hardy and Education." *Thomas Hardy: The Writer and His Background*. Ed. Norman Page. New York: St. Martin's, 1980. 41–75. Print.

Conway, Michelle. *Nineteenth-Century Examination Records*. Message to the author. 22 Aug. 2012. E-mail.

Cooper, Andrew. "Voicing the Language of Literature: Jude's Obscured Labor." *Victorian Literature and Culture* 28.2 (2000): 391–410. Web. 10 Feb. 2015.

Coustillas, Pierre. *George Gissing at Alderley Edge*. London: Enitharmon, 1969. Print.

———. "Gissing, George Robert (1857–1903)." *Oxford Dictionary of National Biography*. Online ed. Ed. Lawrence Goldman. Oxford: Oxford UP, 2004. 27 June 2015. <http://www.oxforddnb.com/view/article/33416>.

———. *The Heroic Life of George Gissing, Part I: 1857–1888*. London: Pickering & Chatto, 2011. Print.

Coutts, Elizabeth. "Buss, Frances Mary (1827–1894)." *Oxford Dictionary of National Biography*. Ed. H. C.G. Matthew and Brian Harrison. Oxford: Oxford UP, 2004. Online ed. Ed. Lawrence Goldman. Jan. 2006. 27 June 2015. <http://www.oxforddnb.com/view/article/37249>.

"cram, v." *OED Online*. Oxford UP, June 2015. Web. 27 June 2015. <http://www.oed.com/view/Entry/43742?rskey=DsaDUL&result=2&isAdvanced=false#eid>.

Crewe Mechanics Institution. "Letter." *Cambridge University Reporter* 31 Jan. 1872: 142–3. Print.

Cuddy-Keane, Melba. *Virginia Woolf, the Intellectual, and the Public Sphere*. New York: Cambridge UP, 2003. Print.

Curthoys, Judith. *RE: C19 Curriculum*. Message to the author. 22 Aug. 2012. E-mail.

Curthoys, M.C. "The Examination System." *The History of the University of Oxford: Nineteenth-Century Oxford*, Part 1. Ed. M.G. Brock and M.C. Curthoys. Oxford: Clarendon, 1997. 339–374. Print.

Dalgarno, Emily. *Virginia Woolf and the Migrations of Language*. New York: Cambridge UP, 2012. Print.

Dalley, Lana L. "The Least 'Angelical' Poem in the Language: Political Economy, Gender, and the Heritage of Aurora Leigh." *Victorian Poetry* 44.4 (2006): 525–42. Print.

Dames, Nicholas. *The Physiology of the Novel: Reading, Neural Science, and the Form of Victorian Fiction*. New York: Oxford UP, 2007. Print.

———. "Why Bother?" *n+1* 11 (2011): 161–8. Print.

Darwall-Smith, Robin. *A History of University College, Oxford*. Oxford: Oxford UP, 2008. Print.

———. *Re: Typical 19th-Century Curriculum*. Message to the author. 22 July 2012. E-mail.

Davidson, Jenny. *Breeding: A Partial History of the Eighteenth Century*. New York: Columbia UP, 2009. Print.

De Bellaigue, Christina. *Educating Women: Schooling and Identity in England and France, 1800–1867*. Oxford: Oxford UP, 2007. Print.

Delany, Paul. *George Gissing: A Life*. London: Weidenfeld & Nicolson, 2008. Print.

Deslandes, Paul R. *Oxbridge Men: British Masculinity and the Undergraduate Experience, 1850–1920*. Bloomington: Indiana UP, 2005. Print.

Desmond, Adrian James Moore and Janet Browne. "Darwin, Charles Robert (1809–1882)." *Oxford Dictionary of National Biography*. Ed. H.C.G. Matthew and Brian Harrison. Oxford: Oxford UP, 2004. Online ed. Ed. Lawrence Goldman. May 2015. 27 June 2015. <http://www.oxforddnb.com/view/article/7176>.

Devlin, D.D. *Jane Austen and Education*. New York: Barnes and Noble, 1975. Print.

Dickens, Charles. *Hard Times*. Ed. Fred Kaplan. New York: Norton, 2001. Print.

———. *Nicholas Nickleby*. New York: Penguin, 1978. Print.
———. *Our Mutual Friend*. Ed. Adrian Poole. New York: Penguin, 1997. Print.
———. *The Personal History of David Copperfield*. New York: Oxford UP, 1966. Print.
"Disadvantages Arising from Misconduct at Oxford, in a Letter from H. Homely." *The Loiterer* 8 (1789): 1–12. Print.
Dodgson, Charles. *The Letters of Lewis Carroll, Vol. 1: 1837–1885*. Ed. Morton N. Cohen. New York: Oxford UP, 1979. Print.
"The Education of the People." *The Popular Educator* 1 (1852): 97. Print.
Eiland, Howard. "Reception in Distraction." *boundary* 2 30.1 (2003): 51–66. Print.
Eliot, George. *The Mill on the Floss*. Ed. Carol T. Christ. New York: Norton, 1994. Print.
Evans, G.R. *The University of Oxford: A New History*. London: I.B. Tauris, 2010. Print.
"experiential, adj." *OED Online*. Oxford UP, June 2015. Web. 27 June 2015. <http://www.oed.com/view/Entry/66528?redirectedFrom=experiential#eid>.
Feather, John. *A History of British Publishing*. 2nd ed. New York: Routledge, 2006. Print.
Flint, Kate. *The Woman Reader, 1837–1914*. New York: Oxford UP, 1993. Print.
Frost, Ginger S. *Victorian Childhoods*. Westport: Praeger, 2009. Print.
Froula, Christine. *Virginia Woolf and the Bloomsbury Avant-Garde: War, Civilization, Modernity*. New York: Columbia UP, 2007. Print.
Gardner, Howard. *Frames of Mind: The Theory of Multiple Intelligences*. New York: Basic Books, 1983. Print.
Gargano, Elizabeth. *Reading Victorian Schoolrooms: Childhood and Education in Nineteenth-Century Fiction*. New York: Routledge, 2008. Print.
Gilbert, Sandra M. and Susan Gubar. *The Madwoman in the Attic: The Woman Writer and the Nineteenth-Century Literary Imagination*. New Haven: Yale UP, 1979. Print.
Gissing, George. *The Collected Letters of George Gissing, Vol. 1: 1863–1880*. Ed. Paul F. Mattheisen, Arthur C. Young, and Pierre Coustillas. Athens: Ohio UP, 1990. Print.
———. *Demos: A Story of English Socialism*. Ed. Debbie Harrison. Brighton: Victorian Secrets, 2011. Print.
———. *George Gissing's Commonplace Book*. Ed. Jacob Korg. New York: New York Public Library, 1962. Print.
———. *London and the Life of Literature in Late Victorian England: The Diary of George Gissing, Novelist*. Ed. Pierre Coustillas. Lewisburg: Bucknell UP, 1978.
———. *New Grub Street*. New York: Modern Library, 2002. Print.
———. *The Odd Women*. Ed. Patricia Ingham. New York: Oxford UP, 2000. Print.
———. *Thyrza*. Ed. Pierre Coustillas. Brighton: Victorian Secrets, 2013. Print.
———. *The Whirlpool*. Ed. Patrick Parrinder. Rutherford: Fairleigh Dickinson UP, 1977. Print.
Gordon, Lyndall. *Virginia Woolf: A Writer's Life*. New York: Norton, 1984. Print.
Green, Laura. *Educating Women: Cultural Conflict and Victorian Literature*. Athens: Ohio UP, 2001. Print.
Greenslade, William. "Women and the Disease of Civilization: George Gissing's 'The Whirlpool.'" *Victorian Studies* 32.4 (1989): 507–23. *JSTOR*. Web. 24 June 2014.
Guillory, John. *Cultural Capital: The Problem of Literary Canon Formation*. Chicago: U of Chicago P, 1995. Print.
Hall, Lynda A. "Jane Fairfax's Choice: The Sale of Human Flesh Or Human Intellect." *Persuasions: The Jane Austen Journal On-Line* 28.1 (2007). Web. 25 Jan. 2016. <http://www.jasna.org/persuasions/on-line/vol28no1/hall.htm>.
Hansard, British Parliament. Tran. House of Commons. London: 1857. Vol. 146, column 409. Web. 30 July 2012. <http://hansard.millbanksystems.com/commons/1857/jun/25/supply-miscellaneous-estimates#S3V0146P0_18570625_HOC_85>.

150 *Works Cited*

———. Tran. House of Commons. Vol. 345, column 186. London: 1890. Web. 30 July 2012. <http://hansard.millbanksystems.com/commons/1890/jun/06/class-iv-education-science-and-art>.

———. Tran. House of Commons. Vol. 166, column 1268. London: 1862. Web. 30 July 2012. <http://hansard.millbanksystems.com/commons/1862/may/05/committee>.

Hardy, Thomas. *The Collected Letters of Thomas Hardy, Vol. 1: 1840–1892*. Ed. Richard Little Purdy and Michael Millgate. 8 Vols. New York: Clarendon, 1978. Print.

———. *The Collected Letters of Thomas Hardy, Vol. 2: 1893–1901*. Ed. Richard Little Purdy and Michael Millgate. 8 Vols. New York: Clarendon, 1980. Print.

———. *The Collected Letters of Thomas Hardy, Vol. 6: 1920–1925*. Ed. Richard Little Purdy and Michael Millgate. 8 Vols. New York: Clarendon, 1987. Print.

———. *Jude the Obscure*. Ed. Norman Page. New York: Norton, 1999. Print.

———. *A Pair of Blue Eyes*. New York: Macmillan, 1975. Print.

———. *Tess of the d'Urbervilles*. New York: Bantam, 1992. Print.

———. *Thomas Hardy's Public Voice: The Essays, Speeches, and Miscellaneous Prose*. Ed. Michael Millgate. Oxford: Clarendon, 2001. Print.

———. *Thomas Hardy's 'Studies, Specimens &c.' Notebook*. Ed. Pamela Dalziel and Michael Millgate. New York: Oxford UP, 1994. Print.

———. *The Woodlanders*. New York: Oxford UP, 2009. Print.

Hardy, Thomas and Florence Emily Hardy. *The Life of Thomas Hardy*. Hamden: Archon, 1970. Print.

Henchman, Anna. *The Starry Sky Within: Astronomy and the Reach of the Mind in Victorian Literature*. New York: Oxford UP, 2014. Print.

Hilton, Mary and Pam Hirsch, eds. *Practical Visionaries: Women, Education, and Social Progress, 1790–1930*. Harlow: Longman, 2000. Print.

"History of the Victoria University of Manchester." *The University of Manchester*, n.d. Web. 27 June 2015. <http://www.manchester.ac.uk/discover/history-heritage/history/victoria/>.

Holmes, Richard. *The Age of Wonder: How the Romantic Generation Discovered the Beauty and Terror of Science*. New York: Pantheon, 2008. Print.

Honan, Park. *Jane Austen: Her Life*. New York: St. Martin's, 1987. Print.

Horwitz, Barbara. *Jane Austen and the Question of Women's Education*. New York: Lang, 1991. Print.

Hughes, Kathryn. *The Victorian Governess*. London: Hambledon, 2001. Print.

Hughes, Linda K. "Elizabeth Barrett Browning, *Aurora Leigh*." *The Cambridge Introduction to Victorian Poetry*. Ed. Linda K. Hughes. New York: Cambridge UP, 2010. 261–75. Print.

Hughes, Thomas. *Tom Brown's Schooldays*. New York: Oxford UP, 1999. Print.

Hurt, J.S. *Elementary Schooling and the Working Classes 1860–1918*. Buffalo: U of Toronto P, 1979.

Huxley, Thomas H. "A Liberal Education; and Where to Find It." *Science and Education: Essays*. Ed. Thomas H. Huxley. New York: D. Appleton, 1899. 76–110. Print.

Jameson, Fredric. *The Political Unconscious: Narrative as a Socially Symbolic Act*. Ithaca: Cornell UP, 1981. Print.

Jenkins, Alice. *Space and the "March of Mind": Literature and the Physical Sciences in Britain, 1815–1850*. New York: Oxford UP, 2007. Print.

Jenkins, Elizabeth. *Jane Austen*. New York: Pellegrini & Cudahy, 1949. Print.

Juvenal in Oxford. Oxford: G. Shrimpton, 1877. Print.

Karlin, Daniel. "Victorian Poetry of the City: Elizabeth Barrett Browning's *Aurora Leigh*." *Babylon Or New Jerusalem? Perceptions of the City in Literature*. Ed. Valeria Tinkler-Villani. New York: Rodopi, 2005. 113–24. Print.

Kent, Christopher. "Learning History with, and from, Jane Austen." *Jane Austen's Beginnings: The Juvenilia and Lady Susan.* Ed. J. David Grey. Ann Arbor: UMI, 1989. 59–72. Print.

Kenyon Jones, Christine and Anna Snaith. "'Tilting at Universities': Woolf at King's College London." *Woolf Studies Annual* 16 (2010): 1–44. Print.

Knox, Marisa Palacios. "'The Valley of the Shadow of Books': George Gissing, New Women, and Morbid Literary Detachment." *Nineteenth-Century Literature* 69.1 (2014): 92–122. *JSTOR.* Web. 13 Aug. 2014.

Lee, Hermione. *Virginia Woolf.* New York: Vintage, 1996. Print.

Lelchuk, Alan. "'Demos': The Ordeal of the Two Gissings." *Victorian Studies* 12.3 (1969): 357–74. *JSTOR.* Web. 13 Aug. 2014.

"Lessons in Moral Science—no. VI: The Kind of Indifference which has been Considered Essential to Free Agency." *The Popular Educator* 6 (1855): 494–7. Print.

Liggins, Emma. *George Gissing, the Working Woman, and Urban Culture.* Burlington: Ashgate, 2006. Print.

Lightman, Bernard. *Victorian Popularizers of Science: Designing Nature for New Audiences.* Chicago: U of Chicago P, 2009. Print.

Lloyd, Anna. *Anna Lloyd (1837–1925): A Memoir.* Ed. Edith M. Lloyd. London: Cayme, 1928. Print.

"machinery, n." *OED Online.* Oxford UP, March 2015. Web. 27 June 2015. <http://www.oed.com/view/Entry/111856?redirectedFrom=machinery#eid>.

Macleod, Elizabeth. "A Day at Girton." *The Macleod Family Magazine—Motley* 1.11 (1881). Print.

Maclure, J. Stuart, ed. *Educational Documents: England and Wales 1816–1967.* London: Chapman & Hall, 1968. Print.

Major, J.R., ed. *Examination Papers: Consisting of Passages Selected from Greek and Latin Authors, Prose and Verse; with Questions on the Subject-Matter, History, Grammar &c.* Oxford: John Henry and James Parker, 1856. Print.

Maltz, Diana. "Practical Aesthetics and Decadent Rationale in George Gissing." *Victorian Literature and Culture* 28.1 (2000): 55–71. *JSTOR.* Web. 24 June 2014.

"manner, n. (and int.)." *OED Online.* Oxford UP, March 2015. Web. 27 June 2015. <http://www.oed.com/view/Entry/113569?redirectedFrom=manner#eid>.

Martinez, Michele. *Elizabeth Barrett Browning's Aurora Leigh: A Reader's Guide.* Edinburgh: Edinburgh UP, 2012. Print.

Mattison, Jane. *Knowledge and Survival in the Novels of Thomas Hardy.* Stockholm: Lund Studies in English, 2002. Print.

Maynard, Constance Louisa. "One Page of Girton's History Anticipated Or the Savage and Triumphant Progress of the Classical Tripos Over Two of Her Loftiest Students." *The Girton Review* Feb. 1875. Print.

Mermin, Dorothy. *Elizabeth Barrett Browning: The Origins of a New Poetry.* Chicago: U of Chicago P. 1989. Print.

Mill, John Stuart. *Autobiography of John Stuart Mill.* New York: Columbia UP, 1960. Print.

Millgate, Michael. "Introduction." *Thomas Hardy's Public Voice: The Essays, Speeches, and Miscellaneous Prose.* Ed. Michael Millgate. New York: Oxford UP, 2001. Print.

———. *Thomas Hardy: A Biography Revisited.* New York: Oxford UP, 2004. Print.

Mitchell, Charlotte. "Hughes, Thomas (1822–1896)." *Oxford Dictionary of National Biography.* Ed. H.C.G. Matthew and Brian Harrison. Oxford: Oxford UP, 2004. Online ed. Ed. Lawrence Goldman. Jan. 2012. 27 June 2015. <http://www.oxforddnb.com/view/article/14091>.

More, Hannah. *Essays on Various Subjects, Principally Designed for Young Ladies*. London: Dobson, 1787. Print.

———. *Hints Towards Forming the Characters of a Young Princess*. London: Cadell, 1805. Print.

———. *Strictures on the Modern System of Female Education*. London: Strahan, 1800. Print.

Morley College. "Our History—London College Courses." *Short and Part Time Courses London—Morley College*, 2015. Web. 22 May 2015. <http://www.morleycollege.ac.uk/history>.

Morris, Mowbray. "Culture and Anarchy." *Thomas Hardy: The Critical Heritage*. Ed. R.G. Cox. New York: Barnes & Noble, 1970. 214–21. Print.

National Home Reading Union. *Summer Assembly*. Blackpool: National Home Reading Union, 1890. Print.

Newman, John Henry. *Apologia Pro Vita Sua*. Ed. David J. DeLaura. New York: Norton, 1968. Print.

Olson, Kirsten. *Wounded by School: Recapturing the Joy in Learning and Standing Up to Old School Culture*. New York: Teachers College, 2009. Print.

Open University. "The OU Story." Open University, 2015. Web. 25 May 2015. <http://www.open.ac.uk/about/main/strategy/ou-story>.

"Overwork." *The Girton Review* March 1883: 16. Print.

"Oxbridge, n. and adj." *OED Online*. Oxford UP, Dec. 2014. Web. 27 June 2015. <http://www.oed.com/view/Entry/135559?redirectedFrom=oxbridge#eid>.

Oxford University. *The Student's Handbook to the University and Colleges of Oxford*. Oxford: Clarendon, 1873. Print.

Oxford University Commission. *Report of Her Majesty's Commissioners Appointed to Inquire into the State, Discipline, Studies, and Revenues of the University and Colleges of Oxford Together with the Evidence, and an Appendix*. London: W. Clowes and Sons, 1852. Print.

Parrinder, Patrick. "The Voice of the Unclassed: Gissing and Twentieth-Century English Fiction." *George Gissing: Voices of the Unclassed*. Ed. Martin H. Ryle and Jenny Bourne Taylor. Burlington: Ashgate, 2005. 145–58. Print.

Parry, Jonathan. "Lowe, Robert, Viscount Sherbrooke (1811–1892)." *Oxford Dictionary of National Biography*. Ed. H.C.G. Matthew and Brian Harrison. Oxford: Oxford UP, 2004. Online ed. Ed. Lawrence Goldman. May 2011. 27 June 2015. <http://www.oxforddnb.com/view/article/17088>.

Perry, Ruth. *Novel Relations: The Transformation of Kinship in English Literature and Culture, 1748–1818*. New York: Cambridge UP, 2004. Print.

Peterson, Linda. "'For My Better Self': Auto/biographies of the Poetess, the *Prelude* of the Poet Laureate, and Elizabeth Barrett Browning's *Aurora Leigh*." *Traditions of Victorian Women's Autobiography: The Poetics and Politics of Life Writing*. Charlottesville: U of Virginia P, 2001. 109–45. Print.

Phegley, Jennifer. *Educating the Proper Woman Reader*. Columbus: Ohio State UP, 2004. Print.

Playfair, Lyon. *Technical Education on the Continent*. London: George E. Eyre and William Spottiswode, 1852. Print.

The Popular Educator. Vol. 1.2. London: John Cassell, 1855. Print.

The Popular Educator. Vol. 6. London: John Cassell, 1855. Print.

Potolsky, Matthew. "Hardy, Shaftesbury, and Aesthetic Education." *Studies in English Literature 1500–1900* 46.4 (2006): 863–78. Web. 10 Feb. 2015.

Preston, Carrie J. *Modernism's Mythic Pose: Gender, Genre, Solo Performance*. New York: Oxford UP, 2011. Print.
Price, Leah. *How to Do Things with Books in Victorian Britain*. Princeton: Princeton UP, 2012. Print.
"The Provisional Committee to Further University Education in the South-West." *Times Educational Supplement* 18 Oct. 1917: 400. Print.
Radin, Grace. *Virginia Woolf's The Years: The Evolution of a Novel*. Knoxville: U of Tennessee P, 1981. Print.
The Reason Why? A Careful Collection of some Hundreds of Reasons for Things which, Though Generally Known, are Imperfectly Understood. London: Houlston, 1856. Print.
Reid, Julian. *RE: C19 Curriculum*. Message to the author. 28 Aug. 2012. E-mail.
Robinson, Jane. *Bluestockings: The Remarkable Story of the First Women to Fight for an Education*. London: Penguin, 2010. Print.
Robson, Catherine. *Heart Beats: Everyday Life and the Memorized Poem*. Princeton: Princeton UP, 2012. Print.
———. "Reciting Alice: What Is the Use of a Book without Poems?" *The Feeling of Reading: Affective Experience and Victorian Literature*. Ed. Rachel Ablow. Ann Arbor: U of Michigan P, 2010. 93–113. Print.
Roebuck, Janet. *The Making of Modern English Society from 1850*. London: Routledge, 1982. Print.
Rose, Jonathan. *The Intellectual Life of the British Working Classes*. New Haven: Yale UP, 2001. Print.
Rothblatt, Sheldon. *The Modern University and Its Discontents: The Fate of Newman's Legacies in Britain and America*. New York: Cambridge UP, 1997. Print.
Rousseau, Jean-Jacques. *Émile, Or Treatise on Education*. Trans. William H. Payne. Amherst: Prometheus, 2003. Print.
Rudy, Jason. *Electric Meters: Victorian Physiological Poetics*. Athens: Ohio UP, 2009. Print.
Ruskin, John. *Sesame and Lilies*. Ed. Deborah Epstein Nord. New Haven: Yale UP, 2002. Print.
Russell, Willy. "Educating Rita." *Plays*. Vol. 1. London: Methuen, 1996. 269–359. Print.
Ryle, Martin H. "'To show a Man of Letters': Gissing, Cultural Authority and Literary Modernism." In *George Gissing: Voices of the Unclassed*, Ed. Martin H. Ryle and Jenny Bourne Taylor. Burlington: Ashgate, 2005. 119–32. Print.
Sadler, M.E. *Oxford and Working-Class Education: Being the Report of a Joint Committee of University Working-Class Representatives on the Relation of the University to the Higher Education of Workpeople*. Oxford: Clarendon, 1908. Print.
Sander, Anna. *RE: Request to Consult the "Student Life/Studies/Records of Collection" Archive*. Message to the author. 20 July 2012. E-mail.
"scramble, v." *OED Online*. Oxford UP, March 2015. Web. 27 June 2015. <http://www.oed.com/search?searchType=dictionary&q=scramble&_searchBtn=Search>.
Shakespeare, William. *Macbeth*. New York: Folger–Simon & Schuster, 2003. Print.
Shuman, Cathy. *Pedagogical Economies: The Examination and the Victorian Literary Man*. Stanford: Stanford UP, 2000. Print.
"Sixteenth Annual Report of the Local Examinations Syndicate." *Cambridge University Reporter* 31 Mar. 1874: 294–9. Print.
Sloan, John. *George Gissing: The Cultural Challenge*. New York: St. Martin's, 1989. Print.
Smith, Charles H. "Wallace, Alfred Russel (1823–1913)." *Oxford Dictionary of National Biography*. Ed. H.C.G. Matthew and Brian Harrison. Oxford: Oxford UP, 2004. Online

ed. Ed. Lawrence Goldman. Jan. 2011. 27 June 2015. <http://www.oxforddnb.com/view/article/36700>.

Stewart, Garrett. *Dear Reader: The Conscripted Audience in Nineteenth-Century British Fiction*. Baltimore: Johns Hopkins UP, 1996. Print.

Stone, Marjorie. *Elizabeth Barrett Browning*. New York: St. Martin's, 1995. Print.

———. "Genre Subversion and Gender Inversion: *The Princess* and *Aurora Leigh*." *Victorian Poetry* 25.2 (1987): 101–27. Web. 21 Oct. 2014.

"The Study of History." *Fritillary* 12 Dec. 1897: 1. Print.

Taylor, Beverly. "Elizabeth Barrett Browning and the Politics of Childhood." *Victorian Poetry* 46.4 (2008): 405–27. Web. 5 Feb. 2015.

———. "'School-Miss Alfred' and 'Materfamilias': Female Sexuality and Poetic Voice in *The Princess* and *Aurora Leigh*." *Gender and Discourse in Victorian Literature and Art*. Ed. Anthony H. Harrison and Beverly Taylor. DeKalb: Northern Illinois UP, 1992. 5–29. Print.

Taylor, Jenny Bourne. "The Strange Case of Godwin Peak: Double Consciousness in *Born in Exile*." *George Gissing: Voices of the Unclassed*. Ed. Martin H. Ryle and Jenny Bourne Taylor. Burlington: Ashgate, 2005. 61–75. Print.

Tennyson, Alfred, Lord. *The Letters of Alfred Lord Tennyson, Vol. 1: 1821–1850*. Ed. Cecil Y. Lang and Edgar F. Shannon Jr. Cambridge: Harvard UP, 1981. Print.

"Thoughts on Education—A New System Recommended." *The Loiterer* 27 (1789): 157–64. Print.

Tomalin, Claire. *Thomas Hardy*. New York: Penguin, 2007. Print.

Tucker, Herbert. "An Ebigrammar of Motives; Or, Ba for Short." *Victorian Poetry* 44.4 (2006): 445–65. Web. 21 Oct. 2014.

University of Oxford. *New Examination Statutes: Abstracts of Their Principal Provisions, with a Catalogue of Books, Either Expressly Mentioned, or Treating of the Subjects Required*. Oxford: John Henry Parker, 1851. Print.

———. *Epic: Britain's Heroic Muse, 1790–1910*. New York: Oxford UP, 2008. Print.

UK Parliament. "Extension of Education." *Going to School*. U.K. Parliament, n.d. Web. 12 June 2015. <http://www.parliament.uk/about/living-heritage/transformingsociety/livinglearning/school/overview/1914-39/>.

———. "Further Reform, 1902–1914." *Going to School*. U.K. Parliament, n.d. Web. 12 June 2015. <http://www.parliament.uk/about/living-heritage/transformingsociety/livinglearning/school/overview/reform1902-14/>.

Vincent, David. *Literacy and Popular Culture: England 1750–1914*. Cambridge: Cambridge UP, 1989. Print.

Wadham College. *Examination Papers, Wadham College*. Oxford University, 1835–1853. Print.

White, Laura Mooneyham. *Romance, Language and Education in Jane Austen's Novels*. Basingstoke: Macmillan, 1988. Print.

Williams, Raymond. *The Country and the City*. New York: Oxford UP, 1973. Print.

Wollstonecraft, Mary. *A Vindication of the Rights of Woman*. Ed. Deidre Shauna Lynch. New York: Norton, 2009. Print.

Woods, Alice. *Educational Experiments in England*. London: Methuen, 1920. Print.

Woolf, Virginia. "Aurora Leigh." *Aurora Leigh*. Ed. Margaret Reynolds. New York: Norton, 1996. 439–46. Print.

———. *The Letters of Virginia Woolf, Vol. 5: 1932–1935*. Ed. Nigel Nicolson and Joanne Trautmann. New York: Harcourt Brace Jovanovich, 1979. Print.

———. *The Pargiters, the Novel-Essay Portion of the Years*. Ed. Mitchell Leaska. New York: New York Public Library, 1977. Print.

———. *A Passionate Apprentice: The Early Journals 1897–1909*. Ed. Mitchell A. Leaska. San Diego: Harcourt, 1990. Print.

———. "Report on Teaching at Morley College." *Virginia Woolf: A Biography*. Ed. Quentin Bell. New York: Harcourt Brace Jovanovich, 1972. 202–4. Print.

———. *A Room of One's Own*. Orlando: Harvest, 2005. Print.

———. *Three Guineas*. Orlando: Harcourt, 2006. Print.

———. *To the Lighthouse*. San Diego: Harcourt Brace Jovanovitch, 1955. Print.

———. *The Waves*. San Diego: Harcourt, 1959. Print.

———. "A Woman's College from Outside." *The Complete Shorter Fiction of Virginia Woolf*. Ed. Susan Dick. 2nd ed. New York: Harcourt, 1989. 145–8. Print.

———. *A Writer's Diary*. Ed. Leonard Woolf. London: Hogarth, 1969. Print.

———. *The Years*. London: Penguin, 1998. Print.

Woolford, John. "Elizabeth Barrett and the Wordsworthian Sublime." *Essays in Criticism* 45.1 (1995): 36–56. Print.

Wordsworth, William. *The Prelude, 1799, 1805, 1850: Authoritative Texts, Context and Reception, Recent Critical Essays*. Ed. Jonathan Wordsworth, M.H. Abrams, and Stephen Gill. 1st ed. New York: Norton, 1979. Print.

———. "The Tables Turned." *The Norton Anthology of Poetry*. Ed. Margaret Ferguson, Mary Jo Salter, and Jon Stallworthy. New York: Norton, 2004. 457. Print.

Index

Ablow, Rachel 19*n*7, 57*n*6
ABRACADABRA: A Fragment of University History 15
accidental reading/learning: Arnold on 7; Gissing on 54–5, 94–5; Mill on 6–7, 19*n*8, 74; Newman on 6–7, 19*n*8, 74; *see also Aurora Leigh*, radical education in (Barrett Browning)
accomplishments, in girls' education: Austen on 22–3, 32, 34–9, 43; Barrett Browning on 17, 43, 48–50, 57*n*10; De Bellaigue on 48, 57*n*11
affective reading 93, 95, 96
alienated intellectuals (Jameson) 83–4, 97
Altick, Richard 7, 53
American education 12, 18, 85–6, 99*n*9, 112–13
Apology for Poetry (Sidney) 90
Armstrong, Isobel 52
Arnold, Matthew 5, 7, 8, 10, 19*n*8, 21*n*25, 47, 107
Art of Pluck, The (Caswall) 14–15, 107
Art of Reasoning, The: A Popular Exposition of the Principles of Logic (Neil) 63
"Aurora Leigh" (Woolf) 49–50
Aurora Leigh, radical education in (Barrett Browning) 1, 9, 17, 45–58; introduction 17, 45–6; book learning and belatedness 46–8, 57*n*9; education through stray odd volumes 52–6; experiential learning and headlong reading 17, 45–6, 50–2, 57*n*5, 96; a girl's education like water-torture 48–50
Austen, George 28
Austen, Henry 26
Austen, James 26
Austen, Jane 1, 2; anticipated Carlyle 3, 22, 24, 31, 43; critique of girls' schools education of accomplishments 22–3, 32, 34–9, 43; education of 25, 27–8; *Emma* 17, 23, 27, 34–6, 41–2, 96; *History of England* 17, 23, 27, 29, 30–1, 34; *Mansfield Park* 9, 17, 22, 23–4, 28, 34, 36–43; *My Dear Cassandra* 28–9, 32; *Northanger Abbey* 17, 26, 29–30, 31, 33, 96; Austen's Oxbridge connections 25–31; *Persuasion* 17, 31, 34; "Plan of a Novel" 31–3; *Pride and Prejudice* 17, 24, 27, 37, 40, 42; regenerative education 35, 36, 40–2; resisted Wollstonecraft's ideas about women's education 16–17, 22, 24, 25, 46; *Sense and Sensibility* 28; *see also* scrambling type of learning (Austen)
Autobiography (Mill) 5–6, 94
autodidact culture (Hardy) 59–81; introduction 17, 59–62; critique of Hardy as autodidact 62–8; doing without Cambridge in *Tess of the D'Urbervilles* 61, 76–9, 81*nn*21–22; *Jude the Obscure* as autodidact 72–6, 81*n*17; National Home Reading Union 17, 66–7, *66, 137–140*; *A Pair of Blue Eyes* and Oxbridge 60–1, 67–71, 80*nn*13–14; *The Popular Educator* 17, 60, 63–8, *65*, 80*nn*11–12, *126–36*

Barnes, Martha McCullough 86
Barrett Browning, Elizabeth 2, 3; *Aurora Leigh* 1, 9, 17; critique of girls' schools education of accomplishments 17, 43, 48–50, 57*n*10; "The Cry of the Children" 53; education of 46–7; model of education for women of different classes 9, 44*n*14, 45–6, 50, 52–5; summary conclusion 110–12; *see also Aurora Leigh*, radical education in (Barrett Browning); headlong reading (Barrett Browning)

Beale, Dorothea 9
Bell, Andrew 4
Bloomsbury Group 100, 101
Bodichon, Barbara Leigh Smith 2, 45
Bourdieu, Pierre 3, 62, 73, 74
Brown, Julia Prewitt 44n17
"Buried Life, The" (Arnold) 5, 47
Burrows, Montagu 11–12, 20n18
Buss, Frances 9

Cambridge University: Girton College 9, 107–10, 114n18; women's colleges 106–12, 114n14; Woolf's association with 101
Carlyle, Thomas 3, 4, 7, 8, 22, 24, 31, 43, 57n4
Cassell, John 64
Caswall, Edward 14–15, 107
Cheltenham Ladies College 9
Christian self-government *see* scrambling type of learning (Austen)
Clarke, James Stanier 28–9, 31
classism in education: Barrett Browning on 9, 44n14, 45–6, 50, 52–6; and ease (Bourdieu) 3; Gissing on 82–4, 89–92; Hardy on 59–60, 61–2, 67–71, 76–9; and *The Popular Educator* critique of 17, 60, 63–8, *65*, 80nn11–12, *126–36*; and working classes 7–10, 19n11, 59–61, 64
Collet, Clara 2, 45
Collins, Philip 80n8
Colquhoun, Patrick 4
Cooper, Andrew 73
Coustillas, Pierre 83, 89–90, 98n4
cramming for tests 107–9; critiques of 6, 14–16, 20n21; Dodgson on 9–10; in Gissing's own education 85; at Oxbridge 12–16; *The Popular Educator* on 64; student comments on 9, 20n21, 107–10, *108*; use of term 20n23; *see also* Revised Code; rote learning; University of Oxford
"Cry of the Children, The" (Barrett Browning) 53
cultural capital (Bourdieu and Guillory) 62

Dalgarno, Emily 101
Dalziel, Pamela 63
Dames, Nicholas ix, 2–3, 18n4
David Copperfield (Dickens) 86
Davies, Emily 9
"Day at Girton, A" (Macleod) 109
De Bellaigue, Christina 48, 57n8, 57n11

democratization of education (Gissing) 82–99; introduction 17–18, 82–4; educational ideas in *Thyrza* 82–3, 84, 87, 88–92, 97, 98; summary conclusion 96–8; and unteaching in *Thyrza* 90, 92–6
Demos (Gissing) 83, 96, 99nn12–13
Dickens, Charles 7, 19n10, 30, 61, 86
"Disadvantages arising from misconduct at Oxford, in a letter from H. Homely" (*The Loiterer*) 26
displaced intellectuals (Greenslade) 83–4, 89, 102
divining, learning as 74–5; *see also* autodidact culture (Hardy)
Dodgson, Charles 9–10, 107
Duff, Grant 97

ease (Bourdieu) 3, 73, 74
"Ebbigrammar of Motives, An; or, Ba for Short" (Tucker) 56n3
"Economic Position of Educated Working Women, The" (Collet) 45
Educating Rita (Russell) 112
Education Act of 1870 59, 98n4
educational machinery, during nineteenth century 1–21; critiques of rote learning/cramming 14–16, 20n21; and educational outliers 2–3; literature that unteaches readers 4–7; mechanization of education 3–4; pedagogical legacy of Oxbridge 10–14; rote learning and exams at Oxbridge 12–14, 20n18, 44n14; summary conclusion 16–18; and working classes 7–10, 19n11
educational outliers 1–3, 19n10, 100; *see also* Austen, Jane; Barrett Browning, Elizabeth; Gissing, George; Hardy, Thomas
"Education of the People, The" (*The Popular Educator*) 65–6
Eliot, George 84
embodied knowledge *see Aurora Leigh*, radical education in (Barrett Browning)
Emma (Austen) 17, 23, 27, 34–6, 41–2, 96
emotional intelligence *see Aurora Leigh*, radical education in (Barrett Browning)
English literature, institutionalization of 82
Essays on Various Subjects, Principally Designed for Young Ladies (More) 24
Examination Papers: Consisting of Passages selected from Greek and Latin Authors, Prose and Verse; with Questions on the Subject-Matter, History, Grammar &c 13–14

Examination Statutes 12–13
experiential learning 17, 45–6, 50–2, 57*n*5, 96

Flint, Kate 51
Fritillary, The (magazine) 110; excerpted page from *111*

Gardner, Howard 112
George Gissing's Commonplace Book (Gissing) 89; excerpts from 87–8
Girton College 9, 107–10, 114*n*18
Girton Review, The (magazine) 107–10
"Girton's History Anticipated or The Savage and Triumphant Progress of the Classical Tripos over Two of her Loftiest Students" (Maynard) 107–9; excerpted page from *108*
Gissing, George 1, 2, 3; *Demos* 83, 96, 99*nn*12–13; education of 84–5; *George Gissing's Commonplace Book* 87–8, 89; *New Grub Street* 17, 82, 87, 97, 98; *The Odd Women* 83; regenerative education 91; as teacher in American high school 18, 83, 84–6, 87, 99*n*9; *Thyrza* 17–18, 52, 54, 82–3, 84, 87, 88–96, 97, 98, 137–41; as tutor 83, 84, 85–8; *The Whirlpool* 83; *see also* democratization of education (Gissing)
Grahame, Walter 87
Green, Laura 18*n*3, 62, 79*n*3, 81*n*14, 81*n*16
Greenslade, William 83–4
Guillory, John 62

Hackett, Sarah 27
hands-on learning *see* scrambling type of learning (Austen)
Hard Times (Dickens) 7, 30
Hardy, Thomas 2, 3, 44*n*14; education of 61, 63–4, 79, 80*n*9; influence on education 80*n*4; *Jude the Obscure* 10, 17, 55, 59, 62, 64, 71, 72–6, 81*n*17, 96; *A Pair of Blue Eyes* 17, 60–1, 62, 67–71, 80*nn*13–14; received honorary college degrees 61; regenerative education 70; *Tess of the D'Urbervilles* 1, 17, 61, 71, 76–9, 81*nn*21–22; *Thomas Hardy's 'Studies, Specimens &c.' Notebook* 63; *The Woodlanders* 17, 62, 70–1; *see also* autodidact culture (Hardy)
Harrison, John 64
headlong reading (Barrett Browning) 17, 45–6, 50–2, 57*n*5, 96; *see also Aurora Leigh*, radical education in (Barrett Browning)
heart and brain reading (Gissing) 95, 96, 139; *see also* affective reading; democratization of education (Gissing); headlong reading (Barrett Browning)
Heine, Heinrich 93–4
Henchman, Anna 63–4
Hints Towards Forming the Character of a Young Princess (More) 24
History of England (Austen) 17, 23, 27, 29, 30–1, 34
Hughes, Thomas 9

indefinable tentative process (Carlyle) 22, 24, 31
inner life, development of *see Aurora Leigh*, radical education in (Barrett Browning)
insider/outsider binary, breakdown of *see* democratization of education (Gissing)
institutional outsiders: Austen 1, 29, 90; Barrett Browning 1, 90; and early women's college writers 106–12; experimentation in *The Pargiters* 18, 102–6; Gissing 1, 17–18, 82–4, 90, 97–8; Hardy 1, 60, 72, 76, 79; introduction 18, 100–2; modern historically excluded insiders 112–13; "A Woman's College from Outside" 102; Woolf 18, 100–14; *see also* Austen, Jane; Barrett Browning, Elizabeth; Gissing, George; Hardy, Thomas; Woolf, Virginia

Jameson, Fredric 83–4, 97
Jenkins, Alice 49
Jude the Obscure (Hardy) 10, 17, 55, 59, 62, 64, 71, 72–6, 81*n*17, 96; Mechanics' Institutes 73; *see also* autodidact culture (Hardy); Oxbridge, use of term
judgment, development of *see* scrambling type of learning (Austen)
"Juvenal in Oxford" (poem) 15–16

Kenyon Jones, Christine 101
King's College 100

Lancaster, Joseph 3, 4, 19*n*5
Lawrence, D.H. 84
Lelchuk, Alan 84
Lighthouse, To the (Woolf) 100, 105
Lindow Grove school 85
Lloyd, Anna 16, 107, 109–10
Locke, John 64

Loiterer, The 17, 23, 43; "Disadvantages arising from misconduct at Oxford, in a letter from H. Homely" 26–7; excerpted pages from *115–25*; "Thoughts on Education—A new System recommended" 27
Lowe, Robert 4, 7–8
Lyell, Charles 19*n*8

machinery, use of term 8
Macleod, Elizabeth 109
male autodidact culture *see* autodidact culture (Hardy)
Mansfield Park (Austen) 9, 17, 22, 23, 24, 28, 34, 36–43
marriage market, education for 9, 16, 50; *see also* scrambling type of learning (Austen)
mass education 46, 113; *see also* educational machinery, during nineteenth century
Maurice, Frederick Denison 9
Maynard, Constance Louisa 107–9
McCulloch, John Ramsay 63
Mechanics' Institutes 73
Menand, Louis 18*n*4
Mill, John Stuart 4, 5–7, 54, 55, 74, 92, 93, 94, 95
Millgate, Michael 63, 80*n*6, 81*n*22
Milton, John 53, 54
monitorial system (Lancaster) 3, 19*n*5
More, Hannah 16, 24
Morley College 104–5
Morris, Mowbray 62
multimodal learning 112–13
My Dear Cassandra (Austen) 28–9, 32
Mystery of Udolpho, The (Radcliffe) 31

National Home Reading Union 66–7; excerpted page from *66*; Summer Assembly program 17; excerpted pages *137–140*
Neil, Samuel 63
New and Appropriate System of Education for the Labouring People, A (Colquhoun) 4
New Grub Street (Gissing) 17, 82, 87, 97, 98
Newman, John Henry 5–7, 54, 74
Newnham College 101, 102, 112, 114*n*16
New Woman tradition 99*n*14
Nicholas Nickleby (Dickens) 7
Northanger Abbey (Austen) 17, 26, 29–30, 31, 33, 96

North London Collegiate School for Ladies 9
novel, as education for girls 28, 33
Nussbaum, Martha 18*n*4

Odd Women, The (Gissing) 83
Open University 112
Our Mutual Friend (Dickens) 7
outsiders within *see* women's college writers
"Overwork" (*The Girton Review*) 110, 114*n*18
Owens College 85, 89–90
Oxbridge, use of term 2
Oxford and Working-class Education (Sadler) 60

Pair of Blue Eyes, A (Hardy) 17, 60–1, 62, 67–71, 80*nn*13–14
Pargiters, The (Woolf) 18, 102–6
Pass and Class, An Oxford guide-book through the courses of literae humaniores, mathematics, natural science, and law and modern history (Burrows) 11–12
payment by results system (Lowe) 7–8, 113
Perry, Ruth 34
Persuasion (Austen) 17, 31, 34
Place, Francis 61
"Plan of a Novel" (Austen) 31–3
political careerists *see* democratization of education (Gissing)
Popular Educator, The (1852) 17, 60, 63–8, 80*nn*11–12; excerpted pages from *65, 126–36*
Prelude, The (Wordsworth) 4
Price, Leah 2–3, 58*n*14
Pride and Prejudice (Austen) 17, 24, 27, 37, 40, 42
Princess, The (Tennyson) 46
Principles of Political Economy (McCulloch) 63
Proposed National Arrangements for Primary Education (8–9

Radcliffe, Ann 31
Reading Ladies Boarding School 27
reading theories *see* theories of reading
Reason Why, The? A Careful Collection of Some Hundreds of Reasons for Things Which, Though Generally Known, Are Imperfectly Understood 67

regenerative education: Austen on 35, 36, 40–2; Gissing on 91; Hardy on 70
religion and education *see* scrambling type of learning (Austen)
Revised Code 7–8, 12
Robson, Catherine 20*n*13
Romantic tradition and education 56*n*2
Room of One's Own, A (Woolf) 100
Rose, Jonathan 53, 62
rote learning: critiques of 14–16, 20*n*21; at Oxbridge 12–14, 20*n*18, 44*n*14; women's college writers critique of 106–12; *see also* autodidact culture (Hardy); cramming for tests
Rousseau, Jean-Jacques 4, 45, 56*n*2
Royal Commission of Oxford 11–12, 13, 14, 21*n*25
Rudy, Jason 46
Ruskin, John 30
Russell, Willy 112

Sadler, M.E. 60
"Scholar-Gipsy, The" (Arnold) 5
Schools Inquiry Commission 47
sciences and scientists 19*n*8, 82, 85
scramble, to (defined) 23
scrambling type of learning (Austen) 22–44; introduction 16–17, 22–5; in *Emma* 23, 27, 34–6, 41–2; fake scrambling 33–40; in *Mansfield Park* 23–4, 28, 34, 36–43; "Plan of a Novel" 31–3; in *Pride and Prejudice* 24, 42; scrambling in Austen 40–3; in *Sense and Sensibility* 28
self-directed learning *see Aurora Leigh*, radical education in (Barrett Browning); scrambling type of learning (Austen)
self-education *see Aurora Leigh*, radical education in (Barrett Browning); autodidact culture (Hardy); democratization of education (Gissing); Hardy, Thomas; scrambling type of learning (Austen)
Sense and Sensibility (Austen) 28
Sesame and Lilies (Ruskin) 30
Shakespeare 53, 54, 55, 63
Sidney, Philip 90, 95–6
"Signs of the Times" (Carlyle) 3, 22, 57*n*4
Sloan, John 90, 98*n*2, 99*nn*12–13
Snaith, Anna 101
spasmody (Tucker) 50–1, 57*n*6
spatial imagination (Jenkins) 49
Spectator (magazine) 33

standardized testing 13–14, 112–13; at Oxbridge 16, 20*n*18, 21*n*25, 113; *see also* test preparation industry
Stanford University 113
"Stanzas from the Grande Chartreuse" (Arnold) 5
Stephen, Katherine 101
Stephenson, George 64–6
Strictures on the Modern System of Female Education (More) 24
"Study of History, The" (The Fritillary) 110; excerpted page from *111*
suffering, learning from *see* scrambling type of learning (Austen)

"Tables Turned, The" (Wordsworth) 4, 51
Tennyson, Alfred Lord 5, 46
Tess of the D'Urbervilles (Hardy) 1, 17, 61, 71, 76–9, 81*nn*21–22
test preparation industry 13–14
theories of reading 2–3, 19*n*7, 57*n*6, 58*n*14
Thomas Hardy's Studies, Specimens &c. Notebook (Hardy) 63
"Thoughts on Education—A new System recommended" (*The Loiterer*) 27
Three Guineas (Woolf) 100, 102
Thyrza (Gissing) 17–18, 52, 54, 82–3, 84, 87, 88–96, 97, 98; excerpts from *141*
Tomalin, Claire 80*n*9
Tucker, Herbert 50–1, 56*n*3, 57*n*6
tutored education: of Austen 29; in Austen's novels 32, 34–5, 37–42; offered by Dodgson 9–10; offered by Gissing 83, 84, 85–8; within Oxbridge education 11–13, 16; of Woolf 113*n*3; *see also* accomplishments, in girls' education

uncribbed (Hardy) 77
University of Oxford: Arnold on 5; entrance and curriculum requirements 10–11; *Examination Papers* 13–14; *Royal Commission of Oxford, 1852 report* 11–12, 13, 14, *21n25*; students' resistance to curriculum and testing 5, 10, 15–16, 21*n*25; student writings 26, 106–7, 110–12; Tennyson on stifling effects of 5; University Extension movement 9, 59–60; women's colleges 18, 106–12, 114*n*14
unlearned concept *see* scrambling type of learning (Austen)

unteaching, use of term 1–2, 4–7; *see also* democratization of education (Gissing)

Vindication of the Rights of Woman, A (Wollstonecraft) 22
Virgil (Dryden) 63

Waltham High School, Massachusetts 85–6
Waves, The (Woolf) 105
Wells, H.G. 84–5
Whirlpool, The (Gissing) 83
Whitman, Walt 78, 83, 90, 92–6
Williams, Raymond 62–3
Wilson, J.M. 13
Wollstonecraft, Mary 16, 22, 24, 25, 46
Woman Reader, The, 1837–1913 (Flint) 51
"Woman's College from Outside, A" (Woolf) 18, 102
"Women and Work" (Bodichon) 45
women's colleges 59, 106–12, 114*n*14
women's college writers: critique of rote education 106–12; *The Fritillary* (magazine) 110, *111*; *The Girton Review* (magazine) 107–10; outsiders within 101–2

women's education reform 9–10, *see also Aurora Leigh*, radical education in (Barrett Browning); scrambling type of learning (Austen)
Wood, James 85
Woodlanders, The (Hardy) 17, 62, 70–1
Woolf, Virginia: attended King's College 100, 101, 106, 113*n*5; "Aurora Leigh" 49–50; education of 100–1, 113*n*3; "Essay-novel" (unpublished) 102–3; *To the Lighthouse* 100, 105; *The Pargiters* 18, 102–6; *A Room of One's Own* 100; taught at Morley College 104–5; *Three Guineas* 100, 102; *The Waves* 105; "A Woman's College from Outside" 18, 102; on writing of *The Years* 114*n*8; *The Years* 18, 103, 105–6, 114*n*8; *see also* institutional outsiders (Woolf)
Wordsworth, William 4, 6, 45, 56*n*2, 63, 92, 94
working-class men, education for 7–9; *see also* democratization of education (Gissing)
working-class readers 53
Working Men's College 9, 59

Years, The (Woolf) 18, 103, 105–6, 114*n*8